Working with Carers

Working with Carers

Christine Heron

Jessica Kingsley Publishers
London and Bristol, Pennsylvania

First published in the United Kingdom in 1998 by
Jessica Kingsley Publishers Ltd
116 Pentonville Road
London N1 9JB, England
and
1900 Frost Road, Suite 101
Bristol, PA 19007, U S A

Copyright © 1998 Christine Heron

Library of Congress Cataloging in Publication Data
A CIP catalogue record for this book is available from the Library of Congress

British Library Cataloguing in Publication Data
A CIP catalogue record for this book is available from the British Library

ISBN 1 85302 562 3

Printed and Bound in Great Britain by
Athenaeum Press, Gateshead, Tyne and Wear

Contents

Acknowledgements

My thanks to the following people who helped towards the completion of this book: David Pye for proofreading and putting up with me. Gary Morris, Anne Torley and Jane Vickers for providing information and their perspective on carers. Alex Murphy, Information Officer from the Scottish Office of the Carers National Association, for explaining the differences in legislation between England and Scotland. Sue Walsh for providing literature. All colleagues, service users and carers who have contributed to my understanding of carers' issues, in particular members of Wirral Carers Development Group.

This book is dedicated to the memory of Maurice Heron who died in the way he would have wished, independently, without needing anyone's care.

Introduction

In recent years there has been considerable interest in the role of carers in social care provision. Research studies, the carers' movement, social policy developments such as community care, and legislation resulting in specific responsibilities for local authorities have all contributed to new ways of working with carers.

These approaches are reflected in two main ways:

- The work of individual practitioners in their relationships with carers through activities such as assessment, care planning, groupwork and individual support

- The work of managers within social care organisations in the development of strategies for carers such as involvement and consultation, information and improved service delivery.

This book is a guide for managers and practitioners, discussing the major developments in practice and service planning and suggesting approaches for future work. It is of relevance to workers who have an interest in carers from both statutory and independent organisations and to carers themselves. The first chapter discusses the background to the phenomenal rise in the profile of carers, setting this in the context of social policy, legislation, demographic trends and changes in society. In Chapter 2 the point is made that carers are not a homogenous group, rather the concept of the carer is an overall category about which some generalisations can be made, but within which there are many differences that practitioners need to take into account. Chapter 3 examines the impact of caring and suggests a framework for describing the support that carers require.

Chapters 4 to 9 examine a number of practical approaches to supporting carers, applying general theories of assessment, groupwork, stress management, problem solving and the like to working with carers. In many ways this has been a neglected area, and it is one which will undoubtedly be developed further as working with carers becomes increasingly prevalent. This section is designed to be of use to practitioners with varying levels of experience, from unqualified carer support workers to qualified social workers with extensive experience in social care, though not necessarily with carers.

The approaches in chapters 4 to 9 will generally apply to all groups of carers, particularly those from the largest group – people caring for older people who have an illness or disability. There are, however, groups of carers who have particular issues which need special consideration. Chapter 10 considers approaches to working with young carers, carers under 18 who may fall between the provision of adults' and children's services. Chapters 11 and 12 respectively examine ways of working with carers of people with mental health problems and parents of children with disabilities. Historically, these two areas have seen the greatest amount of interest in carers, and practice developments within them are accordingly more advanced. In some ways they can be taken as models for other areas of work with carers. The final section considers potential future developments in policy and practice.

There are a number of general points to be made about the approach of this book. Since its subject is carers, and in order to redress the strong emphasis on service users which has prevailed in social care, the approach taken has been to 'think carer'. If, at any stage, this seems as if the role or rights of service users are being ignored this is unintentional. My belief is that the rights of service users and carers are both important. Service users should always be the main focus of social care support, but the needs and role of carers must also be considered.

The importance of good housing, income and health service support is as essential for carers as it is for service users. This book emphasises multi-agency work throughout, however the focus is on social care support rather than that from other areas.

Of all the topics in social care, caring is the most universal; practitioners, policy makers and members of the general public may all become carers. In some situations, service users are also carers. Caring is not limited to a particular group of people, it can literally happen to anyone. As an only child with no extended family I have always been aware of the possibility that I may become a carer. When I started this book I had parents in their seventies for whom I was a helper. In the course of writing, my father, who suffered from glaucoma, died of a heart attack, days before going in for yet another eye operation. He died in the way many of us would wish, instantaneously without suffering. In many ways his death was a release; his eyesight was deteriorating rapidly and without sight he would have been completely helpless. As someone who was fiercely independent, undoubtedly he would have made a singularly intolerant person requiring care! My helper role to my mother has now increased. If I become a carer and need statutory services, I expect my knowledge and understanding should help me to achieve what I need; however I do not expect it to be easy!

I

Carers in Context

'My mother was a carer, she looked after dad who had multiple sclerosis for 15 years 'til he died. Of course in those days there was no such thing as being a carer, she just saw herself as his wife.' (A carer)

Although people have been looking after and caring for others throughout history, the term 'carer' was unknown until recent years. It was only in the late 1970s that it started to appear in social care literature, while its first dictionary entry was as late as 1984 (Pahl 1994). Once discovered, however, it has more than made up for its slow start by becoming a focus of great interest to social policy makers, researchers and practitioners. In this chapter we examine the rise of the concept of the carer and the main factors which have contributed to its development.

Defining the carer

The word 'carer' involves a number of levels of meaning. Most significantly it is a political term which unites carers into a group of people who have particular issues in common and who require some form of policy response. On a personal level it also provides an identity for individuals, giving them an additional role in society and membership of a wider group of people with similar concerns and needs. It has now passed into common usage in a number of significant areas, being accepted in the field of social policy where carers' issues have taken an increasingly prominent role. Similarly it is used by health and social care practitioners and by carers' groups and organisations. Sometimes the term 'informal carer' has been used to indicate the distinction between paid workers or those who undertake caring as part of organised voluntary work, and carers who support others because of connections of family or friendship. The carer is also now becoming increasingly well known within society as a whole. The term appears regularly in the media, carers are the subject of national and local charities, and businesses are interested in sponsoring these charities. In 1996, carers were one of the priority groups for funding from the British National Lottery.

However, there still remains a lack of clarity about the term and it has not completely passed into general use. A recent questionnaire about community care services asked respondents to identify themselves as service users, carers, or workers (Heron 1995). It was clear that a number of the people who ticked the box marked 'carer' were actually proprietors of independent sector residential and nursing homes. Similarly, there is a tendency to refer to support workers who are employed by private individuals to provide personal care as 'carers'. There is also a small number of books and articles on social care which still use 'carer' as a general term to encompass paid workers, volunteers and family members.

Conversely, a number of people who would be considered to be carers dislike the term and will not accept its being applied to them. This is often because they view caring as part of their responsibilities as spouse, parent or relative and do not want to be perceived as carers in addition to this role. In this case, people are generally objecting to the application of the term to themselves as individuals, rather than its use as a category to improve services for carers in general. Some people have also questioned the suitability of the term because of its emotional content. Being a carer implies that an individual 'cares' so if someone gives up being a carer there is a feeling that they may be perceived as no longer 'caring' for that person. Confusion about the term 'carer' has been exacerbated by the fact that, until recently, there has been a lack of clarity about exactly to whom it refers. However, it is important that the term becomes used in a standard way in order to promote consistency and so that the needs of carers remain high on the social care agenda.

The Carers (Recognition and Services) Act 1995 has gone some way to addressing these issues by providing a definition of a carer within the context of statutory provision of assessment of need. Under the terms of the Act, carers 'provide or intend to provide a substantial amount of care on a regular basis' (Department of Health 1996a, p.2). Carers may be adults, or children and young people under the age of 18. Parent carers who care for disabled children on a substantial and regular basis are also included. Carers do not have to be related to the person they care for, nor do they have to be living with them. Volunteers working for an organisation are excluded from the definition, as is anyone who receives any form of payment for providing help.

The definition in the Act is generally helpful, in that it provides some clarification on who would be included within the concept of carer. Its focus is upon carers who have a major commitment to care as opposed to those who have been defined as 'helpers' – people who provide some limited support. The role of young carers – children or young people under 18 who provide care – is specifically recognised, thus raising the profile of the young carer. Guidance to the Act (Doh 1996a; b)acknowledges the fact that while many parents of children with disabilities would regard themselves primarily as parents rather than carers, their needs may be similar to those of other carers. Although all forms of parenting involve substantial and regular care, this will generally decrease as children become older and more independent. Parents of children with severe disabilities are likely to be involved in providing care for a much longer period of time, if not indefinitely. In addition to parents, siblings of disabled children may also be considered as having a caring role.

However, the Act cannot be regarded as providing a comprehensive definition, since 'substantial' and 'regular' are not further defined and are left for interpretation 'in their everyday sense' (Department of Health 1996a, p.4). Local authorities who have a duty to implement the Act will therefore need to establish their own criteria on who is to qualify as a carer. To this end, 20 hours per week is often quoted as indicating that someone is providing substantial and regular care (Social Services Inspectorate 1995a). In fairness to the legislation, it is difficult to see how a definition could have been more specific without arbitrarily excluding some carers who need support and including others whose needs may not be so great. Similarly, some flexibility is required in order that carers of people with mental health problems or people experiencing drugs or alcohol problems, who may not provide substantial and regular care but who nevertheless have a great supervisory responsibility, will be included.

A profile of carers

Based on figures from the 1990 General Household Survey, there are around 6.8 million carers in Britain which amounts to approximately ten per cent of the population. It is estimated that 15 per cent of all adults have some caring responsibilities. Of these, the majority are 'helpers', but approximately 1.6 million people care for more than 20 hours per week and would be likely to fall into the category of providing substantial and regular care. Some are caring for over 100 hours per week (Office of Population Censuses and Surveys (OPCS) 1992). Similarly, almost 1.3 million people provide personal care, the type of care most associated with high dependency (Parker and Lawton 1994).

These are obviously not inconsiderable figures and indicate the extent of support offered to people in the community by carers. An earlier survey indicated that around 20 per cent of households involved a carer. Furthermore a fifth of all carers had been involved in long-term care for the same person for ten or more years. The majority of carers are women (Green 1988). Generally both policy makers and practitioners are mainly concerned with people who are heavily involved in caring on a long-term basis. These individuals will be most likely to have reached the stage of requesting support and of meeting increasingly tight eligibility criteria for services. The numbers of substantial carers appear to be increasing, especially older carers and women looking after older people who are experiencing confusion or have mental health problems (Parker and Lawton 1994).

One of the major reasons for these increases, and indeed one of the most crucial issues in social policy at this time, is the demographic trend towards an ageing population. There are approximately 6.5 million people over 70 in Britain and the figure is set to rise to ten million in the next millennium. Similarly the numbers of those over 85 has risen by 46 per cent (OPCS 1987). It is this latter group which has the highest requirements for social and medical care. In fact it is estimated that 41 per cent of people over 85 need support in basic living tasks (OPCS 1982). Older people constitute the main group who require the support of carers and, moreover, a large number of carers are themselves older people. Based on figures from the 1985 General Household Survey, of those providing care for more than 20 hours per week, 26 per cent were over 65 (Green 1988). It is obvious that many carers will themselves come to need services to continue with their caring tasks and even to maintain their own independence.

A similar situation exists in relation to parents of adults with severe physical or learning disabilities who have not been able to live independently, but due to medical advances are now able to live for years longer than would have been expected. Many such carers are now becoming elderly and need support to continue to care for their children. While the numbers of such carers are far fewer than those involved with older people, nevertheless their needs are having a significant effect on required resources. The situation, then, is that from a relatively stable population, the numbers of carers requiring support is increasing and will continue to do so. For many western countries this trend is set to continue well into the next millennium.

Carers in social policy

While demographic trends are important factors contributing to the high profile of carers, it is the international move towards care in the community which has been the major influence. Indeed, it is since community care developments accelerated in the 1980s that carers have risen from a marginal role to a place close to the top of the social care agenda. The NHS and Community Care Act 1990, which gave local authority social services departments the responsibility of assessing and financing people who require community care services, has proved a milestone for carers as well as users of services.

Carers and community care are inextricably linked. Short of massive state provision for all people who need care, it is only with the support of carers that many people are able to remain in the community. Realistically, in many cases community care could be relabelled 'carer care'. While policy documents are careful to include friends and neighbours as part of an individual's network of support, such people are rarely involved at the heavy end of caring. Friends may provide a sitting service, they may undertake errands or organise outings; but they are unlikely to be willing or able to provide 24-hour supervision for someone who is suicidally depressed or wash and toilet an adult with a physical disability on a daily basis.

If we examine recent legislation and policy documents, the growing emphasis on the needs of carers is clear. The NHS Act 1977 and the Local Government Act 1972 *allowed* the NHS and local authorities to provide support services for carers, such as information and support groups. But discretionary powers inevitably resulted in piecemeal provision which varied according to the enthusiasm of key personnel in local areas. For the first time, local authorities were *required* to take the ability of a carer to provide support into account when undertaking an assessment of disabled people under the Disabled Persons (Services, Consultation and Representation) Act 1986. However, the emphasis of this legislation was very much concerned with the rights of disabled people themselves; carers were still mainly regarded as an adjunct to the needs of service users, rather than having separate needs of their own.

It is not until the documents culminating in the NHS and Community Care Act 1990 that carers' needs come to the forefront of service provision. In the Griffiths Report (Griffiths 1988), which formed the basis of the Act, informal care from relatives and neighbours was seen as the first and most important level of community care. The White Paper *Caring for People* (Department of Health 1989) repeatedly emphasised the role of carers and indicated that supporting carers was a key responsibility for statutory service providers. Furthermore, the Act itself required local authorities to take into account the needs of carers when undertaking assessments. The move had now been made beyond providing information and support to carers, to regarding them as integral to service provision. At this time many local authority social services departments followed Department of Health Guidance and introduced carer assessments to accompany the community care assessments that they were obliged to undertake under the Act (Department of Health 1990).

Although undoubtedly a significant step forward for carers, many felt that the legislation did not go far enough in recognising the contribution of carers and addressing their needs. Social services departments have been almost universally criticised by carers' organisations for not informing carers of the availability of separate assessments and failing to take their needs into account, but since this was not a legal requirement, there was little organisations could do to improve this situation.

As an answer to these issues, the Carers (Recognition and Services) Act 1995 is extremely significant for carers in that, for the first time, they have legislation devoted specifically to their cause. In terms of recognition alone, this is a major advance. Originally a private member's bill, it had all-party support and eventually gained the agreement of the government to grant the parliamentary time to enable it pass into statute.

The main implications of the Act are that social services departments now have a *duty* to offer a separate assessment to carers and to reflect the results of this assessment in subsequent service provision. Thus the needs of carers must formally be taken into account in the assessment process. In many ways the Act is not ground-breaking, rather it makes mandatory the current practice of many social services departments. 'As many authorities already offer carers an assessment, the legislation in effect enshrines good practice into statute' (Department of Health 1996a, p.3). The fact that this is now a requirement means that it will be possible for carers and their organisations to challenge authorities if they are not taking the needs of carers into account.

The Act is also limited in two main ways, being confined to carers within the definition discussed earlier and to situations where people are eligible for an assessment under the NHS and Community Care Act, the Children Act 1989 or Section 2 of the Chronically Sick and Disabled Persons Act 1970. Thus it gives rights to carers who are most heavily involved in caring. While few would argue that this is where the highest levels of need lie, there is a concern that authorities will focus all their resources on these carers and neglect others who may well be the substantial carers of the future. This will confirm the experiences of many carers who state that once they are in the system, help and support are available – the problem is crossing the threshold into that system! As with other areas of social care, limited resources mean that preventative work takes on a lower priority.

Furthermore, while authorities are compelled to assess carers' needs this does not include any guarantee of services. A variety of legislation requires authorities to provide certain services for categories of people in need. Without a similar duty in relation to carers it is not difficult to imagine that people supported by carers will receive significantly less services than those who are not. This will not repeat the situation that existed some years ago when many organisations operated the policy that people with carers should not receive services. Rather it will be with regret that, where resources are limited, the principle of managing risk will always mean that people living with carers are less vulnerable than those on their own.

Probably most carers and their proponents would regard the Act as a good start, but in a race which still has a long way to go. In the words of the Carers National Association:

> The Carers Act is an extremely important brick in the wall of rights which is gradually being built up for carers, but it is against a background of 'eligibility criteria', charging for services, more demands for services and less cash to provide them. (Carers National Association 1994/95)

Tensions in social policy

Community care is a policy which creaks and groans in a number of areas and the role of carers is not the least of these. An important area which needs to be clarified is that of the relative rights and responsibilities of carers, service users and the state. Currently, the balance between rights and responsibilities is constantly shifting under social and economic pressures both at the levels of national policy and of local social care practice. In most western countries, there appears to be tacit agreement between policy makers and citizens that caring is a personal responsibility belonging to the relatives of people in need. Carers have always cared and appear willing to continue to do so. At the same time, there has been increasing recognition that they also require support, and that the state is obliged to take on responsibility to provide care in certain circumstances. Just what these circumstances are is less than clear and appears largely based upon economic variables.

For instance, until the NHS and Community Care Act (1990), carers and users were able to access private residential or nursing home care, with comparative ease. When social services departments took on the responsibility for assessing need and *paying for the care*, local eligibility criteria immediately limited the numbers of people able to access these services. Of course, few people would agree with the indiscriminate use of residential care, indeed some would go further and say that, in some cases, carers using residential or nursing home care for unwilling relatives could be a form of abuse (Pritchard 1995). However this development had a strong economic significance as a method of controlling escalating central government spending by giving the responsibility for residential and nursing home placements to local authorities.

The use of residential accommodation by carers for respite care has also been curtailed by the legislation. In a Carers National Association survey of the effects of community care, 45 per cent of the sample believed that access to residential or nursing home care was more difficult than before the legislation was passed (Warner 1994). So while carers' legal rights have undoubtedly been strengthened, the gate-keeping role of social services for access to services has also been increased. Basically, the situation is that if an individual requires state support then the decision as to whether they will receive that service is made by a representative of the state. In order to maintain the balance of power in such situations, formal complaints procedures have been made mandatory so that workers are clearly accountable for their decisions. However, significantly, reports consistently indicate that many carers are not being informed about the availability of complaints procedures (Warner 1994, 1995; Social Services Inspectorate 1995a).

There have been a number of attempts to calculate the amount that it would cost the state to care for people in the community if carers did not take on this role. Currently this is thought to be over £30 billion a year (Nuttall *et al.* 1993). This is used as an argument for a number of measures to compensate carers for what they do. The main thrust of campaigning organisations is to gain increasing recognition for carers and to win practical support, such as improved finances and services. Their rationale is that carers are in fact saving the state money. However, interestingly, this argument depends on the perception of the relative responsibilities between carer and state. In contrast to Britain, some countries require people to provide support to relatives in need. For instance, in France there is the '*obligation alimentaire*' in which relatives with sufficient resources have a duty to provide for those who require support. Currently this obligation is most often called upon for the funding of older people in residential care (Twigg and Grand 1996). Children in Belgium and Italy also have an ultimate responsibility for the care of their parents (Help the Aged 1995). In Germany the principle of 'subsidiarity' requires people needing care to demonstrate that they have tried unsuccessfully to gain help from their family before applying for state care (Jamieson and Illsley 1990).

So while one option for central government might be to increase state support for carers, it is also not inconceivable that an alternative could be to formalise some of the responsibilities of carers. There are a number of social trends which are likely to put increasing pressure on community services and this might affect the balance of responsibilities. For instance, the increasing divorce rate and the move to smaller nuclear families are likely to have an effect on the numbers of people available to be carers, once the participants in these changes reach the age of requiring care.

And what of the relative rights and responsibilities between users and carers? Does an adult child have a responsibility to care for a parent? If so, what is the extent of that responsibility and would it alter, if, say, the child was now bringing up their own family? There are also the well-documented tensions that arise between the need a carer has for a break and the preferences of the service user. Does the carer have a right to respite or does the user have a right to remain within their home? Similarly, a user residing with a carer may prefer to have personal care undertaken by a paid worker rather than a son or daughter. Would this be accepted by care purchasers?

There are substantial tensions between the relative rights and responsibilities of all parties involved in the care of people in need. In all events, the role of the carer in relation to the state is certainly not a closed chapter, and changes are likely to occur in years to come.

Carers in social care practice

Just as the role of carers in relation to social policy has developed substantially, so the effects of this are being reflected in social care practice. Up to a few years ago, a review of practice in relation to carers would have resulted in a poor show of results. Lack of awareness, few specialist initiatives and an extreme lack of 'carer friendliness' in mainstream services would have been the findings in most areas. Even the prominence of the user empowerment movement was not particularly helpful towards the cause of carers. Although carers were sometimes included in this, often it was as if they were tacked on as an afterthought – as in 'user *and carer* involvement'. Carers Impact (described below) indicates how this made their task of developing carers' services in specific areas more difficult to achieve. 'A focus upon the user was built into the organisation of services at every level and permeated staff attitudes: as a result the needs and views of carers were marginalised.' One of the tasks of Carers Impact became to help agencies to 'think carer' (Unell 1996, p.7).

Today we have a very different picture; while the situation is certainly not ideal, all agencies have made significant progress in the above areas. There is awareness of the needs of carers, and recognition that they should have access both to core services and specialist support. Along the way a number of factors both signalled and contributed to these developments. Here we discuss some of the most significant.

A substantial body of research has accumulated around the area of carers, covering virtually all aspects of this area of work. These include analyses of General Household Surveys – the first to focus on carers took place in 1985; studies on the effects of caring; research into trends in caring; and evaluations of services for carers. The results of research indicate a consistent picture of the needs of carers which has been used by carers' groups, policy makers and practitioners alike.

A number of Department of Health-sponsored initiatives took place in selected areas to stimulate interest in and development of carers' issues in local authorities and health authorities, with results being disseminated throughout relevant agencies. The early 'Demonstration Districts for Informal Carers' was an evaluative project which had the aim of stimulating services for carers within the voluntary sector. Each of the areas involved appointed a multi-agency consortium and was allocated funding of £200,000 to develop services for carers. Forty-three new services were developed over the three areas including family support workers for carers of people suffering from schizophrenia, extension of hours of day centres, telephone advice lines, advocacy, carer centres, weekend clubs for children with disabilities and sitting services. The majority of services proved popular with carers, and 35 of the 43 were able to continue with local authority funding at the end of the project (Department of Health 1991). Accompanying this, the companion volume *Getting it Right for Carers* was an early attempt to give guidance on improving services for carers (Haffenden 1991).

The later Carers Impact experiment, managed by the Kings Fund, involved advisors supporting multi-agency steering groups in selected areas with the aims of creating a strategy for carers, promoting carer involvement, increasing awareness of carers in organisations and developing services for black carers. The overall context was to develop core services rather than specialist developments such as newsletters. The evaluation of this project indicated some positive developments such as increased awareness, improved involvement of carers in planning, better collaborative work between agencies and some measurable service developments. It also encountered a number of problems, such as poor relationships between Health and Social Services and confusion about the remit of Carers Impact (Unell 1996).

Between 1994 and 1995, the Social Services Inspectorate undertook a national inspection of a selection of local authorities to determine how they were implementing *Caring for People* (Department of Health 1989) in relation to supporting carers. The inspection focused on issues such as involvement and consultation, assessment and care planning, services, support and information. The Inspection Reports (Social Services Inspectorate 1995a, 1995b, 1995c) indicated that all the authorities had developed their services and planning arrangements to take into account the needs of carers, but this differed widely between areas. Some, for instance, had a clear planning strategy while others had allowed developments to occur on an *ad hoc* basis. A number of recommendations for policy and practice were made, including: the importance of a written strategy on support for carers; the need to develop criteria for carers' assessments and the involvement of carers in planning mechanisms.

The Carers National Association have carried out regular surveys into the effects of the Community Care Act, looking at information, assessment, services and charging policies (Warner 1994; 1995). Overall the majority of carers in the surveys appear to indicate that community care has either made no difference to the services they receive or the situation has actually deteriorated.

In terms of social care support for carers at the level of individual practitioners, there are considerable differences in development between different areas corresponding to service user groups. For instance, work with families of people with mental health problems and parents of children with disabilities is advanced both in research and practice developments, with a variety of well-documented methods of supportive intervention. In contrast, approaches to working with other groups of carers and carers in general are much less developed, focusing around issues such as self-help groups. With the continuing raised profile of carers, this area is likely to see continuing development, particularly in light of the emphasis on carers' assessments.

Carers speaking out

Finally, one of the most significant developments for carers in recent years has been the emergence of a campaigning arm, which has proved extremely effective in raising the profile of carers. The large numbers of different organisations representing people with physical disabilities has often been cited as a reason why disabled people's issues have not figured more prominently on social and political agendas. However, although carers are in many ways an equally diverse category involved in supporting carers of all the service user groups, they have achieved sufficient unity for a national voice.

In Britain the Carers National Association (CNA) is the most prominent national organisation with a remit to develop policy and service for all carers. Sir Roy Griffiths, in the foreword to *Community Care: Just a Fairy Tale* (Warner 1994), emphasised the role of the CNA in promoting recognition for carers. This was a prophecy of things to come, since, in association with other organisations such as the Alzheimer's Disease Society, the CNA were responsible for initiating and promoting the Carers Act through lobbying and campaigning. They were also involved in negotiations about the content of the Act. For instance, it appears that the government believed initially that the needs of young carers and parent carers were covered by the Children's Act of 1989 and therefore did not need to be included (Carers National Association 1994).

While carers are speaking out on a national level, it is important not to forget that a similar move is taking place in local areas, where carers and their organisations are increasingly involved in the planning and development of services. Including carers in this way is becoming standard practice within social care agencies. Carers are involved on an individual basis in decisions made about the support for the people they care for and they are also consulted as a group in terms of the planning and delivery of services. Methods of involving carers at all levels of service delivery are increasingly important for managers and practitioners and are discussed in Chapter 9.

In addition to the carers' movements, it is worth mentioning that another group have had a prominent role in providing a critique of community care and the role of carers within this policy. Feminist writers, basing their theories on the fact that the majority of carers are women, have contended that community care is a way of exploiting women as a massive source of unpaid labour, condemned to poverty through their caring role.

To some extent there is a shared vision between carers organisations and feminists. Certainly there would seem to be general agreement that carers should not be compelled to care if they do not wish to do so and that, as a group, they require adequate financial recognition for what they do. However, in recent years, feminists, particularly those with the more extreme solutions, have fallen foul of other women's groups and carers. One of the most telling criticisms is that such writers are so aligned with the carers point of view that they are acting in a discriminatory manner against service users, many of whom are also women. The proposal by some feminists that residential care is a positive alternative to enable carers to be free of the burden of caring is unlikely to be embraced by the people who would be on the receiving end of this policy, nor indeed by most carers. Similarly there is a feeling that carers who enjoy what they do should be valued rather than undermined. It has also been pointed out that while women do indeed form the majority of carers, the number of male carers is hardly insubstantial (Morris 1993).

As we have seen, one of the most far-reaching aims of carers' groups is in the area of carers' rights: specifically, to achieve practical benefits for carers. To summarise these briefly, they consist of rights to an adequate income and rights to services, both of which would have substantial financial implications if adopted. In terms of income, organisations are looking for a method of compensating carers for the work they undertake, and ensuring that caring does not lead them into poverty. For instance, Caring Costs (1994), a campaign organised by the Caring Costs Alliance which is made up of over 40 leading voluntary organisations, suggests an income policy for carers which gives both carers and people they support sufficient income, related to national average earnings, so that they are not dependent on each other's benefits and so that carers are compensated for loss of earnings. In addition, the campaign advocates improved conditions for carers who are able to work, such as statutory opportunities for job share, time off for caring responsibilities, and flexitime arrangements. Another suggestion relating to income involves an insurance scheme linked to benefits for carers which would enable them to contribute towards a pension fund.

In relation to services, there are calls for certain services to be allocated to carers as of right and free of charge, including a guaranteed break each year, and an allocated hourly amount of respite during the week. These aims must be regarded as long-term in nature, since they do not conform to the overwhelming majority of British social care policy which seldom gives people rights to specific services and rarely stipulates the level or amount of services to be provided.

Conclusion

Within twenty years the concept of the carer has developed to become a key area in health and social care. One interpretation of this is that carers have now become one of the main 'service user groups.' Since the days of the Poor Law when individuals requiring state care were classified by the authorities under categories such as paupers and mental defectives, grouping people together in relation to common need has always been useful to policy makers and practitioners. The main groups in current use within adult social care include: older people, people with mental health problems, people with learning disabilities and people with physical disabilities. Carers are a common denominator running through all these groups and now have a separate identity of their own. Research into carers' issues continues at a great pace, and for every research finding and policy development, practitioners are required to adjust and develop the way they approach their everyday work. In the chapters that follow we will examine the main professional issues that people working with carers need to consider and build into their practice.

2

Carers are...

'Carers have got quite enough to do looking after the person they care for, without being involved in planning services.' (A carer's representative)

Generalised statements about carers are not uncommon in both carers' literature and in everyday social care practice. As we have seen, in one respect this is a positive development, indicating that carers are gaining increasing recognition as a group who have distinct care needs. On the other hand, there is a danger that carers' individual needs will be overlooked in a mass approach to carers as a homogeneous group. It is generally useful to scrutinise statements which begin 'carers are...' or 'carers like...' and ask the question: does this really apply to all carers? If so, on what evidence is this based? If not, does it apply to a significant number or does it need to be amended so that it more meaningfully reflects the situation?

For instance, the statement 'carers are fed up with questionnaires' may be an accurate reflection of what a number of carers have indicated. But if we take this at face value there is the danger that this can be used as a reason not to undertake consultation. By examining the situation in more depth we may find a number of important variables: perhaps we need to change our methods of consultation; perhaps we ought to ensure we give feedback on questionnaires; it may be that a quiet majority of carers are prepared to continue with questionnaires and that the statement is not representative; possibly the group we are consulting with is exhausted and we need to find a larger catchment; or finally, indeed, carers are saying 'don't ask us anything else!'.

Practitioners will be aware that carers may have only one thing in common – the fact that they are providing support for another person. How they approach this care, the impact on their lives, the relationship with the person they care for and many other factors will all differ between individual carers. At the same time there are a number of themes which consistently occur and which can be used to categorise carers in terms of shared needs. This chapter will examine a number of these themes which can be taken into account when assessing the needs of individual carers and for overall planning of services. It is important that workers achieve a balance between taking account of trends which apply to large numbers of carers and maintaining an individual approach in which specific needs can be addressed.

Family relationship

The family relationship between carer and cared for can have implications which practitioners will need to consider. Approximately four out of five carers will be family members (Green 1988). Most commonly, they will be spouses, adult children or parents, but they may also be young children, siblings, extended family, daughters-in-law or close friends. It is generally the case that the closer the kin relationship the greater the sense of responsibility for looking after the person, and the greater the public expectation that this will take place.

Partners or spouses

Spouses are generally the largest group of carers, mainly made up of people caring for older people, people with a disability and people with a mental health problem. The nature of a partnership, in particular marriage, is that a contract has been established between the two people with a commitment to help each other throughout all life's circumstances. Spouses usually take on the caring role automatically and may have less ambivalence towards this than other relatives, especially where there was a positive emotional relationship prior to the need for care. In many situations there may have been an assumption that at some stage, the relationship would involve caring. At the same time the pressure of expectations can lead to a great deal of personal stress for the carer. Spouses can feel a huge obligation to continue to care, throughout the most difficult circumstances. This is particularly acute where the relationship had underlying difficulties prior to taking on a caring aspect. While some marital relationships involving carers break down, research into whether there is a higher level of marital split in relationships where one partner is a carer has proved inconclusive. However, it certainly does not appear that the rate is any lower than for the population as a whole.

In terms of the types of care undertaken, spouses will often be involved in a range of activities including the most intimate care tasks such as toileting, bathing and nursing tasks. The physical aspect of partnerships induces a general acceptance by carers and workers that all these tasks are appropriate. Practitioners need to be mindful, however, that this might not always be the choice of the people involved, and that wherever possible this should be taken into account.

Parents

While parent carers may be fewer in numbers than those who are spouses, there is an even stronger expectation that they will care for their children with special needs, due to the general acceptance that parents should look after their children.

Parents may become carers if their child is born with a disability, or if they become disabled later in life through illness or accident and have not yet established their own nuclear family. Parents are also likely to be involved in physical care tasks, since this is an expectation of the usual parent–child relationship. The significant difference is, of course, that the care for a non-disabled child will decrease as the child becomes more independent and is able to undertake more tasks for themselves, while this may not be the case for children with disabilities. As they become older, the aspect of physical care becomes more problematic, and this is especially the case for people who have become disabled as adults. Intimate, physical care is part of the relationship between young children and their parents, and indicates helplessness and dependency. It can therefore be inappropriate for adults wishing to gain or regain independence. Practitioners will need to listen to the views of the user and wherever possible arrange for independent care.

Children

Adult children who provide care for their older relatives form another significant group of carers. In this case, however, while there is still a strong cultural emphasis on responsibility to provide care, this may be regarded as less unconditional than for the two groups cited above. For example, a study of approximately 1000 adults in the north west of England indicated that while adult children were still expected to care for their parents, the perceived obligation was considerably less if the children had their own family responsibilities and where they were requested to provide financial help for non-essential tasks (Finch and Mason 1993). Contributing to their parent's personal care is likely to be a new experience for adult children and their parents and may not be comfortable for either party. Practitioners need to be aware of this and enable families to discuss any problems this involves; wherever possible alternative sources of care should be provided.

The expectations that certain people have a responsibility to provide care has implications for practitioners. Both workers and carers must be particularly vigilant that carers with a close kin relationship are not considered as able to cope with more than other carers. Being married does not mean that an individual can lift a heavier weight than someone who is an in-law, nor is a parent carer less likely to suffer from stress or need less time out. In assessing for need for services the assessment should be based on extent of need, without judgement about the extent of an individual's 'obligation'. This attitude needs to be present both in individual workers and in the organisation as a whole. If this is not the case then resources may be directed towards carers who have less need, while those with greater needs are passed over.

Gender

Gender in relation to caring is an area which has aroused a great deal of interest. Research has focused on the ratio of female to male carers and how issues of gender affect the way in which people accept the carer role. It has also been targeted at gender in relation to access to services. Most studies indicate that there are higher proportions of women carers. Figures from the General Household Survey in 1990 indicate an approximate ratio of 57 per cent women to 43 per cent men (OPCS 1992). However, while the figures for male carers may appear high, there are substantially more women at the heavy end of caring, undertaking personal care, while men tend to be more involved in practical support (Parker and Lawton 1994).

The reasons for this imbalance are a complicated interplay of historical, social and psychological factors which are difficult to separate. Traditionally women, with their nurturing child-rearing role, have taken on tasks of caring for other family members, particularly elders, when this was required. To a large extent the assumptions about this role continue and in addition to external pressure from family and friends, women may internalise these demands so that the expectation to care can become connected with their own sense of identity and self-worth. Of course this is not to say that women become carers simply because of pressures they are under. As with any carer, motivation to care usually involves a combination of duty, regard for the person in need and personal satisfaction – the relative proportions of which will vary with individual carers and their relationship with the person they care for.

Practitioners need to be aware that, because of the mixture of social and personal expectation, women often experience guilt if they are finding difficulties in coping. They may also be reluctant to ask for help, perceiving this as a sign that they have let the person down. Such factors can be especially strong within cultures which reinforce the woman's role as care giver. At the same time it is not uncommon for women to have considerable feelings of resentment and anger about being a carer. Sometimes they have taken on the role unquestioningly, then, as its effects on their lives become more marked, they become increasingly trapped and helpless. Feelings of frustration often concern the restrictions that they experience. These can include inability to pursue a career, conflicting demands from other family members and lack of time for themselves.

It can be useful for practitioners to explore how much informed choice went into the decision to take on caring. In a study of co-resident daughters who were carers, the majority of women drifted into care, with few consciously coming to a decision to take this on (Lewis and Meredith 1988). A similar situation can occur when an elderly relative comes to live in the home of a daughter, or daughter-in-law. Here there will have been more of a conscious decision for this move to take place, but this may not have involved an informed choice: sometimes a woman will be the only person available to care; on occasion she may be the most logical choice; but often she becomes a carer when there are a number of other options that are simply not considered. Practitioners can take women back to the point at which they began to be engaged in caring and explore the processes that were happening at that time, with a view to re-evaluating their current role and examining solutions to improve their situation. For instance, sometimes the person requiring care is part of a larger network of potential carers, but the care focuses on one woman.

Example

Lorna is a single woman caring at home for her mother who has advanced dementia. Lorna has a part-time job, corresponding to the time when her mother attends a day centre. Apart from the time she spends at work, Lorna gets no relief from looking after her mother. Her social activities are focused on the home — her boyfriend comes round at weekends and occasionally other friends will visit. She finds this quite stressful as she is never quite sure how her mother is going to react with people she does not know, and fears people will be embarrassed by 'strange' behaviour.

Lorna's brother Keith lives a few miles away with his wife and children. Keith's contact with his mother is not great; although he pops in for regular visits these are not planned in advance and may last as little as ten minutes. Lorna is annoyed by the fact that their mother usually recognises Keith and sometimes knows his name, whereas she does not recognise Lorna. She also complains that Keith offers no help and that on the few occasions she has asked him to sit for their mother so she can go out, he has been totally unreliable.

Keith feels that Lorna needs to get out more. She is spending too much time at home and thinks she is the only person who can do anything right. He says that he is always willing to look after their mother, but Lorna puts obstacles in his way. She criticises what he does and says her mother is more agitated when she gets back. He admits that a couple of times he was late turning up for a sitting session but this was because he had work or family commitments and he did explain this to his sister.

In this not untypical situation the main carer has invested considerable energy into her relationship with her mother. She has ambivalence about leaving the house for social reasons, and about leaving her brother to cope. Her lack of confidence in his ability to care appears to be fuelled by feelings of resentment about his commitment to caring. In his turn, Keith may have used Lorna's attitude as a means of keeping his role casual, and on his terms. To address this situation the worker was able to spend some time with Lorna working through her feelings towards her mother, her brother and being a carer. As a second stage, by improving communication between Lorna, Keith and his family, more regular periods of respite care were organised. Although this was not in any sense shared caring, there was some redistribution of caring responsibilities between sister and brother to an extent which was acceptable to both.

Although women remain in the majority as carers, the role of male carers is a significant issue which should not be neglected. Research indicates that the ratio of men to women in spouse carers is much closer than for other categories, with a number of studies indicating that the gender balance in this area is approximately equal. The imbalance appears in other categories: there are slightly more unmarried daughters caring for parents than sons, but significantly more married daughters (Arber and Gilbert 1993). This is confirmed in a Carers National Association study in which only one out of nine males were caring for parents or disabled children (Warner 1994). Similarly, it appears that, after a spouse, daughters are the preferred choice to take on the role of carer (Qureshi and Walker 1986).

On the other hand, it is important not to oversimplify issues of gender; in the study by Finch and Mason (1993) sons, rather than daughters, were the preferred choice to care for their fathers. Daughters were a significant second choice, but in the reverse situation of caring for their mothers, daughters were the preferred choice and sons were barely mentioned. From this, it seems that daughters are deemed suitable to care for either parent, while sons are seen as mainly appropriate to care for their fathers.

Some of the fiercest gender battles have been fought in the area of access to services. In relation to care in the home, early research indicated that services were more likely to be offered if a male carer was involved (Equal Opportunities Commission 1980). Interestingly though, research by Arber and Gilbert (1993) indicates that while the tendency to provide more support to male carers still exists, it appears to be a marginal imbalance. A more significant factor is the lack of support offered when an older person resides with their *married* children. Since the majority of those who care for their parents are daughters it could appear that some form of institutional sexism is at work. Many of these women will also have responsibilities in relation to child-rearing, household management and even employment; therefore it can be seen that they are facing substantial responsibilities. On the other hand, it is possible that other factors are operating; for instance, married women may be less inclined to request help from service providers or to value interventions by workers in their home. In a detailed analysis of the 1985 General Household Survey Parker and Lawton (1994) concluded that there was little evidence of discrimination against women, but again, services were less where carers were resident and where carers were relatives.

One interesting finding which suggests that it might be appropriate to target some resources at male carers, is that where men supporting older relatives with dementia received home care services, there was a reduced chance of the older person entering residential care. Where the carer was a woman the individual was unlikely to go into care regardless of whether the carer received home care support. The implication is that some male carers will benefit from the support offered by home care services in a way which some women may not (Levin, Sinclair and Gorbach 1989). Of course any such positive discrimination should be approached with extreme caution to ensure that the needs of women carers are not being neglected.

The area of gender in relation to carers is problematic, and organisations need to be careful that they have not built bias into their systems of service allocation, unless this is based on defined need and the wishes of carers. Practitioners also need to ensure that as individuals they are not being influenced by any personal ideas about women's role as carers or their ability to cope, particularly in relation to married women who undertake care. Conversely, organisations could benefit from examining services, particularly home support services, to ensure that they are operating in a way which is acceptable to women householders. From an organisational point of view, services should be monitored and analysed in relation to their levels of take-up to ensure that they are being allocated fairly in terms of individual need.

Residence

Whether the person needing care lives with the carer or separately is another issue to be considered. Where the carer and the person needing care live apart, the pressures on the carer may be both greater and less than in co-resident situations. While the carer may have more of a break from caring through living in another location, they may experience anxiety about the safety of their relative when they are not there, about conflicting demands from other family members who do not understand the amount of time they spend away from the family home, and about the time spent travelling between sites.

While only 25 per cent of carers overall live in the same household as the person needing care, this rises to 68 per cent for people who require personal care (Parker and Lawton 1994). Generally speaking, people needing care who live alone are likely to have lower levels of care needs than those who live with carers. At the same time, some research suggests that older people living alone receive substantially more services than those living with carers (Levin et al. 1989). There are likely to be a number of factors contributing to this situation: people living on their own are perceived as at greater risk by service providers and therefore will attract services; carers who are living with the person they are caring for may not wish for a higher level of service for a variety of reasons. But it still appears that there may be an imbalance in the way services are allocated, with an expectation that co-resident carers will take on higher levels of care.

When a member of an established family group who live together needs long-term care, there is a period of adjustment when family members come to terms with changes in relationships, roles and routines within the family. However, when the person needing care comes to live with the carer and, in some cases, their family, substantial adjustment will need to take place on both sides. There can be issues of territoriality, with other members feeling their private space has been invaded. Sometimes this may be a literal problem, as for instance a younger family member may be forced to share their bedroom with a sibling to make room for a grandparent. There may also be tensions as routines are altered to fit in with the caring tasks and as the person requiring care adjusts to living in an unfamiliar situation, having probably given up their own home. Obviously the level of tension will depend on factors such as whether the relationships between people involved are generally positive or negative, whether people are willing to compromise and whether the person requiring care exhibits challenging behaviour.

Support from practitioners at the time in which a move into the carer's home is being considered can be very beneficial. Sometimes both the carer and the person needing care have ambivalent feelings about this move, but this takes place in a way which is not talked through or planned. The role of the worker can be to discuss the benefits and counter indications of such a move, with all parties involved. This should mean that people are clear about the reasons for a move, which should never be carried out as a knee-jerk approach to a crisis or with an assumption that 'it's the right thing to do'. Certainly a move in which people have had a chance to consider the options, make an informed choice and discuss ways of overcoming potential problems is much more likely to be successful.

Age

Age has also been found to be a pertinent factor in relation to caring. The stage of life which an individual has reached will have an effect on their willingness and ability to be a carer. While the main group of carers are currently in the 43 – 64 age band (OPCS 1990), there has been a greater focus on both very young and older carers, groups which are viewed as needing particular support (young carers are considered separately in chapter 10).

Older carers

Older carers can loosely be defined as people who are 70 years old plus. Often they will be caring for spouses of a similar age, sometimes for middle-aged children. From a practical and emotional point of view people in this age-group often find it easier to take on a caring role. This can be attributed to the fact that they are at a time of life when they may have less commitments, when there is an expectation of illness or disability in the lives of their contemporaries and there is no requirement to earn a living. At the same time there may be great concern about what will happen to the person they care for if they themselves become unable to care through illness or death.

The ageing population of carers is a significant factor for organisations planning service provision, since extra resources will be needed to take over the care previously provided by the carer. The ethos of the organisation needs to be such that practitioners involved with older carers are mindful not only of any support which individuals may need in order to continue in their role as carer, but also of assistance which the person may require in their own right. Particular sensitivity is often required when long-term carers start to lose their ability to fulfil a role which has been integral to their sense of identity for many years. Carers may find it particularly difficult to accept that they need to reduce their input, even to receive care themselves. Ideally, it will have been possible for a worker to discuss these issues with the carer and the person they care for and to plan for this event. It will also be increasingly necessary that practitioners look for creative solutions to benefit both parties when caring is breaking down.

Example

Jean, 88 years old, had cared for her son Tony on her own since the death of her husband ten years previously. Tony himself was 60 years old and had learning disabilities which meant he required help with dressing, washing and getting ready for bed. The extent of Jean's involvement with services had been that Tony attended a day centre three days a week. Jean was suffering from arthritis which made it increasingly difficult to get Tony dressed ready for the centre. Jean resisted the suggestion of a home support worker vigorously, disliking the idea of a stranger coming into her house. However, eventually she accepted that she had little alternative and agreed to the service. As Jean's mobility decreased, the work of the support worker was extended to some personal care tasks for herself. This situation was handled sensitively and Jean maintained the lead role in caring for her son. Finally, since Jean had occasional periods of ill health due to physical exhaustion a system of respite was introduced in which both Jean and Tony were able to attend a residential unit together for fortnightly breaks. Both were satisfied with this arrangement and Jean's only worry was that they may not have two permanent vacancies within the establishment when she and her son needed permanent care.

Race

Carers from ethnic minority groups, particularly black carers, are likely to experience all the problems which white carers encounter but are also likely to be further disadvantaged in terms of accessing services and support. The reasons for this are many and complex and dependent on the circumstances of individual families and particular ethnic minority groups. They can however be summarised in the following way:

- Communication difficulties are a significant factor prohibiting people from knowing what support is available and how to access it. In many situations this is due to the fact that adult family members are unable to speak English to obtain relevant information. Studies consistently show that those least likely to be fluent in English are older people and women – those who are more likely to become involved in a caring role (Baker 1991). For example, approximately 70 per cent of first generation Chinese cannot speak or read English. Similarly, 60 per cent of carers in a study in Liverpool were unable to communicate in English (Wing Kwong and Kerrie 1992).

- Where language is not the primary obstacle, lack of familiarity with the culture and the mechanisms of accessing information can be equally detrimental. Low self-confidence and lack of trust in bureaucratic organisations may also prevent people from coming forward to seek help. Other factors may also be operating – some people who are legally resident in this country may still have doubts about their status and therefore will not contact services for fear of drawing attention to themselves. Some individuals may be from a culture in which self-help is a strong social norm and may struggle on through extremely difficult circumstances to the point of putting their own safety and that of the person they are caring for at risk. Others may be working long and unsociable hours which make it difficult to find out how to access services. Specifically in relation to carers, people from some ethnic minority groups may not have this concept in their language and culture, and therefore may find it hard to relate to.

- People from ethnic minority groups are likely to encounter discriminatory responses from workers and organisations. This can take the form of racial stereotyping, in which workers make incorrect and untested assumptions about people based on their views of a culture. A common assumption is that Asian carers receive support from their extended families and the wider community and therefore do not require support. Discrimination is also apparent in services which are not sensitive to cultural or religious needs and are therefore inappropriate for ethnic groups. In addition, black carers are likely to face racism in their everyday lives.

While there has been little extensive research into black carers, the small-scale studies which have taken place indicate that the numbers and patterns of these are likely to follow broadly similar patterns to the white population. For example, overall, the majority of carers are women. In the Liverpool study into Chinese carers, 75 per cent were women and over 50 per cent were over 65. Similarly, in relation to spouse carers, a study into the health needs of Afro-Caribbean elders indicated an almost equal split between male and female (Squires 1991). Black carers also tend to undertake the same range of caring tasks as white carers, and will care for similar lengths of time. Of course, there may be differences in relation to particular groups. In demographic terms, information from the 1991 census indicates that the proportion of black people above pensionable age is significantly less than the white population – 3.22 per cent as opposed to 16.80 per cent. However, numbers are increasing and it is likely that their health and social care needs may be greater than their white counterparts (Butt and Mirza 1996). Organisations need to consider local conditions before making decisions about resource allocation.

Many black carers will experience compounded disadvantages associated with not being able to access appropriate services, particularly benefits and social care or health support. Some will be living in poverty within poor housing conditions and will thus have burdens additional to their caring responsibilities. These issues will be explored in later chapters, with practical suggestions on how people from ethnic minority groups can access services more equitably.

Single carers, primary carers and shared caring

Studies of patterns of caring often indicate that it is common for one person to take on the main responsibility for the person needing care. The principal or primary carer is the person with whom professionals will liaise over the services to be provided for the service user. In some cases the primary carer is the spokesperson for other carers or family members. Sometimes the primary carer will be a *single carer* operating in isolation; perhaps an only child is caring for her parents, or a father is left to care for a child with physical disabilities following the death of his wife. For single carers there may literally be no one else with whom they can share the impact of care, since long-term caring is often an extremely isolating occupation which does not facilitate people to make and maintain social relationships.

The single carer takes on a role of great significance from the perspective of care workers. In many ways it can be easier to relate to one individual than to a family. They may be a point of focus, making it easier to share information. If there are different points of view, these will be between service user and carer rather than a complicated network of people with conflicting opinions. The single carer is also crucial in that if they are unable to care, the individual will require services, therefore there are clear benefits in enabling them to continue. From the carer's point of view there appear to be both positive and negative elements to being a single carer. Some recount that they prefer the clarity of role which accompanies total responsibility. They also indicate that there are no problems of arguments or disputes about responsibility which often occur when shared caring takes place. On the other hand there are problems involved in caring alone – the difficulties of isolation, stress and having no one with whom to share physical tasks or emotional concerns are likely to be much more acute for these carers, and might be areas which require the support of practitioners.

The level of support offered to primary carers from other family members will vary according to the nature of the family relationships. If the primary carer has taken over the role through choice and is sensitively and substantially supported by others, this is an ideal situation for caring. In this scenario families come together and work out, with the person needing care if at all possible, the relative responsibilities of all concerned. They then carry out these tasks, ensuring that the needs of the primary carer are met by providing reliable respite, holidays and sitting so that they have freedom to lead their own life. There is strong mutual support and little chance of the system breaking down. Unfortunately, as an ideal this is not always met in reality. In some situations, families can become factionised, arguing about who should do what and criticising individual's contributions. Chapter 7 indicates methods which practitioners can use to support families in working more closely together.

Situations in which care is shared between family members without there being a primary carer are less often encountered. An example of this would be older parents still living in their own home, supported by a number of their adult children and in-laws. As a system this has the same potential for success and difficulties as the model above. The advantage of shared caring when working well is that there is true acceptance of mutual responsibility so that no individual is left feeling that they are holding the responsibility alone. The disadvantage is that where one person does not have an overview there can be much greater potential for mistakes in organisation and for care not to be provided. Practitioners may have experienced crisis situations where a person needing support has been put at risk by family members each assuming it was another's turn to provide the care. Similarly, without a focal person it can be difficult for workers to engage the family in any coherent way since there may be many conflicting demands. In situations of shared caring, where the service user is unable to provide an overview of the situation, it can be useful for the worker to negotiate for a main contact person within the family.

The nature of the caring tasks

One obvious way of distinguishing between carers is the fact that they look after people with different needs. Carers may be involved in supporting people who have physical disabilities through birth, illness or accident; people with learning disabilities; people with mental health problems; people whose mental abilities have been affected by illness or injury; and people whose functioning is impaired through substance abuse. The nature of the disability of the person requiring care will obviously have great implications for the carer and the tasks they will need to undertake. While the image of a carer is often of someone who pushes a relative in their wheelchair or who provides personal care, in reality what they are required to do may be much more varied. Practitioners need to have a thorough understanding of what carers' responsibilities may be, so that they can make accurate assessments of need. Below are outlined some of the most significant tasks which carers may undertake.

Personal care

Personal care may encompass any or all of the following: help with washing, bathing, going to the toilet, cleaning teeth or dentures, cutting nails, hair care, skin care. There are degrees to all of these tasks. For instance, one person with disability may need minimal support, perhaps help with underclothes when going to the toilet; another may also need help with wiping; while someone who is severely confused may need constant prompting as well as physical help.

Health care

Competent relatives often carry out nursing tasks under the supervision of a qualified nursing practitioner. Thus they may be involved in the administration of medication, changing dressings, giving eye and ear drops, applying ointments and lotions and a wide range of other tasks.

Support with mobility

People may have mobility needs within the home, such as steadying or support to get from room to room, help to sit down or get up and help in and out of bed. They may also need help with turning while in bed to prevent pressure sores. Outside the home, people may require to be pushed in a wheelchair. Obviously the greater the physical demands on the carer the more they are liable to physical strain and other health problems.

Domestic tasks

Carers may have responsibility for all household tasks, from cooking and cleaning through to house maintenance and gardening. They will also need to undertake activities such as shopping or collecting pensions. If the person they are caring for has a mental disability the carer may become solely responsible for decisions about finances and other important issues in the family's future. Where the carer has other responsibilities – work, children or caring for other relatives – their responsibilities will be even greater.

Monitoring / supervising

A significant responsibility for some carers will be the amount of time they need to spend monitoring or supervising the person they care for. Again, this may involve different levels of input. Some people needing care will require periodic checking to find out whether they need anything or to ensure they have not fallen. Others may need supervision for the majority of the time – such as someone with severe dementia who is constantly at risk with household objects. In these cases, the carer will need to give repeated guidance and instruction. Some supervision will be regular but not daily, for instance the parent of someone with a learning disability living independently may spend time with them going over their finances. Supervision may involve a great deal of distress for the carer, such as when a person with a mental health problem is behaving in a bizarre or threatening fashion.

Spending time with the person needing care

Carers also spend significant amounts of time with the person needing care which do not involve any of the practical tasks described above, such as time spent listening, or undertaking leisure or social activities. Such activities may be part of a carer's responsibilities because they still involve caring tasks. The carer of a person with a mental health problem may spend time listening to their fears or worries; for the carer of a disabled person, going to see a film may involve ordering specialist transport, pushing the wheelchair and finding the disabled entrance to the cinema.

Rehabilitation

Finally, carers may also be involved in activities which contribute towards the person they care for's recovering, or gaining more independence. This may be under the guidance of a worker such as a speech therapist or psychiatrist, and can involve a diverse range of tasks, from helping someone who has had a stroke to regain some speech, or helping someone with a visual impairment to become more mobile, to carrying out a behavioural programme to encourage an autistic child to relate to others. Generally, this can be an aspect of care about which carers express satisfaction, particularly if they see that the person is making progress and where they have established a good relationship with practitioners which makes them feel involved, useful and 'part of a team'.

Phases and duration of care

A number of 'stage' models have been applied to carers, generally based upon the stages associated with bereavement or managing change. While stages should be viewed with some caution – people seldom follow these faithfully and chronologically – they can be useful for an overall framework in which to assess carers' needs and to suggest appropriate interventions. The most basic categories are the beginning, middle and end phases of caring. All carers will go through these phases, although obviously phases will be of a different duration for each individual carer.

The initial stage of caring is crucial for the carer. It is during this time that the need to care becomes obvious. Often this will be because of a sudden illness or disability of the person needing care, and the focus is completely on that person and their needs. People who experience disability are perceived as going through a number of emotional reactions at this time – confusion, denial, anger, grief, reluctant acceptance. Carers, especially those who have a strong emotional investment with the other person, are likely to share the feelings in this process. At the same time they may feel that they need to be strong to support the other person. Because of the emotional and social pressures operating at this stage carers may often take on the role without adequate consideration or planning. Support for the carer in terms of counselling, useful information and future planning can be helpful to ensure that they are, so far as possible, making informed choices, and are approaching caring with some understanding of what is involved.

The middle phase of caring can be of any duration, lasting from a number of weeks to decades. As people live longer, however, it is likely that people will also be caring for longer. It is during this time that carers adjust to their caring role, becoming familiar with the responsibilities involved and, ideally, having a good knowledge of where to access support and services. During this phase there is likely to be more acceptance of caring and the emotional aspects may become less acute. At the same time, there may be a number of life events which can precipitate the confusion and emotion of the first stage once again. A deterioration in the condition of the person being cared for; major changes such as moving house, bereavement or change of employment; illness in the carer – all these can cause a carer to re-evaluate their situation. It is during these times that carers need access to support and guidance.

Unless the person receiving care has recovered, the final stages of caring are likely to be as emotionally charged as the first. People stop being an active carer in a number of ways: they may die or the person they are caring for may die; the needs of the person requiring care may become too great to be coped with at home; or the carer may be unable to carry on caring, perhaps because of illness, other commitments or exhaustion. This can be a long, drawn-out process with a deterioration which can last months or even years. One common pattern is that increasing services are put into the situation and residential respite is used more and more until the transition to full care becomes complete. Alternatively it can be a sudden change due to an immediate deterioration or a crisis.

Unfortunately this is often the time in which carers can become neglected, while the attention focuses on the needs of the person requiring care. In reality, particularly where people have cared for a number of years, this transition can be a time of great upheaval and the carer's life can be turned upside down quite as much as when they began caring. While, in the long term, the majority of carers eventually experience relief at no longer having their responsibilities, in the short term they may be feeling lonely, guilty, and fearful. It can be helpful to contrast the life of a current carer with what happens when their responsibilities come to an end. The person they care for is constantly present, their time is almost fully taken up with tasks and they may be in contact with a number of practitioners – then everything stops.

Therefore it is important that the needs of carers at this stage are recognised. Ideally, they will receive support to enable them to express how they are feeling and to plan for what they are going to do in the future. Some organisations undertake specific interventions to support carers at this stage, such as courses or individual work to help them to review their time as a carer and to consider what to do next. Simple contact and interest is also very beneficial. The day centre worker or home support who telephones or visits to find out how the carer is doing will be highly appreciated.

Carers and professionals

As we shall see in later chapters, carers have definite views on how the workers they come into contact with should act! Here, however, the emphasis is on how workers may consider the role of the carer in relation to their own role and to the person requiring care. One useful distinction is that workers may regard carers as either co-workers, resources or co-clients (Twigg 1989). As a co-worker, the practitioner views the carer as someone with whom they can work to support the person requiring care. While carers may welcome a partnership approach, the danger is that their own needs may become overlooked. Workers who view carers as a resource will tend to focus on the tasks that the carer does in relation to the service user and again may lose sight of their needs, and may take their contribution for granted. As a co-client, carers are considered from the point of view of their own needs as well as that of the person they are looking after and the boundary between carer and cared for becomes less distinct. While this may be warranted when carers have substantial personal needs and require support and services in their own right, in other situations it can lead to problems of undervaluing the carer's role.

It is helpful for practitioners to undertake a self-evaluation exercise to determine how they view the role of carers. Possibly most workers do not have one simple way of regarding all carers, rather this varies according to individual circumstances. It is, however, important that workers are clear in their own minds about how they view carers, and that they adopt an approach which emphasises valuing their role, without losing sight of the fact that they may also require support. Of course, this distinction also operates at the level of organisation as a whole, in terms of how the role of carers is perceived, which may determine the resources allocated to carers' needs.

Checklist of considerations relating to distinctions between carers

- Factors which practitioners need to be aware of to ensure that services are allocated equitably and in relation to need include: the familial relationship between carer and person requiring care; the carer's age, sex, race, place of residence; whether the carer is caring alone or with help; the service user group of the person requiring support; the tasks the carer undertakes.

- What measures does the organisation have in place to support carers at the beginning, middle and end phases of care?

- How does the organisation perceive the role of the carer and is this reflected in service provision?

3

The Impact of Caring

'He asked me to help him with his homework and I said I was sorry I couldn't because I had to look after his grandad. He said he understood, but I don't think he should have to understand. He's losing out and so am I.' (A carer)

Anyone who provides care for another person will find that their life alters due to the responsibilities they have assumed, and those who give substantial and regular care are likely to experience great changes. Originating in the field of mental health, the term 'family burden' has been used to describe the effects of caring on the carer and their family (Grad and Sainsbury 1968). This is an emotive term which has been disputed by workers, carers and people who are cared for. In common usage, burden is a negative concept and in this context gives an image of someone being borne down by a heavy load, struggling against a dead weight. As such it does not encompass the positive experiences that can accompany caring. It also portrays the cared-for person as someone useless and unproductive and is therefore discriminatory.

Of course, this is not to deny that many carers experience great problems and limitations due to their role. Most practitioners come across carers when they are at the stage of requiring support so tend to be involved in situations at the heavier end of caring. However it is important that there is an acknowledgement that the caring role does not have an inevitable negative effect on people's lives. Rather it is complicated, with elements which can be constructive and positive as well as limiting. As an alternative, the term 'impact' can be used to give a more objective description (Perring, Twigg and Atkin 1990).

Although there is general agreement about the factors which impact on carers, there are a number of different methods of categorising these. A common division, again from the field of mental health, is that between subjective burden – the psychological effects of caring – and objective burden – practical difficulties such as loss of income or having to undertake additional household tasks. The difficulty of any categorisation is that factors are generally interconnected; practical problems result in emotional distress, while this in its turn makes it harder to cope with practicalities. Here, the impact on carers is examined from three perspectives which attempt to reflect the way carers themselves describe their concerns; these are *stress, limitations* and *emotional impact.* These categories should in no way be seen as independent but as interrelating elements which affect and reinforce each other. It is only by considering the range of ways in which caring can impact on people's lives that practitioners will gain understanding of how to support carers. Therefore the final part of this chapter builds on carers' experiences to suggest a framework of need which can be used as the basis for interventions to support carers.

Stress

Stress can be defined as a physiological and psychological state of arousal which occurs when an individual is subject to external or internal pressures. Physiological changes that can occur when someone is under stress include increased heart rate, faster breathing, and release of adrenaline into the bloodstream. Normally a state of stress would be a temporary event, rapidly followed by relaxation. However, people have the ability to remain in an almost constant state of arousal, either because they are faced by repeated stressful events, or because they have used their creative abilities to convince themselves that this is the case. On a psychological level, stress manifests in states such as anxiety, worry, depression and hopelessness and in behavioural terms this can result in irritability, being forgetful, being critical or being over-protective. Of course, most people experience some stress in their lives and carers do not have a monopoly on this. However the responsibilities of caring involve a significant number of potential stressors – life situations which can incline an individual to experience stress.

Overburden and burn-out

Caring may involve a real danger of overwork. Some carers are in full or part-time employment and when they return home move straight into their caring responsibilities. Others will not be able to undertake paid work because of the extent of their caring commitments: many carers work 14 hours a day, seven days a week; some are also disturbed in the night. Physical exhaustion can be a real problem for carers, especially if they are older people or not in good health. Some caring tasks, such as lifting someone who is heavy, pushing someone in a wheelchair and extra washing, all of which are undertaken day in day out, can be physically strenuous. Carers remark how sometimes, when workers become involved, they will insist on having two people to do activities such as lifting, while the untrained carer is expected to cope on her own. Besides physical exhaustion, carers who have to undertake a supervisory or monitoring role often experience mental strain due to having to be constantly alert to what the person they are caring for is doing.

The carer's workload will also increase if they have to take on the responsibilities which were once carried out by the person they care for. In some cases a carer may have to take on the roles of both parents in bringing up children as well as supporting their spouse. They may also have to deal with household finances or house maintenance. Sometimes this involves learning new skills at a time when the individual's energy is already stretched through caring.

Stress is believed to have an addictive quality due to the biochemical changes which occur when people are in this state; people who lead busy lives with high levels of responsibility can become accustomed to living in this way and find it difficult to let go of all the tasks they feel they need to accomplish. This phenomenon can be seen in carers who may be unable or unwilling to relax, take a break or ask for help. It can be difficult to tease out the factors which contribute to this situation. A sense of commitment to the individual, a feeling of duty and a need to be needed may all be significant. It may also be the case that some carers experience their main sense of self-worth from the caring role and feel lost without it. Practitioners will be aware of carers doggedly coping with extremely stressful situations where help is clearly needed. Some carers will refuse external support completely, others may accept it but will find reasons why it should not actually happen. For instance, they may refuse to let someone go into respite care even though this has been demonstrated to be flexible and will meet needs of the person they care for. Carers who fall into any of these categories may suffer from burn-out: a condition of physical or mental exhaustion, in which they are unable to continue caring – a condition not unfamiliar to health and social care workers!

Stressful relationships

Another significant stress factor in caring is the effect it can have on relationships between family members. This can become manifest in any number of ways. Common examples include: resentment from other family members about the time spent with the person needing care; lack of privacy; insufficient understanding of the nature of the illness; disagreements about the way to deliver care; and conflict about relative responsibilities. Such differences cause a background of disharmony which can adversely affect relationships in the family.

One of the most crucial elements in caring, and one which has a great impact on the levels of stress experienced by the carer, is the relationship between the carer and the person they care for. The potential tensions involved in being a carer and a dependant are substantial and will test a relationship even when this is based on affection and goodwill. Where a negative relationship is involved, these tensions can become insupportable. Although this book concentrates on the needs of carers, it is important not to forget that if the disability is recent the person being supported is likely to be experiencing severe distress. Whatever their disability they are likely to be facing permanent limitations to their lives. They may be trying to come to terms with a great sense of fear, anger, shattered hopes and frustration. In addition to this they have to adjust to a new relationship with the carer, one in which they have a dependent role. All of this can lead to considerable pressure.

The point is also often made that a bad-tempered, selfish young person does not become pleasant and considerate just because they have become older and now need care. People take their personality traits into the caring situation and it is unlikely, although not impossible, that this situation, fraught with potential stressors, will bring out the best in them. Occasionally and anecdotally one comes across an example where caring actually improves a relationship, as in the following situation.

Example

Gillian had always had a poor relationship with her husband's mother, Alice, whom she felt had all the characteristics of a stereotypical mother-in-law. Whenever Alice visited she criticised. The house was too warm or too cold. The meals were not nutritious – meat and two veg was better than all this rice and pasta. The children were badly behaved. Gillian dreaded the visits and when Alice had a stroke and could no longer live alone it was only a strong sense of duty which led her to agree to her coming to live with them. Initially the situation was as bad as she feared. Her mother-in-law complained constantly and Gillian's husband trod an uneasy line between them trying to keep the peace. He began to spend longer hours at work, which only fuelled Gillian's resentment. Then one day when she was helping Alice into her chair, as she sat down she said 'thank you, dear'. For the first time Gillian saw Alice as old, frail and defeated. From that moment her attitude to her mother-in-law changed. She felt herself becoming more sympathetic and patient while, in turn, Alice's criticisms reduced and she expressed appreciation for what Gillian did for her. Over time the two women became friends.

Health problems

A number of studies have indicated that caring can be bad for people's health. Information from the 1985 General Household Survey (GHS) indicated that 50 per cent of carers over 65 had a chronic illness, while 37 per cent of carers over 45 who provided more than 20 care hours a week had experienced a disabling illness in the past year (Green 1988). In contrast, Parker and Lawton (1994) in a secondary analysis of the GHS question the connection between caring and health problems and suggest that the effects may be due to the fact that the majority of carers are older people, and women who, statistically, already have poorer health. However studies which ask carers about their health consistently show that carers *believe* their health has been affected. One survey by the Carers

National Association indicated that 60 per cent of carers believed that their own health had suffered as a result of their responsibilities (Carers National Association 1992). Another showed that the main problems carers encounter are exhaustion, back troubles, sleep problems and depression (Lamb and Layzell 1995). Practitioners may encounter a range of health-related problems in carers, not simply in terms of illness but also physical disturbances such as eating problems or lack of sexual functioning.

Limitations

A sense of limitation and missed opportunities is often expressed by carers when they talk about their lives. For some people there is a feeling that their life has taken a different course from that which they would have chosen had they not had the responsibility of caring. For others the effects may be less far-reaching, but focus on the quality of their everyday lives and the restrictions caring imposes. Limitations may affect any sphere of life and often involve issues such as employment and career, finance, and opportunities for relationships, having children and social contacts.

Limitations on employment

A number of carers will not have had the opportunity to go to work, or will have had to give up working in order to care. People who would have preferred to work may experience a great amount of regret and dissatisfaction at not being able to pursue a career. This will be particularly acute if the caring role is not satisfying to the individual. There can be a sense of a life wasted or potential unfulfilled. In some circumstances there may be anger and resentment against the person they are caring for. Sometimes this is expressed openly, more often it surfaces as irritation and short temper, and sometimes it is only shared when the person being cared for has died or moves to permanent care.

> I gave up work in my forties to care for my wife who has what they call early-onset dementia. Eventually it was a choice – either she went into a home or I stayed at home and looked after her. I know I did the right thing, but sometimes I look at her and think about all that I gave up to care for someone who doesn't even recognise me any more. (A carer)

Where carers are able to work, this is generally limited by their caring responsibilities meaning that they can only undertake part-time work or restricted hours which are likely to be low paid. This means that carers are caught in a trap of being unable to afford to purchase relief care to enable them to have improved, more highly paid work options.

A survey by the Caring Costs Alliance (1996) of over 1000 'heavy end' carers gives graphic figures to illustrate these points. Over half the carers had had to give up their employment, while 20 per cent had reduced the time they worked. Twenty per cent of those unemployed said they had not started a career because of their caring responsibilities – these were mainly women. Of those working, nearly three-quarters indicated that their earnings had been substantially affected by their caring responsibilities, with a calculation of an annual lost income of £5625 per individual.

One particularly alarming finding was that half of those in work also spent over 100 hours per week on caring responsibilities. The levels of stress experienced by these individuals was considerable. Perhaps surprisingly, carers in the sample indicated that the biggest loss they had experienced from giving up employment was that of social contact with colleagues, which rated higher than financial considerations. This result is probably indication of the general loneliness and isolation of caring.

Limitations on finance

The financial effects of being a carer are now well documented through a number of studies. For instance, it has been estimated that a quarter of all carers live in poverty, a figure which increases to 40 per cent for carers above pensionable age (Evandrou 1990). Benefit systems often have the effect of making the carer dependent on the person they care for and the benefits they attract. Single carers living with the person needing care are especially likely to be unemployed, dependent on benefits and struggling financially (Glendinning 1992). Not only can there be poverty while the person is caring, but also, should they cease this role, they may find themselves with even greater problems. Many carers are unable to contribute to a pension or other insurance, therefore face old age with basic state provision. Some may have to sell assets, use savings and cash in insurance policies to afford to care for the person. Others, living in a property belonging to the person they care for may find themselves literally homeless if that person should die or need residential care.

A further problem is that not only can caring result in lower than average income, but it can also require additional expenditure. One study indicated that 87 per cent of carers incur extra costs through caring responsibilities, particularly with heating, laundry and adaptations (McLaughlin 1990). In addition the caring role may mean that hidden expenses are incurred. For instance, carers may not have transport and therefore may be dependent on higher prices of goods in local shops. A poverty trap is a very real issue for carers and the longer they take on the caring role the more they are likely to find it difficult to raise their standard of living. When their responsibilities come to an end, carers may find any experience and training they have had is out of date for the economic market. A DSS study showed that former carers aged 50 were much less likely to be in employment than people of the same age who had not been carers (McLaughlin 1990). Often their main work-related experience is as a carer, but although some carers opt for employment in the caring professions which may involve some transferable skills, this will certainly not be everyone's choice.

Limitations on relationships and social contact

A sense of isolation is consistently highlighted by carers as a limitation on their lives. This applies most acutely to single carers, but is also apparent to carers within a family setting. For single carers, isolation can have its basis as a practical problem. Those supplying substantial and regular care may have few opportunities to meet other people and engage in social activity. If they work, they are likely to have used up the respite time allocated by statutory agencies and the goodwill of friends or neighbours to help out during their working hours. If they do not work, but spend most of their time in the home, it may be even more difficult to break out and form social links.

Maintaining contacts with others can be difficult; friends who lack understanding become frustrated when the carer does not respond to their invitations or lets them down at the last minute. Sometimes carers themselves can contribute to this problem by not explaining the true situation to their friends and maintaining a facade that everything is running smoothly. Unless the carer is an extremely outgoing person who finds it easy to make and maintain contact with others they may find socialising increasingly difficult. Carers describe how this situation can creep up on them almost without them noticing it: 'I suddenly thought one day that I hadn't heard from any of my friends for well over six months. It occurred to me then that I wasn't sure whether I still had any friends' (A carer).

Social isolation can also be a problem for primary carers when the conflicting demands of their families and the cared-for person mean that their time is carefully allocated between the two groups, leaving little spare time for making contact with people outside the family boundaries. A related situation can occur when nuclear families are involved in sharing the care. Here, the family may operate an informal caring rota, enabling members to leave the home, but singly rather than together. This can have a particular effect on spouses who may find themselves growing apart and often may not realise this until the caring role is over.

Isolation, however, can go beyond the practical difficulties of socialising. Some carers manage to maintain a level of social contact but still experience a sense of being alone, since they are unable to talk to people about their situation. This is apparent where any carer does not have another person with whom to share the emotional impact of caring. It can also apply to a primary carer whose family does not engage with them on this issue, and even to families that share care if their communications skills are poor. The lack of someone with whom to talk about the experiences of caring can be an extremely stressful factor in a carer's life. Through not talking about the emotional impact of the situation, people may internalise feelings, possibly causing depression or severe anxiety.

However, finding someone to talk to can be a difficult task, especially for someone who may already be socially isolated, and there can also be problems for people who have a good social network. People do not want to talk about their situation in case they bore or annoy the other person. Also although there is often a *quid pro quo* on sharing emotional experiences, especially in close female relationships, carers may be wary about doing this because of the subject matter involved. It is one thing if your concerns are about the state of your marriage and perhaps another if you want to talk about incontinence pads or your son hearing messages through the television. Understanding is also an issue; there is a feeling that unless someone has been involved in caring they cannot really understand what the person is going through. Within families, where it could be expected that people would be able to empathise, there can be a tacit agreement to avoid the subject as much as possible.

> After the first year we never really talked about Simon. Not really *talked*. If he was going through a bad phase there was lots of grumbling, but generally we just got on with things. I think we all thought that if we talked about it, it would make things more real. As if they could have been any realer! (A carer)

An isolating effect that is often experienced by carers of people who have some form of mental dysfunction is the loss of a confiding relationship. If they are caring for a life partner, the very person who could have offered emotional support not only needs care, but may be unable to offer any support in return. In addition to taking on the caring role they are left without their normal sources of help in a situation where there are likely to be restrictions on finding suitable alternatives. Carers in such situations often cite personal loneliness as one of the most difficult aspects of their lives.

For other people, the caring role can mean that they literally do not get the opportunity to establish relationships with other people. This can mean that people who would have wanted to have a long-term partnership, or marriage and children are unable to fulfil these ambitions. Sometimes, even though the opportunity to marry may occur, carers feel that this is incompatible with their caring role and decide against making the change.

Finally, in terms of its effects on people's everyday lives, lack of spontaneity is often cited as a great limitation for carers. Carers indicate that they never have the luxury of deciding to do something on the spur of the moment. Going out involves a great deal of planning – arranging sitters, organising suitable transport, sorting out respite. There is rarely the opportunity to make an instant decision to go shopping or go for a swim. A small factor perhaps, and one shared by people bringing up small children – for carers, however there may be no end in sight.

The emotional effects of caring

The emotional impact of caring varies greatly between individuals. It depends on factors such as: personality of the carer; relationship between carer and cared-for; duration of the caring role; and ability of the carer to access and understand their feelings. There are, however, a number of repeated themes which emerge when carers speak about how the caring role makes them feel. Here we examine the emotional effects of caring through key words which carers often use to describe their circumstances.

Feeling trapped

A feeling of being 'trapped' is often expressed by carers. There is a sense of having no open doors in their lives, no option but to continue with a routine which offers little variety or hope. Unsurprisingly, creative drawing by carers often focuses on objects such as houses with thick, heavy walls, or small, dark rooms which give a shut-in feeling. Carers often speak about the repetition of their lives in which every day has a similar pattern and there is little to look forward to. There may be a very genuine feeling of having no alternatives or meaningful choices, because they could only obtain freedom through giving up caring which they are not prepared to do. In some situations the sense of being trapped can become a psychological condition in which there may be real options in their lives, but they are simply unable to perceive these. Practitioners may also observe how the sense of being trapped can be accompanied by a feeling of safety, when people long accustomed to their role may become threatened by the thought of stepping beyond it.

In extreme forms, the sense of being trapped can become depression and hopelessness. It can also give rise to a feeling of 'powerlessness' in which people lose confidence in themselves. This can make dealing with unfamiliar people or situations increasingly difficult. It certainly means that some carers may have difficulty in asserting themselves with workers from whom they are seeking support. This lack of self-esteem may become particularly telling at the end of a period of caring when people are seeking to re-orientate themselves into an 'ordinary' life but find they have difficulty coping with new demands. It can be easy for workers to view carers as extremely competent, coping people and overlook the fact that under the surface they may feel unsure and afraid.

Example

A home support worker was surprised to find an experienced, competent carer in a state of high anxiety about a questionnaire from the local health authority asking how they could improve their services to carers. The carer had pushed this into a drawer but was aware that the time limit for the questionnaire was nearly up. She had made several attempts to fill in the questions but was worried that she was not doing it right, that if she said the wrong things she might lose a service or get someone into trouble. The care worker was able to sit down with the carer, explain that the questionnaire would have no effect on any individual's service and that filling it in was completely voluntary. On request she helped the carer to fill in the questions.

Feelings of grief and loss

Feelings of grief and loss are prevalent amongst carers, and are particularly acute at the early and final stages of caring. Sadness can be related to many of the aspects of the caring role that have already been discussed. The basic fact that the person needing care is disabled in some way is the starting point for these feelings – it is hardly pleasant to see someone you love or care for facing such problems. A sense of loss is especially relevant in these circumstances. In the early stages of care especially, the carer as well as the person with a disability will experience loss of their previous way of living.

Feeling guilty

Of all the words which carers apply to how they feel about caring, 'guilt' is perhaps one of the most commonly encountered. Guilt can span a variety of contexts in caring. Carers often express feelings of 'not doing enough' even though to the outside world it may be difficult to understand how they could do any more. They may also feel uncomfortable at taking time out in a respite break, giving the reason that the person they are looking after cannot take a day off from their disability, or that they are the carer therefore they should be able to cope. Similarly, some carers doubt their own abilities as a carer and feel guilty that what they are doing is not good enough.

On another level, guilt is often associated with the actual condition of the person they are caring for. Especially if the relationship has been close, the carer may associate themselves with the cause of what happened to the individual. It is important to realise that even though the basis in reality may be extremely tenuous, the impact on carers is extremely real. There are many examples of self-blame: if a man has a stroke, his wife may blame herself for his diet, or for not getting him to relax more; the husband of a woman injured in an accident may feel he should have been driving the car; the mother of a disabled child may feel that the way she looked after herself during pregnancy may have contributed to this condition. Feelings of guilt will be stressful to the individual and almost certainly will affect their relationship with the person they care for and their ability to care.

Feeling angry

Of course, guilt is often only one side of an emotional coin which co-exists with feelings of anger and resentment. Practitioners will have encountered a number of carers, who, rather than directing negative feelings inwards, project anger outwards. Sometimes the anger is directed at the person they are caring for. If this anger is expressed this can lead to further feelings of guilt and a vicious circle of criticism and blame. In extreme circumstances anger can result in abuse of the person cared for. Anger can also be directed towards people or organisations outside the immediate family. For instance, a carer may become angry and intolerant towards workers or organisations providing care, which may be extremely hurtful if workers feel that they are giving their best but being criticised for it. With some carers things are less personal; they may be angry with society, the political system or with God for allowing the problem to occur.

Carers and abuse

There has been increasing recognition that some carers will be involved in the abuse of the person they care for, or conversely, may be abused themselves. Abuse can be divided into the following categories: physical, psychological, financial, sexual and neglect (Biggs, Phillipson and Kingston 1995). A definition of abuse of older people has been made by the Social Services Inspectorate: 'It may be intentional or unintentional or the result of neglect. It causes harm to the older person, either temporarily or over a period of time' (1993, p.3).

A useful distinction in the concept of abuse in relation to carers is that between actions which happen as a result of stress or lack of knowledge and those which involve intentional harm to another person. Any of the factors mentioned earlier in this chapter can contribute to levels in stress in carers which mean they may temporarily lose control. A BBC documentary ('Who Cares?') shown in 1989, based on the pioneering work of Mervyn Eastman in this field, showed carers who had lashed out at the person they care for and were subsequently overcome with horror and guilt about their behaviour. Often such reactions will be triggered by challenging behaviour, such as violence, aggression, or repetitive behaviour of people with dementia. Very often this can be addressed by giving carers appropriate support in terms of respite, counselling, home care or other interventions. Sometimes this might be the stage at which they need to consider having a temporary or permanent break from caring. Pritchard (1995, p.37) indicates five main factors which carers indicate 'pushed them over the edge' – the older person's behaviour, their caring tasks, frustration, isolation and lack of services and support. Carers who are ignorant of good practice in relation to caring for people may also cause them harm. Examples of this include tying relatives to chairs, keeping them in night clothes through the day to avoid dressing them, and not providing a stimulating environment for a child with learning disabilities. Again, such behaviour can often be amended by supporting the carer and helping them to improve their care practices.

Intentional abuse can range from relatively straightforward financial abuse in which a carer cashes their mother's pension and leaves her with insufficient food and heat, to more complex interpersonal situations.

Example

Susan had severe arthritis, was confined to a wheelchair and largely unable to use her hands. She was totally dependent on other people for self-care. Susan's husband, Roy, would ignore her requests to go to the toilet. When Susan was no longer able to hold her urine and soiled herself, Roy would leave her for hours, wet and uncomfortable. Roy would also leave the house with the television remote control out of her reach and with no drinks or food to hand. Roy was extremely unwilling to talk through these problems with a carers' worker, but eventually presented a picture of bitterness and resentment at having to work full-time as well as being a carer. His main anger, however, was that Susan's condition was hereditary and their daughter in her twenties was now showing signs of disability.

Similarly there will be ambiguous cases – is the family who use a child's mobility allowance in the family budget necessarily abusive? And what if they try to discourage her from moving into her own flat so they will not lose this benefit? There may be no easy answers in situations of abuse, and often people on the receiving end of abuse may be determined to take no action to change the *status quo*.

The other side of this is the fact that carers themselves can be the subject of abuse. Violent acts are not uncommon in people with dementia who may, for instance hit out with fists or walking stick. The corollary to carer stress can be service user stress – someone with a physical disability may become abusive because of the problems they face in everyday life. Both these situations may be helped by improved services and support to the service user and carer.

Again, abuse of carers may be intentional, such as the individual who constantly verbally abuses the carer or who misuses the family finance. While the caring role may imply power over another person, this is not necessarily the case, especially in relationships which have a history of violence or other forms of abuse. Members of severely dysfunctional families also become old and require care and the nature of the previous family relationships will influence the 'caring' in these families. Such families are generally the most difficult for practitioners to work with.

The practitioner's response to abuse is largely shaped by organisational procedures. With cases of child abuse there are the highly organised child protection procedures, and with older people most local authorities have introduced policies following the Social Services Inspectorate Guidelines (SSI 1993). At the same time there has been much less focus on abuse of vulnerable adults who are not above pensionable age; this is an area which needs to be addressed, particularly in terms of adults with learning disabilities and mental health problems. A further area for consideration is what action to take if the abused person is the carer – an aspect rarely covered by procedures.

All the above considerations point to the need for qualified and experienced workers to be involved in the assessment of individuals and their carers. In relation to carers it is important that responses to abuse focus wherever possible on support and education to amend behaviour. However, practitioners have a responsibility to safeguard vulnerable individuals, therefore they must be alert to signs of abuse, whether these be against the service user or the carer.

The positive side to care

Finally, to balance the perspective of caring as inherently negative, many carers indicate that their lives are enhanced by this role. Some people get a great deal of personal satisfaction from caring. There is no shortage of people who are enthusiastic about helping other people, a fact exemplified by the numbers who wish to make a career in social work, nursing or the other caring professions. Individuals who have a strong nurturing side to their personality will undoubtedly find caring easier and more pleasurable than those who do not. Indeed, practitioners will be aware of people who seem to thrive on caring for other people, and who often take on responsibility for a number of people in need among their family and friends.

Within a family setting, someone who is cared for may also be a valued and useful family member. A person with limited mobility may still be able to mind children, or help with tasks such as planning meals or finances. Thus they may enable their carers to have more opportunities in their lives rather than limitations. Even if they are very physically confined they may take the role of confidant and friend to other family members. Also, some carers will be able to contribute financially to the family, indeed a number of families may be dependent on that person's contribution to maintain their lifestyle.

Caring can often involve an extremely close relationship. Sometimes there is mutual support between the people involved. Carers express appreciation for the sense of having someone 'always there,' of having someone to talk to and share things with. 'My father and I have separated the house into two flats and he tries to be as independent as possible. It's nice to have someone to come home to, and tell him what's been happening in my day' (A carer). Caring in a relationship between partners or spouses can also be extremely close, particularly when the relationship was established on the basis that one person would need care. Often in such situations the carer will not see themself as a 'carer' but will view any caring tasks as an extension of their partnership. Although they may bring physical care to the relationship they do not regard this as unequal since the other person contributes their own qualities.

Perhaps surprisingly, the sense of closeness is not just confined to situations where the person requiring care is mentally alert. Carers of people with dementia and other mental impairments will also comment about feeling close to the individual, often based on the satisfaction of being needed. Research in the area of mental health seems to indicate that older people may appreciate the fact that adult children have not left home or have returned home because of their illness, thus obviating loneliness, and providing company they may otherwise not have had (Perring *et al.* 1990).

Realistically though, it does seem that the caring role is most pleasurable when the relationship between the people involved is positive, and when the cared-for person is considerate, expresses appreciation for what is being done and is concerned for the carer.

Carers' needs

Information on how caring impacts on carers enables practitioners to understand the factors which are operating in their lives and how they are being affected by what they do. It also allows workers to have some insight into the carer's world view. Impact can then be translated into needs – those areas in which carers may require some form of support in their own right. Needs, in turn, form the basis of strategy, so that when we have a clear picture of carers' main needs we can plan and implement ways of meeting these. Below we examine the principal areas in which carers have expressed the need for support and the implications of these for social care practice.

The need for a break and practical support

Respite care forms the basis for practical support for carers; without this in place other forms of support are likely to be only marginally effective. Appropriate respite will enable a carer to have a break, to enter into employment and in critical cases to regain the strength and will to continue to care. Other practical support, such as help with lifting or bathing is also essential to enable the carer to undertake their tasks.

The need for information

In any survey that asks carers what they need, information is likely to be high on the list of priorities. When people begin caring they are generally uninformed about the condition of the person they are supporting. They also are not aware of what services are available to help that person or themselves. This is variously described as 'being in a vacuum' or 'not even knowing what questions to ask'. By supplying appropriate information, agencies can significantly address the concerns of carers and can reach a large number of carers to ensure that services go to the individuals who are in greatest need. It is important that information delivery involves an inter-agency strategy, based on topics that carers themselves have highlighted as priorities.

The need for training in caring skills

Carers often find themselves in circumstances where, if they were paid staff, they would receive training and support. As carers point out, they are not born knowing how to be a carer and while common sense can carry people through many situations, sometimes this is not enough. Training provides in-depth information and practical coping skills. The list of areas in which carers can benefit from training is large and will depend on the individual needs of the person requiring support. One important area is practical skills such as lifting techniques, to improve the way personal care is delivered and avoid potential harm to the carer or person requiring care. Also useful to carers are skills in rehabilitation to enable the person they care for to learn or relearn skills which would increase their independence, and strategies for managing particular situations which carers find problematic, such as dealing with anger and aggression.

The need for emotional support

The opportunity to talk about caring, off-load worries and share the problems of caring can be extremely useful for many carers. Even those who do not consciously acknowledge the need to talk about how they are feeling may find themselves benefiting greatly from doing just that, if they find themselves in a situation where this is encouraged. In many cases it has been found that when carers' groups first form, the emotional side to caring is generally top of the agenda and has to be addressed before they go on to other issues. There are a number of ways of providing emotional support. Individual counselling, self-help groups, and telephone support all have a role to play in relation to this.

The need for improved communication and problem solving

Lack of communication between carers and the people they care for has been a hidden problem which has rarely been the subject of support interventions. However, problems facing families are often founded in communication difficulties. These can be between the dependant and the carer, between the carer and their families, or practically any combination of the people involved! It is also important not to forget that there may be problems in the relationship between the carer and professional workers. Most people communicate with each other in an automatic way, based on learned behaviour, which can crystallise into inappropriate patterns within the family. All this is within the added stress of a caring situation. Workers can be involved in improving communication in a variety of ways. For instance, they might teach communication skills, problem-solving techniques or assertiveness training. They may also mediate where there are particular problems to be addressed.

The need for stress management

Stress management techniques can directly help carers by teaching strategies which they can utilise to reduce the stress they may be experiencing. Stress management involves understanding stress and how it operates, examining behaviours and attitudes which can exacerbate stress and learning relaxation techniques. Other approaches which can be included under stress management which are particularly useful for carers include techniques for leading a healthy lifestyle, methods of improving social networks, and crisis management.

The need for involvement in the planning and delivery of services

While involvement in planning services is seldom at the top of individual carers' lists of needs, this is an important issue for carers' organisations and is generally recognised as an issue of good practice by service providers. Through involving carers in planning, there is a greater chance that services will be organised in ways which best meet their needs.

Strategy for carers

The above areas of need should not be viewed as definitive; other important needs which go beyond the remit of this book are for an adequate income, financial security and appropriate housing. However, taken together they can be seen as forming the basis for a plan for social care support for carers. The key factors in developing a carers strategy are as follows.

Definition of 'carer'

It will be helpful if authorities explain what definition of carer they are working to. For instance, are they adhering to the Carers Act definition (described in Chapter 1), in which case how do they define substantial and regular? Do they use different definitions in different circumstances?

A local picture of need based on national research

There is a great deal of national research into carers' issues which local areas need to take into account. At the same time, local areas need their own demographic information, in order to have a firm basis for resource allocation. It may be, for example, that an area has a particularly high number of parents over 80 caring for adults with learning disabilities, or that many carers are concentrated in a geographical area.

Main subject areas

The main areas in any carers strategy include: general principles; aims and objectives; a plan for information; eligibility criteria for assessment and services; a plan for consultation and involvement; proposed developments in services; and a method by which the strategy will be monitored. In addition, it can be useful to include information on the training practitioners are given in relation to working with carers and how carers' issues are reflected in departmental policy and guidance. For instance, a department might decide that, in addition to specific carers policies, all policy documents should indicate how they will impact on carers.

Accountability

Strategies should include details of time-scales for implementation, and individual responsibility for particular developments. The most effective strategies appear to be ones which are published in a single document and in which a senior officer has responsibility for carers' developments (Social Services Inspectorate 1995b).

In the following chapters we will examine ways of developing and implementing services within a strategy for carers, first considering the process and methods of assessing the needs of individual carers.

Checklist of considerations for carers' needs

The following factors comprise the main areas of carers' social care needs which should be addressed by appropriate service provision. They include the need for:

- A break
- Practical support
- Information
- Training in caring skills
- Emotional support
- Problem solving and effective communication

- Stress management
- Involvement in the planning and development of services.

Questions the organisation should answer are:

- What services does the organisation provide to meet these needs?
- Is there an overall strategy for carers?

4

Carers' Assessments

'The social worker came into my house and basically took over. I thought, fine, but when you go who will be left looking after George?' (A carer)

Assessment is a key tool in health and social care and forms the basis upon which decisions about services or other interventions can be made. Recognition of the importance of assessment has developed considerably in recent years. At one time it was often undertaken in an *ad hoc* or subjective way; the assessment of a situation might be based on the worker's personal feelings rather than any objective process of forming conclusions based on relevant information. Significantly, until recently, assessment of the needs of adults did not figure strongly as a subject on many social work courses. There was little interest in it as a discipline, and scant analysis of its role and function within social care. Community care developments have triggered a growth of interest in its methods and approaches. Within this overall context, carers' assessments are an even later development and, as such, are largely unexplored. In this chapter we will examine approaches to assessment as they relate to carers and their needs.

Types of assessment

Carers will come across assessment in a number of ways, not all of which will be formally acknowledged as such. Most significant in terms of community support are statutory assessments which local authorities have a duty to provide to eligible people, now including carers. These assessments will generally cover all areas of potential need within a person's life, such as support in personal care, housing requirements, health issues, social support and emotional needs. Statutory assessments will usually be undertaken by a care manager who has the power to purchase or refer to services on behalf of the user or carer. As such, for people who are unable or unwilling to purchase care privately, these are the main means by which they can access community services.

Carers will also encounter specialist assessments, which focus on specific areas of need of the person they care for. Examples of these include assessment by an occupational therapist for mobility equipment, mental health assessments, financial assessments and assessment on the potential for independent living.

Such assessments are usually undertaken by specialist workers who have expertise and qualifications in a particular field. In addition, any agency involved in delivering a service will generally carry out its own form of assessment. For instance, a residential unit for people with learning disabilities may perform an internal assessment to decide whether the individual may benefit from coming to live in the home and in what way they can be helped; home care agencies often undertake an assessment in order to match the home care worker to the service user or carer, and to ascertain the exact nature of the tasks required. In such cases there tends to be a twofold purpose to the assessment. Not only does it provide a method of gaining more detailed information about people's requirements, but it also enables any service to maintain its own boundaries and have the final decision on whom it will support.

A less formal type of assessment will take place if a carer contacts a carers' group or helpline. In fact, some people may not be clear that this also constitutes assessment. It is important for this to be realised because informal sources of support can be the individual's first point of contact for help and the information they receive at this stage can be crucial. Staff or volunteers in these agencies need an understanding of, and training in, basic assessment techniques so they can make appropriate recommendations about what may benefit the carer.

By this time in the process, carers and users may be extremely familiar, not to mention fed up, with assessment. It can seem that there are innumerable hoops to go through in order to access the services they need. This can prove a dilemma for practitioners, since although the different forms of assessment may feel like barriers to carers, in many ways they are requirements of good practice, based on particular areas of expertise. If they did not take place, there would be a danger of a superficial assessment which did not address specific areas. So if, for example, a residential home providing respite for confused older people did not undertake an assessment to find out exactly what individual users and carers required from the service this would become 'warehouse' care. In which case, the carer may quite rightly complain that respite was more trouble than it was worth because their relative returned home in an even more disorientated state.

To address these issues, assessment should be based on principles of good practice. Below are outlined some of the major principles which apply to most forms of social care assessment, with particular reference to the needs of carers.

Principles of good practice in assessment

Assessment should be individual and needs-led

The individual, needs-led assessment has become the foundation of good practice in recent years. This approach is the antithesis of the service-led assessment in which a worker would assess someone in terms of what services were available, rather than on the basis of what their needs were. To take a classic example, the outcome of a service-led assessment could be that an individual requires residential care. The same assessment from a needs-led basis would indicate that the person is not able to get washed and dressed alone; they are unable to use the cooker due to poor mobility in their hands and cannot walk outside the house unaided; they have suffered two recent break-ins and are extremely anxious about the security of their home.

Of course the outcome of both assessments might be the same – residential care – but the second example avoids a leap from need to service provision. It clearly divides the process into two parts: first *gathering* data which indicates what the need is, second *analysing* that data to determine how the need can be met. To put this another way, we initially need to answer 'what' questions – what is the problem, what are the strengths, what people are involved – and only when this has been done do we look at 'how' – how we can address these needs.

While the principle of the needs-led assessment is generally agreed as best practice it is still not particularly well understood. Even where people have a sound grasp of its subtleties it is remarkably easy to slip back into the trap of service-led assessments. Indeed the pressure to do so can often come from carers who have an expectation of a particular service and request it directly. This can be exacerbated where workers are constrained by a lack of flexibility in solutions to care needs, either because of lack of resources or organisational limitations. Thus, in the example above, residential care may not be the best, but the only option available. However, if we deny the principles of needs-led assessment we are in danger of losing its chief benefit – the chance to design creative care solutions which are unique to the individual's situation.

Assessments should be carer and user-led

That assessments should be carer and user-led has become an essential feature of current social care assessment, indicating a shift in approach from a professionally controlled process to one in which the worker takes on the role of facilitator. The principle of carer/user-led assessment has a variety of interconnected meanings all of which need to be applied in practice.

On one level it involves well-established principles of good practice such as trying to look at the situation from the carer's perspective and working at their pace. For instance, it may seem obvious to a worker that a carer's mental health is being threatened by their situation and that if they do not have respite they are in danger of a breakdown. The carer, however may be upset, confused and resistant to accepting help. In this situation, if the worker tries to force the issue of respite they run the risk of increasing the carer's stress and getting a flat refusal to consider options. Looking at things from the point of view of the carer is not only good practice but entirely pragmatic, since effective change can best be achieved by the people involved forming their own decisions.

The concept of carer/user-led assessment, however, has further implications. In this approach the carer is an expert whose views are of equal value to any practitioner. The individual is in control of their own assessment which is no longer done 'to' them but 'with' them. They are given full, relevant information at all stages of the assessment and their permission is required before the worker can contact other people or agencies. Their own perspective on their needs is paramount, as are their wishes and their priorities. In practical terms this means that the practitioner shares everything they write with the user or carer. Alternatively, for people who are able, self-assessment is the ideal, with the user or carer taking responsibility for recording the information, either independently or supported by the worker.

In relation to this, another new development has been to explore the possibilities of the user or carer taking on the role of co-ordinating their own package of care. This is usually best done in partnership between service user and carer, unless the former is unable to take an active role, in which case the carer would take on this responsibility. In some situations this can work extremely well, since both these individuals have the highest investment in ensuring that the services they require are delivered in a way which is suitable for their needs. Instances of this regularly occur on an everyday level. Carers will contact organisations if services do not arrive or if there are problems with their delivery. A carer recently complained that a home care worker was being driven by car from job to job by her father. Not only was this breaching confidentiality but it made the carer feel as if she needed to release the worker early because someone was waiting for her outside. The carer contacted the agency who agreed to change the worker and prevent her from using this mode of transport. With the carer recognised as co-ordinator, such situations would be more formalised. For instance, the carer could have the power to organise respite care and care in the home to suit their own convenience within agreed parameters. This could mean that if the carer was entitled to 24 hours home care per month they would decide when this was most useful for them and would book it accordingly. In many ways this system offers the flexibility of direct payments without the need for money to change hands. Carers can also be involved in organising meetings and reviews.

However there are also a number of potential obstacles to such developments. Most important, some carers may feel this is a huge additional responsibility which they do not wish to shoulder. In this case their wishes need to be respected. Carers may also not have sufficient information to be able to undertake these tasks; they may lack experience in organisation and co-ordination and may need confidence-building to take on a lead role. Many of these issues can be resolved by giving carers relevant information, support and training. An issue which may be more difficult to address is developing the culture of organisations so that the power traditionally held by workers is rebalanced in favour of the carer or user.

Finally, people should have a right to have a friend, relative or advocate present at any interview. It should not be assumed that the carer will take the role of advocate for the service user, since they may be in disagreement or they in their turn may need the support of another person.

Assessments should be based on principles shared across organisations

Principles are important in that they underpin the way practitioners deliver services and give carers a general understanding about what to expect from services they receive. They are particularly important in relatively new areas like work with carers, since such developments often occur in an *ad hoc* way which then need to be considered and evaluated. Developing a system of principles can assist in this process. As an exercise it can help workers, carers and service users to decide what is really important in the assessment process.

Examples of principles which could specifically apply to carers include:

- Carers will not be discriminated against in terms of age, gender or race
- Carer's knowledge and expertise will be valued
- Carers will be supported to enable them to continue to care
- Carers will be supported in considering whether they wish to continue caring
- So far as possible the way carers undertake personal care will be followed by respite workers.

If people are working to an acknowledged set of principles, it is easier to address inconstancies in approach between workers. For instance, the home care worker who ignores the carer's advice and insists on providing personal care in her own way because she is the 'trained expert' would clearly be going against the ethos of the organisation. It is especially important that when a variety of agencies may be providing support to carers, these agencies should share a common value base. Significant differences in approach between workers in different organisations is a serious problem which causes distress and frustration for carers. Of course, a wonderful set of values shared between agencies mean very little unless practitioners own this approach and build it into their work. There also needs to be a way of monitoring whether these principles are being upheld in everyday practice. Similarly, principles need to be publicised so that carers are able to assess their impact on service delivery.

Carers' assessments

A significant development in assessment in recent years has been the change in focus from service user alone, to service user and carer. At one time, in the best scenario, assessment and other interventions were carried out from the perspective of the service user who was seen as at the middle of a network of significant others (in the worst scenario the service user was considered in isolation and solely in terms of what the professional worker could provide for them). The network could include carer, friends, neighbours, employer, colleagues – all of whom provided some support for the individual. But these people were important for the sole reason that they provided care; the focus was clearly on the needs of the service user. Only if there were obvious problems and a potential breakdown to the caring situation would the carer be considered, and then in terms of how they could be helped to continue to care. Latterly, some organisations have developed with a carer focus and operate in the opposite way to those above. Here the carer's needs are paramount, those of the service user secondary and perceived from the perspective of the carer. Midway between these two positions are assessments which involve both users of services and carers, and take an overview of the needs of the family. This approach, which does not view people in isolation but looks at the dynamics of the situation as a whole, is generally accepted as being good practice and is now reflected in the Carers Act.

Guidance to the Act (Department of Health 1996 a & b) clearly states that practitioners should not take it for granted that a carer is willing to continue providing the same level of care, the same type of care or even that they will continue to provide care at all. It also emphasises that practitioners should take the carer's personal situation into account, such as whether they are employed or if they have family commitments, when making the assessment. While the main focus is on a holistic assessment, separate interviews for users and carers are advised as an option in some situations. All these points go a long way to emphasising the needs of carers as separate individuals in their own right, rather than simply connected to the user.

At the same time, as we have seen, under this legislation only carers who are providing substantial and regular care to someone who is eligible for assessment under specific legislation have a *right* to an assessment. Some statutory agencies may adopt some form of screening process to ensure that carers are eligible to receive an assessment. Screening would generally consist of simple questions to establish the following facts:

- Whether the service user is eligible under the NHS and Community Care Act, the Children Act or Section 2 of the Chronically Sick and Disabled Persons Act
- The time a carer spends supporting the individual per day and per week
- The types of task they undertake
- Whether this is a long-term commitment.

Local authorities are not prevented from providing assessments to carers who do not fit the above criteria, but they are not obliged to do so. While 20 hours has been suggested as a guide to whether an individual is providing substantial care, caution should be taken not to use this as a rigid framework. Individual situations will always need to be taken into account.

That carers are not being informed of their right to have an assessment of their needs is a repeated claim by carers and their organisations. In 1997 a survey by the CNA into the effects of the Carers Act found that half of the 1655 carers who replied indicated that they had not been informed about this right (Carers National Association 1997). In many ways it is difficult to gauge whether this information has not been given, or has been given in such a fashion that carers have not retained it. In order to address this, care managers need procedures which make the delivery of this information an organisational requirement. Good practice would indicate that carers should receive clear information about assessment including: its purpose, what to expect in the process, what questions may be asked, their right to have a separate assessment, and eligibility criteria for services. Ideally, this should be presented in written form before the assessment in order to let carers absorb the information and then be repeated by the care manager at the start of the session.

Separate assessments: practice issues

In relation to carer assessments, there appears to be some confusion between an assessment in which the carer's needs are assessed *separately* from those of the service user but both remain present in the interview and a *separate* assessment in which the care manager and the carer have a private meeting. Both are carers' assessments, but using a different process. Carers should be informed of the fact that they are entitled to have their own assessment and that if they wish this can take place in a separate interview. It can be helpful to indicate that there are a number of options for the session: both carer and the person requiring care can be present throughout, and/or either or both of them can speak to the care manager separately. If participants are asked for their preference at the start of the interview they have the option of deciding how they would like it to be managed. The practitioner can raise the issue again at a later stage to check whether they would like to change the format.

In the majority of cases, assessment will take place in a holistic manner with carer, service user and practitioner together contributing to the process. When carers are informed of their right to a separate assessment and have what this means explained to them, many will indicate that they are happy to have the service user present. A few will not want to talk about themselves at all because they view this as an intrusion into their personal life. Situations which can sometimes be problematic are where the carer requires a totally separate discussion. The practitioner needs to exercise sensitivity when approaching this issue and recognise that carers may find it difficult openly to take this offer up. A separate interview can be a cause of conflict between service user and carer, with the person requiring care being suspicious about what the carer may be saying about them. Some also feel that they are the focus of services and that the carer should have no need for separate attention. Of course, many similar issues may occur in reverse if an individual requests a discussion separate from their carer. The practitioner needs to be aware of occasions when a separate discussion is indicated. Such situations include:

- The carer is clearly distressed, exhausted or stressed
- The carer is taking over the interview with their own needs – in which case a separate interview with the person needing care is also indicated
- The carer and service user are in disagreement
- The carer and user appear to agree but the worker perceives signs that there may be underlying conflict
- The carer has special needs through disability or illness and may potentially need services in their own right
- The carer expresses the view that their own needs have not been taken into account in the assessment.

If the practitioner feels that the carer is turning down the opportunity for a discussion when they actually want this opportunity, then they can try gentle encouragement, or invite the carer to contact them at a later stage. In some circumstances it may be appropriate to phone the carer when the user will be out of the house, such as when they are attending a day centre. A practical issue which needs to be resolved is where and when the meeting should take place. It may be sufficient to move to another room in the house, or that the person requiring care leaves the room for a time. Alternatively, if it seems there may be conflict between the two, or the carer has particularly sensitive issues to discuss, it may be better to arrange an appointment when the service user is absent or at a neutral venue such as the worker's office.

The issue of confidentiality becomes acute when a separate discussion takes place. It is not uncommon that at the end of the session the carer will say that nothing can be shared with the service user. This may tie the worker's hands since there may be important practical issues which can only be addressed by acknowledging to the service user some of what the carer has said.

Often this situation can be resolved by talking this through with the carer. If this is the first time they have unburdened themselves, they may be shocked at what they have said, some of which they may not even have admitted to themselves. They may also be worried about the repercussions on their relationship with the person they care for. There are a number of ways of attempting to address this issue. It can be useful to help the carer to explore how they believe the person might react to what the carer has said, because sometimes the fears about someone's reactions bear little relationship to the reality. Another strategy could be to choose one issue which is most important to the carer to share with the user. For instance, it may be that a carer is experiencing many problems in the relationship but their priority is to have a break to do some shopping on their own. Alternatively, it might be preferable to share one area which the carer feels would be most acceptable to the service user and work from this. Of course the final decision on what may be shared rests with the carer; it may be that no resolution is sought at this stage and that this becomes an issue for long-term work.

In terms of recording assessments it is important that the carers' needs are clearly distinguished from those of the service user. Alternative methods for this are to have a section for carers on an overall assessment form or a separate carers' assessment form. It may be useful to have both forms in use – separate forms can be used if there is a need for lengthy information about the carer or where there may be issues of confidentiality. Occasionally there may need to be a separate file for the carer, who would obviously share the same rights as service users to see information about themselves.

Conflict in assessment

Assessment can be an area where conflicts between carers and those needing care, which may have been simmering for years, can become a major issue. This is because when needs are defined, a spotlight is focused on the relationship and tensions become unavoidable. The following are a number of common areas of conflict which can be highlighted by the assessment process:

- The carer requests that the service user receive services which they do not actually want, for instance to go into respite care, to attend a day centre or to have a 'strange' sitter
- The service user wants any of the above so the carer can have a break, but the carer is reluctant
- The carer believes the person they care for can do more for themselves than they are doing and is resentful
- The carer does not understand the person's condition/prognosis and is critical or has unrealistic expectations
- The carer takes over and does things which the individual wishes to do for themselves
- The carer does not allow the user to take risks

- The service user feels the carer should be there to help them and does not accept that they too have needs.

The essence of these situations is that the service user and carer have a conflicting perception of their needs or a difference of opinion on how support should be provided. When faced with such circumstances, practitioners obviously wish to facilitate a positive outcome, which ideally would involve both parties considering each other's position and coming to a compromise which is acceptable to both. Occasionally this ideal can be achieved and the assessment process can lead to improved understanding between carer and the person needing care – extremely satisfying for the practitioner. Sometimes though, the reality may involve reluctant compromises, unspoken resentments, long-term and painstaking work with the people involved, or all-out conflict!

Methods of working to negotiate solutions between carer and cared-for are in many ways a neglected area, and suggestions for undertaking this are detailed in Chapter 7. Sometimes the relationship between carer and service user may be such that more than one worker needs to be involved in the situation. This will most often occur if there is a problematic relationship and the carer has a high level of needs in their own right – for instance where someone is the carer for a person with mental health problems but also has mental health problems themselves. In this situation a different social worker may need to be assigned to work directly with each individual.

Specifically in terms of assessment, occasions in which the worker is unable to obtain any sort of agreement are rare, and generally signal breakdown of the caring relationship. In situations where this occurs they will need to balance a number of factors. The views and wishes of the service user need to be paramount, however consideration will also need to be given to assessment of risk and relative levels of need. The service user may be unable to be aware of the consequences of their actions, which in some cases might result in institutional care. Sometimes decisions need to be taken which are uncomfortable to all parties concerned. A common example of this is when a person with dementia reluctantly attends a day centre to give a carer a desperately needed break. The worker will need to be constantly mindful of the relationship between the rights of individuals and the risks of their actions if they do not compromise their positions, and to address this with those involved.

When it comes to decision making, if there is a disagreement between the carer and the user, the worker will try to come to a consensus of opinion. But if agreement cannot be reached, then the views of both parties should be recorded and the practitioner should specify their reasons for the decisions that have been taken. This process also applies if there is a disagreement between the worker and the carer or service user.

A framework for carers' assessments

This section gives a framework which can form the basis for a carer's assessment. It introduces key topics which enable information to be categorised in a clear and consistent manner. If the categories below are approached flexibly they will be relevant for the majority of situations in which an assessment is being carried out. They can be used both for statutory assessments, where the emphasis may be on eligibility for services and prioritisation of need, and for informal assessments, to gain a general picture of need. They could also be used as sections on a carer's assessment form. They are suitable for situations where the service user is also present or where the interview is private.

Within the topics are some suggestions for questions which have been found to be useful in triggering relevant answers from the carer. Questions are generally open-ended to encourage the carer to express their views freely. Also included are suggestions for tools which might be appropriate at various points in the assessment to gain a full response. While these may be beyond the time for assessment available to care managers, they may be useful for other workers, and in situations where longer-term support is required to maintain the caring relationship. All tools mentioned in this section are explained fully in later chapters. The following has been adapted from suggestions about what a carer's assessment might cover in the Carers Act Practice Guidance (Department of Health 1996b).

Overview

The first part of an assessment interview needs to set the carer at their ease so they gain confidence in the worker and feel more relaxed about subsequent questions. By asking general questions the worker will also gain an overview of the situation and will be able to gauge which are likely to be the most significant areas for the individual. This can determine the order of the interview to come. If, for instance, the relationship with the person they care for is clearly uppermost for the carer and they are willing to speak freely about this then this may be the next item to consider. If, however, the individual presents as someone generally content with what they do, but needing some practical support, questions about impact on their lives and relationship with the cared-for person should still be asked as a double check, but need not be laboured. This section will also enable the worker to gain an idea about the carer's perspective on the situation – whether they understand the condition of the person they are caring for and its prognosis, and the level of general information that they may require.

TRIGGER QUESTIONS

- Could you tell me about the situation as you see it?
- Could you explain about any difficulties you are facing?
- What information have you been given about your wife's condition and what she needs?

The carer's responsibilities

This topic focuses on what the carer does in their caring role and gives the opportunity to describe the practical tasks they undertake. Information is needed in terms of *what sorts* of tasks they perform, *how often* they are required to do these, *how long* they take and whether these are likely to be long-term requirements. Practitioners need to be reasonably specific about what is involved. For instance, in one situation getting someone up in the morning may mean nothing more than prompting them at intervals or helping with zips and buttons; in another it could take two hours of solid work. It can also be useful to try and establish whether the carer is doing tasks because they can do them more quickly or, in their eyes, better, and what the person could actually do for themselves. In relevant situations, the practitioner would look to working with the carer to reduce what they are doing and to support the individual in learning/relearning skills. At the same time it is important not to overburden the carer; in some situations the amount of time spent in encouraging and prompting may be overly intrusive into their already scant spare time.

TRIGGER QUESTIONS

- Tell me what you do in a typical day
- What sort of help does the person you care for need?
- Are there any particular times of the day that are difficult for you?
- Are you disturbed in the night?
- Have you been given any information about what your relative can do for herself?
- Is there anything you think your son could do for himself?

TOOLS

The carer's journal: keeping a journal or diary is a useful method by which carers can discover the extent of their caring responsibilities. It is useful to keep the journal for a week or longer in order to gain a true picture. Journals can then be used as the basis for discussion.

Support from others

Here we ascertain the amount of support the individual is receiving from other people. The practitioner needs to find out the level of the support, who it is from, whether it is regular and frequent and how reliable the helpers are. Again, it helps to be as specific as possible and to be clear about language. The question 'does anyone else help to care for your husband?' might get a negative answer because the carer equates 'caring for' with personal care. In reality, her husband's brother may call round three afternoons a week to take him on an outing. It can also be useful at this stage to establish whether there are any people in the social network who might be potential carers and how the carer feels about this.

TRIGGER QUESTIONS

- Does anyone else help with the person you care for?
- What sort of tasks do they help you with?
- Does anyone else spend any time with the person you care for?
- Is anyone available in an emergency?
- Is there anyone you feel could be able to help more?

TOOLS

The social network map or ecomap (see Chapter 8).

The carer's other commitments

This section enables the worker to find out the extent of the carer's other responsibilities. Typically these would include whether the carer worked or was in education and whether this was full or part-time. Other family commitments would be taken into account, including child care or whether the person was also providing care for other adults. Where resources were limited, the amount of other responsibilities the carer had in their lives would obviously be a factor to take into account when allocating services.

Impact on the carer's life

In this section the carer is encouraged to explore the effects their caring responsibilities are having on their lives. These can be related to:

- Finance: the worker would ascertain whether the individual was facing financial hardship and would be able to advise or refer on for advice on potential benefits.
- Physical health: the worker needs to discover whether the carer has serious or chronic health problems. Many carers are themselves older

people or in ill health and this can be a crucial factor in determining the level of practical support they require.

- Stress and emotional problems: the worker needs to find out whether the carer is under stress. In extreme cases they may be experiencing mental health problems such as severe depression or anxiety and may benefit from talking with a mental health worker.

- Social isolation: the worker would gain information on whether the carer had any emotional support or social outlets.

TRIGGER QUESTIONS

- How much time over a week do you have to yourself?
- How often do you get out to visit friends?
- How do you feel about leaving the person you care for to go out?
- Do you have any problems with your health?
- Are you experiencing any difficulty with your sleeping patterns?
- What things in your life are you happy about?
- Do you feel you have given anything up to be a carer?
- Is there anything in your life that you would like to change?
- Do you have anyone you can talk to about how you feel?

TOOLS

- Carers journal
- Stress assessment (see Chapter 8)
- Social network map (see Chapter 8).

Relationship with the person being cared for

Questions about the quality of the relationship between the carer and the person requiring care may touch on areas which are uncomfortable for the carer. In many cases this issue will be the crux of why they have requested a separate assessment. The worker will need to gauge the seriousness of the problem to decide whether some form of mediation or relationship counselling is required or whether practical solutions may be achieved within the scope of the assessment.

TRIGGER QUESTIONS

- How would you describe your relationship with your father?
- Are there any ways in which you feel the relationship could be improved?
- Is there anything positive in your relationship with your son?
- What could you do to improve relationship?
- What could your daughter do to improve the relationship?

The carer's expertise and strengths

While the positive aspects the carer brings to the situation should be emphasised throughout the discussion, this section ensures that this is definitely covered. Since some people find it difficult to 'praise' themselves the practitioner may need to be gently persistent and focus on practical things the carer feels they do well. If the carer is unable to describe any areas of strength, then the worker needs to ensure that the carer does not start to feel deskilled. Everyone does some things well and the worker can pursue issues raised earlier in the discussion to point this out. It can also be useful to explain that it is quite usual for carers not to recognise their strong points. In joint assessments, service users can usefully point out the carer's strengths.

TRIGGER QUESTIONS

- Have you learnt any skills through being a carer?
- Is there anything you feel you do particularly well?
- Have you found any creative ways to overcome problems?
- You may feel that you aren't coping very well, but before you told me that...

TOOLS

Strengths and needs exercise – workers help the carer to compile a list of their strengths and needs.

What support the carer is looking for

This section enables the carer to explore what type of support they feel they need. In addition to social care support, the practitioner should discover whether the carer has any needs which might be addressed by training or specialist services, such as correct lifting, improved housing, use of equipment, or a medical discussion on the user's needs, in which case a specialist practitioner such as an occupational therapist may need to be involved.

TRIGGER QUESTIONS

- Are there any particular areas you feel that you require help with?
- Are there any tasks that you feel you could do better if you had some training such as…?
- What form of support would be most helpful to you?
- Are there any particular tasks that you feel are particularly difficult for you?

How the carer feels about caring and the future

This section enables the carer to explore how they feel about caring and to consider their future. It also assesses whether the carer is willing to continue to care, to what extent and in what ways – if this has not been covered earlier in the session. This section may prove difficult for practitioners since, although guidance is clear that there should be no automatic assumption that carers will continue to care, they may know that there may be little chance of resources being allocated to enable the carer to give up caring. They will need therefore to find a balance between giving opportunity for discussion and making choices, without raising unrealistic expectations.

TRIGGER QUESTIONS

- How do you see your future as a carer?
- Have you ever considered reducing the amount you do?
- Do you see your needs changing in the near future?

Risk assessment

An area which has not greatly been explored but which could certainly be used with great significance in assessing carers' needs is the concept of a risk assessment. Such assessments could be used where the carer is finding it difficult to cope with aspects of caring, or where the practitioner feels that the carer is not able to carry out their tasks fully. Perhaps a carer may be getting personally frail and can no longer lift the other person safely, or they abuse alcohol and can no longer supervise someone adequately. Risk assessments often have criteria against which the level of risk is measured – perhaps low, medium, or high. For instance, 'the carer needs to lift her husband to get out of his wheelchair' – medium risk. They can prove a reasonably objective basis for discussing the individual's needs and for allocating services. There is also an argument for risk assessment to be standard for carers' assessments – this would address any tendency by organisations to encourage carers to take on more care than they are able and by carers to try and do more than they safely should.

Decision making, establishing priorities and negotiation

The final stage of the assessment is the bridge between the gathering of information and the development of a strategy or care plan to provide support. If the assessment is linked to eligibility criteria, the practitioner needs to make the decision as to whether or not the individual is eligible for services and at what level they need to receive assistance. The Carers Act gives care managers the responsibility to take the carer's needs into account when making a decision about services.

This can mean that the support given to the individual is increased. For instance, in a situation where a carer was coping well with no particular stress, the service user may be offered two days day care in order to promote skill development or socialisation. But if the carer was finding it difficult to cope, then up to five days care could be arranged. In addition, services may be arranged for the carer in their own right such as a sitting service to enable them to have a break, or an introduction to a carers' support group. Practitioners will need to discuss what the priority needs are and how they can best be met.

Where agencies use a system of priority banding to determine access to services, it is important that the needs of carers are reflected in this in order to give guidance to practitioners and information for carers. For instance, the highest priority might include situations where the caring would immediately break down if the carer was not offered relief and a high/medium band might include carers experiencing substantial stress. While this approach might bring the inevitable criticism that carers with lower levels of need will not receive a service, it has the advantage of bringing carers' needs firmly into the priority system and establishing consistency of approach between service users and carers.

Negotiation may be required where services which benefit the carer impact upon the service user. Obviously, the higher the level of agreement between carer and the person they care for, the easier it will be to come to decisions on the care plan. Where there is little agreement, as we have seen, the worker has the task of negotiating with the people involved to attempt to come to a solution which is mutually acceptable.

The care plan

A written care plan summarising the care that service users and carers will be receiving should be a useful document, giving information such as: who is supplying a service, when, for how long, how much they will cost and who to contact in an emergency. Ideally a care plan should also have a summary of the assessment and will indicate the purpose of providing the services. The Social Services Inspectorate (1995a) indicates a number of problems in the way agencies approach care plans. First, service users, service providers and carers do not always receive copies of the care plan, which means that the arrangements basically have to be carried in someone's head; second, carers are not reflected in the care plan. In relation to the latter there are two ways in which carers should be represented: if services are allocated specifically to meet the needs of carers, these should be clearly indicated, and the role of the carer as care provider should also be recognised. It reflects the organisation-centred approach, that a carer who provides 100 hours of care per week may not appear on the care plan, unlike the twice weekly day centre visit or the six hours of home care. There are many good practice reasons for including the carer in the care plan, including recognition for the carer, and promotion of the feeling that the carer is working as part of the team, which is often appreciated by carers as reducing their sense of isolation and increasing self-worth. It will also provide information for organisations on the amount of care which is being provided by carers.

Reviewing the care plan

The importance of monitoring and reviewing care plans to ensure that they continue to meet need is acknowledged, but many social services departments struggle to meet their commitment to reviews while fulfilling their obligation to undertake new assessments. If authorities are unable to hold regular reviews in all situations it may be useful if they design criteria for priority reviews, such as if the needs of the user or carer are likely to change quickly, or if carers are under particular stress.

Good practice would indicate that a review at the end of the first month of services, as undertaken for people entering residential or nursing home care, should be applied to people in the community. Initial assessments may be made under time-pressured conditions with the carer and service user not knowing what to expect. An initial short-term review may present a much more accurate picture of need which may result in amendments to the care plan.

Under the Carers Act, carers have a right to a re-assessment if their circumstances or those of the person they care for change. This mechanism could prove useful to trigger reviews, and carers should be informed of this in their written information on assessment.

Monitoring carers' assessments

In light of the comparatively recent development of carers' assessments it is essential that all agencies should undertake training for staff who will be involved in making assessments. Also, because of repeated claims that carers are not regularly offered the opportunity for an assessment, and may not be clear about whether an assessment has taken place, some means must be found to monitor the process. This should include a mechanism to ascertain if and how assessments are offered and whether there are any particular patterns in their take-up. Such methods could involve requesting carers to sign an assessment form to indicate that their needs have been assessed, or that they were offered an assessment but did not wish to take this up. Numbers of those opting for a 'private' assessment should also be noted. Compiling such monitoring information will enable the agency to develop a profile of carers' assessments.

Assessment for people from ethnic minority groups

When assessing people from ethnic minorities all the above principles apply. It is, however, particularly important that practitioners also have an understanding of the needs and circumstances of people from ethnic minority groups. In recent years, knowledge and understanding of these issues have grown considerably and, particularly within areas with high ethnic populations, specialist services and bilingual workers are available. At the same time the needs of people from ethnic minorities are likely to be significantly acute due to the disadvantages they may face in accessing appropriate support and services through language or cultural barriers. Organisations and practitioners need to strive continually to develop good practice in relation to these groups, particularly in areas where there are low numbers of people from ethnic minorities where there is likely to be less understanding and experience of their needs.

The following can be seen as principles of good practice when undertaking assessment of need with carers from ethnic minorities.

Individual approach

Practitioners should ensure that they are not working to racial stereotypes but focusing on the needs of individuals within their own situation. In particular they should be wary of any cultural assumptions which would lead to individuals receiving less of a service, such as 'Asian carers are well supported by their extended family', 'Chinese families will not accept any services' or 'Afro-Caribbean carers will not want a separate carers' assessment'. Sometimes the extended family and community network in some cultures does mean that carers are supported and require minimal or no external support. But while higher numbers of Asian and Chinese people live in multi-generational households than white or Afro-Caribbean people, this does not necessarily mean that appropriate care is taking place or that support is not needed. It may be found that people are living together for financial reasons rather than ties of kinship and affection, or that the help the carer receives is given by people who are themselves working hugely long hours, or the person needing care is becoming confused and unmanageable by being helped by a number of different people.

In some situations, the stereotyped view of the Asian community looking after its own members is the very opposite of the truth. Some families live with high degrees of social isolation, perhaps because of immigration factors. Other cultures may have an emphasis on self-reliance and not accepting help from their community. These carers are likely to have high levels of need for support. It is important not to underestimate the silent desperation that some black carers may be experiencing in their lives. In a study in Liverpool, 80 per cent of Chinese carers interviewed had never been able to take a holiday because they had no one to take over the care and 70 per cent felt they did not receive enough help from family and community. Many expressed depression, helplessness and anger. Also, significantly, a number of carers had been uneasy about sharing their own views in front of the person requiring care (Wing Kwong and Kerrie 1992).

Example 1

Rabindra was living in London with a two-year-old child with learning disabilities. She was separated from her husband who had gone to live in the north of England and had no family of her own in this country. Rabindra spoke no English and worked long hours as a cleaner. She had been taken in by a family who looked after the child in the day, but who took nearly all of her wages in payment. A bilingual health visitor had been appointed who had arranged for the child to attend a playgroup for disabled children. The health visitor reported that Rabindra had little understanding of her child's condition and that she suffered from depression.

Example 2

Mr and Mrs Kim had been caring for their daughter who had been diagnosed with schizophrenia for six years. Mrs Kim spoke no English while her husband spoke a few words but had difficulty in communicating. Their daughter was fluent in English, had attended university and had been the main person to help the Kims cope with official English correspondence. The Kims had their own business in which they worked long hours. They were unclear about the nature of their daughter's illness and hoped that one day she would be cured. Mr Kim had seen her psychiatrist and community psychiatric nurse (CPN) but had not been able to understand much of what they told him. Recently her behaviour had become aggressive. She had smashed items in their shop and was demanding money from her parents. Mr Kim contacted the CPN who told him there was nothing he could do. The Kims have withdrawn from most contact with the local Chinese community because they feel people are criticising them for their daughter's condition.

At the same time, it is important that another myth does not emerge – that black people do not take on caring responsibilities. In fact, as we have seen, patterns of caring in all communities are broadly similar.

Understanding religions and cultures

Practitioners will benefit from a sound background knowledge of the cultures of the people they are seeking to support. There are now a number of manuals which give a good explanation of the significant factors in cultures and religions. See, for instance, CENTRA (1994) *Customs and Cultures.* In addition, practitioners can contact community workers in regions which have a large number of people from that background, where knowledge and information is likely to be highly developed. It is particularly important that workers should have an understanding of how to behave appropriately when visiting people's houses and of potential areas for confusion and misunderstanding in language and behaviour. Practitioners will need to develop skills in understanding how particular ethnic minorities communicate in a non-verbal way so that actions such as smiling or nodding are not misinterpreted. However, such information should be used as signposts only – people and families are above all individual. For instance, there is likely to be a great difference in the attitudes of a fundamentalist Muslim to one who is non-practising. Background knowledge should never take the place of active listening to, and observation of, individuals and families.

There are also a number of relevant themes which practitioners need to keep in mind in case they are operating within the family they are assessing. A number of cultures believe that families should be independent and feel there is shame in accepting help, particularly monetary benefits. Such individuals may need a great deal of explanation and convincing about the role of benefits. A feeling of personal pride may also mean that people are particularly concerned that other members of their community should not be aware of what is occurring in their family. Confidentiality is essential; woe betide any practitioner who contacts the local community worker without checking out that this is acceptable to the individual concerned. Gender issues will also be important and a choice may need to be made to use either male or female workers in particular situations.

Using an interpreter

Using an interpreter is essential in circumstances where service users and carers are unable to understand and speak English, or have difficulties in doing this, and where the worker is not fluent in their language. The provision of interpreters will vary between areas depending on the numbers of resident ethnic minority groups. In areas with high numbers the authority will be likely to employ interpreters or bilingual workers in the dominant languages. Localities where the ethnic minority population is small are more likely to use sessional interpreters. However, even in areas with large populations, the span of languages is likely to be so great that sessional workers will need to be used in some circumstances.

Interpreting and working with an interpreter are acknowledged as potentially difficult processes. In the ideal situation interpreters will be qualified, skilled in working within health or social care and there will be an established relationship between the interpreter and the practitioner, who will also have received training in working with an interpreter. The nightmare scenario is an untrained interpreter with no understanding of social care, working with a practitioner whom they do not know and who has no knowledge or experience of such co-working. Potential problems include: the interpreter refusing to interpret material which they find morally wrong; value judgements; mistranslations; collusion with families; and the practitioner ignoring the interpreter. At the very least, organisations need to ensure that the interpreters they use are qualified and familiar with the subject matter, that practitioners are trained to work with interpreters and that procedures exist for this process. These should include written information to people in their own language indicating what to expect from having an interpreter and what to do if they are not happy with the service they get.

It is generally agreed that children within the family should not be used as interpreters and that it is preferable to use professional interpreters rather than other family members. In a small study in Southall, 29 of the 32 people approached indicated that they would prefer a Social Services interpreter to a family member or community organisation for reasons of confidentiality, training and experience, and to co-ordinate appointments (Baker 1991). Wherever possible carers should not be used as interpreters for service users. There are a number of reasons for this; the carer may not be skilled at putting across what the person wants to say, the carer's own needs cannot be looked at so easily if they are in the role of interpreter and finally the carer and the user may actually be in conflict. Of course it can be extremely difficult for a worker who does not understand the language to pick up on any of these variables. Wherever possible, unless all parties clearly prefer to keep the discussion within the family, an interpreter who is qualified and skilled in the area of social care should be used.

Taking time and planning

It also needs to be acknowledged that assessment of people from ethnic minorities may be more time-consuming than usual, with more preparation required in terms of such things as employing interpreters, gaining the trust of the carer and making sure the correct information is being exchanged. It is essential that practitioners do not assume that mutual understanding is taking place. The potential for misunderstanding is great – for example, the belief that cancer is a contagious illness, that a particular medication will cure a condition or that respite care is compulsory may all occur. Spending time checking out whether people understand what has been said and its implications is essential. Particular care must be taken to ensure that people have a good understanding of complex legal and medical issues. It can be useful to ask people to say what they have understood by the discussion, and actively to encourage people to ask questions.

Finally, if it is found that carers are reluctant to accept services, a sensitive approach must be taken to ensure that this is because they truly do not require or want these, rather than because of any other factor. For instance, they may have misunderstood what is on offer through language difficulties, they may fear that the service is not culturally acceptable or they may have concerns about what other members of their community may think. Practitioners need to be able to check out these options without appearing to force services on the family.

Checklist of considerations for carers' assessments

- Is a multi-agency approach to ensure that assessments interconnect without duplication in place?
- Are there agreed multi-agency principles for carers' assessments?
- What measures are in place to ensure that practitioners operate from a carer/user-led perspective?
- To what definition of 'regular and substantial' care is the agency operating?
- Are guidelines in place for care managers undertaking carers' assessments?
- Is written information for carers about their rights to assessment and the process involved given to all carers prior to assessment?
- What methods are in place to monitor the take-up of carers' assessments?
- What methods are in place to check that carers receive copies of care plans?
- Are carers' needs and role both reflected in the care plan?
- Are interpreters available, practitioners trained to work with them and stated standards available for users and carers on what to expect from interpreting?

5

Providing Services that Carers Want

'It's as good as winning the lottery for me. I look forward to those weeks when I am free of pressure and stress all year. My arthritis gets better and I come back prepared to look after my husband for the next few months.' (A carer)

A considerable amount of research has been undertaken into the types of services that carers indicate would be most useful to them, with considerable agreement on what sort of services are needed and the approach that services need to adopt in order to be carer-friendly. Service providers, therefore, need be in little doubt about what carers are saying they require. Here we examine the key components in making up a strategy for providing services for carers.

Respite care

Respite care is a general term for any service which enables a carer to have time away from the responsibilities of caring. Of all the forms of support for carers, it is one of the most appreciated and most essential to enable people to maintain a caring role. Traditionally, respite care meant short-term hospital or residential care for service users, but its meaning has gradually been extended to cover any service which offers a break to carers, reflecting the flexibility of approach which carers now require. Therefore respite may take place within the individual's own home as well as in a variety of external locations. Similarly, respite may cover reasonably long periods of time – three weeks to enable a carer to go on holiday; shorter periods – a weekend or bed and breakfast service so the carer can have a night out; or short, regular interventions such as an afternoon of day care to enable the carer to go shopping. The term 'respite' has always had a sense of offering carers a 'relief' from caring, but this might not be for a break or for social activities but to allow them to go out to work or undertake other forms of responsibility.

In many ways, respite care is not so much a *type* of service, but the *purpose* behind a service. For instance, a day care placement may be made from the point of view of the service user, to enable them to regain skills such as cooking or writing. It may also be made from the point of view of the carer, so they can have respite. Ideally, there will be a dual purpose behind any placement, so that both carer and user experience benefits.

Types of respite
HOME-BASED RESPITE

Respite within the home may involve a sitting service in which a volunteer or a paid worker spends social time with the individual. Such arrangements may also include personal care or meal provision, when the sitter actually takes over the role of the carer – volunteers are less frequently used in such circumstances. The extent of respite provided will depend on the needs of an individual, and can vary from 24-hour care to a visiting service. Thus, a sitter may stay overnight with someone with dementia to enable their carer to have an evening out. Alternatively, a worker may visit a disabled person three times a day over a fortnightly period to provide meals and personal care to enable their carer to have a holiday away.

RESPITE OUTSIDE THE HOME

Respite outside the home generally involves day, residential or nursing home care. There are a variety of different day services, from day centres and day hospitals to social clubs and specialist, activity-based venues. Types of provision might include a day centre for people with learning disabilities, a day hospital for older people with a physical disability, a gymnastic club for children with learning disabilities, a series of day trips for people with dementia, and a reading club for people who have had a stroke. Care within a residential setting will be dependent on relating an individual's need to the registration category of the home under the Registered Homes Act 1984; for instance, there are different homes for people over 65 and for younger people with a physical disability. Some homes cater specifically for short-term, respite care while others may provide this in addition to long-term, permanent care. The practice of offering respite in a hospital setting has decreased significantly in recent years due to changes in health priorities and a consensus from carers that hospitals rarely offer the type of homely environment, stimulation and individual care their relatives require. Of course one problem with this for carers is that as an NHS service there was no charge for hospital respite, whereas respite through social services departments is generally charged for. Finance is likely to be a significant factor in choosing residential over other forms of respite care; for those with substantial needs it is likely to be prohibitively expensive to put a 24-hour care worker in someone's home.

FAMILY-BASED RESPITE

Respite in a family setting has been used successfully in a number of areas. In this type of service, individuals spend their respite time with a family with whom they have been 'matched'. Such arrangements have proved successful with both carers and service users. Family homes can provide individual attention in a non-institutional environment. The best situations are those which develop over time, where the carer, service user and the host family get to know each other well so that, for the person needing care, the experience is like a second home. This type of service can be truly flexible for carers, depending on the family's ability to take their relative at short notice. At the same time, the success of such projects are dependent on the ability to match families and service users with each other. They are generally less suitable for people with a high level of need or challenging behaviour, since support families may be unable to cope with this or their home may lack the adaptations to be suitable. A variety of family placement or shared caring schemes operate throughout the country.

JOINT RESPITE

In joint respite the carer and person cared for get to spend time together, but with the carer freed from practical responsibilities. This form of respite is ideal in situations where the carer needs a break from the physical strain of providing care, but where service user and carer want to remain together. Some organisations have specialised in providing holiday accommodation where the carer and the person they care for can both attend together, and in which personal care is provided by care assistants. A less extensive version of this is the social club where groups of carers and service users meet together with the support of paid or volunteer workers. For instance, a swimming club for children with autism who are supervised by swimming instructors while parents are able to join in the swimming or socialise with other parents. Joint respite provides an environment in which the relationship between carer and the person they care for can take on a different form. Carers and service users have pointed out how they feel more relaxed after such a break and how being able to have fun together improves the way they relate to each other at home.

From the above it can be seen that, because the concept of respite can cover so many services, it is essential that organisations which provide respite should work together to a common definition. Without this, carers, service users and workers are likely to encounter considerable confusion. An example of this would be where a health authority is working to a definition which includes unplanned, emergency situations as respite while social services considers respite to include all services for carers using residential or nursing homes or home care and the independent sector views respite as any service which offers planned breaks. In this situation workers will be literally speaking a different language. Relevant agencies in every local area need to agree on a definition and to publicise this to all interested parties.

Generally, it will be helpful if the definition of respite is as wide and inclusive as possible to reflect the fact that respite services need to be varied and flexible.

From the point of view of individual practitioners, it is important that workers are able to be creative about what forms a respite service. For instance, some carers do not want to leave their home during their respite time. They may prefer to stay and get on with some uninterrupted housework while the person they care for is being looked after. Similarly, some may appreciate a night sitting service in order to enable them to have a good night's sleep in their own bed.

Caution over respite

While respite is undoubtedly of great value to carers, it should not be regarded as a panacea since it can involve problems of its own. There can be difficulties for both service user and carer in deciding on respite. Leaving your own home to visit a day centre, let alone spending two weeks in a nursing home, may feel like rejection to both parties – with the user feeling resentful and the carer guilty. On the other hand, home-based respite may feel like an invasion into people's private space. Practitioners can help in this process by working with the family to decide what is the most appropriate form of respite for them, and in enabling them to discuss any practical or emotional difficulties which may arise. Thorough preparation, with visits to residential establishments, or meetings with the home support worker, will ease the process and help adjustment.

Also of note to respite purchasers is the fact that while research tends to indicate that respite delays the need for residential care, one study has shown that some forms may actually be associated with earlier admission to residential care. Thus, for older people with dementia, attending residential respite may increase their likelihood of going into permanent care (Levin *et al.* 1989). Conversely there is also a danger that respite can be used to keep caring situations together when they are clearly untenable for the carer and service user and where breakdown is inevitable in the long term. In such situations it may be more appropriate to work towards a permanent solution.

Other home-based services

Another extremely important category of services is support which is given to the carer within their home to enable them to carry out their caring tasks. Examples of this include district nursing, meals on wheels, support with such tasks as bathing, lifting, toileting and a mobile incontinence laundry service which collects dirty clothes, towels and bedding. It is an arguable point whether these services can be classified as respite care and, once again, this may depend on the purpose for which they are allocated. For instance, if a home care worker visits to help bath someone because they are too heavy for the carer to manage, this is not strictly speaking respite care because the purpose is not to give the carer a break. Alternatively, if the same service is provided because the carer is becoming physically tired and needs a break it could be considered to be respite care. Whichever way these services are classified, the points made below will apply to all services for carers.

What carers and users want from respite and other services

Flexibility

The key word when carers are asked how they would like respite services to be is *flexible*, by which they mean a service which as far as possible can fit with their individual needs and requirements. Conversely, the main criticism about respite services is that they are just not flexible, rather they are rigid, predetermined and 'take it or leave it' in attitude. Managers may well agree with this view of the situation but point out that the logistics of providing a service which meets everyone's needs within constrained budgets are impossible to achieve. The challenge for those who organise services is to achieve the maximum achievable level of flexibility while ensuring that carers with the highest priority needs receive the service. This is particularly pertinent for residential services, which generally have the most difficulty in providing a flexible response.

While carers agree that respite should be flexible, it is evident that within this overall concept, there are infinite numbers of individual needs. Research commissioned by Wirral Health Authority asked carers and service users how they would like to see respite organised in terms of length and frequency of support (Cuthbert 1996). The following comments were obtained: more weekend residential care, overnight residential care, care in the home; three weeks of care in a residential setting rather than two; breaks at short notice for special occasions; to be able to plan breaks up to a year in advance; not to have to plan breaks a long time in advance; more frequent short stays; less frequent but longer stays; weeks spaced throughout the year; seasonal preferences such as longer breaks in summer or shorter blocks of time plus weekends.

It is evident from the variety of responses that, truly to meet carers' needs, the service needs to be entirely individualised. If we examine how residential respite care is organised within specialist respite units, this generally involves an allocation of time to carers and a rota worked out some time in advance. Within this there may be a variety of approaches: carers may be allocated the same number of weeks per year or alternatively each carer may be eligible for a different amount; the time may be allocated in regular blocks, such as two weeks on a regular basis, or, again, may be customised to fit the individual, so one person may get two weeks, another one week and a weekend.

The more standardised approaches to allocating time have been widely used because they are administratively more simple. Other advantages are that they may be perceived as fairer by carers in that everyone receives equal time and they allow for clear, advance planning. Indeed, this sort of approach may suit relatively stable populations of users, where there is unlikely to be a surge of new need or a large turnover, such as for children with learning disabilities, who may have formed friendships and wish to go into respite at the same time as their friends. It also maximises the use of respite beds, which are booked in advance and therefore, barring cancellations, will be in constant use. There are, however, considerable disadvantages to this approach; not only does it fail to give carers the flexibility they require, but it may also fail to distinguish between levels of need. In a situation where resources are limited it is clearly inappropriate to allocate time on an equal shares basis, when, to one carer respite may mean a well-earned interlude, while to another it is the difference between surviving and breaking down.

For all organisations involved in organising this form of respite the challenge is to find a system which is as responsive as possible to carer's needs, but at the same time is an efficient use of resources. For instance, while the carer might wish to be able to access respite at short notice it is uneconomic to have empty beds waiting for this eventuality. Therefore, rather than a rota based on set periods of time, it is preferable to organise this according to the needs of individual carers and service users. Thus, the time-table may include a seven day slot for one carer while another bed is occupied during the week by one individual and at the weekend by another. This form of organisation is more complicated but still manageable. In order to implement it effectively a number of elements need to be in place. Firstly, it is extremely beneficial to consult with users and carers about their preferred pattern of respite. It may be that the particular group using the resource are agreed on the approach which would be most useful to them, which can form the basis of the system. For instance, perhaps they may prefer a rota to be organised on a six-month or a two-month basis. Of course this exercise would need to be repeated regularly, and if the population changes.

It is also essential to have effective assessment procedures so that carers who have the highest priority needs receive an appropriate service. Eligibility criteria need to be clearly publicised to carers and users so that myths do not develop about the organisation, for instance that everyone is entitled to a set number of days per year, and so that people do not become resentful of others who may receive more care. It is essential that there is openness and thorough explanation of these issues because while this arrangement is undoubtedly the most fair in situations where resources are limited, carers do not welcome repeated reassessment of their needs and the feeling that they must justify every service they receive.

In addition, those responsible for organising rotas must work under the ethos of maximising use of beds and making every effort to fit in with the requests of carers. In practical terms this may mean establishing carers who would be willing to receive respite at short notice and calling these people if a vacancy should occur, or being willing to attempt to rearrange rotas at short notice. This means establishing close contact and a good relationship with carers and service users. If possible, one or two beds could be outside the rota to enable short-notice placements to be made for special occasions or crisis care; again, if not called upon, these could be used by carers willing to take respite at short notice. At the same time, carers need to take on a firm responsibility to let respite agencies know about any changes in their plans.

One of the main problems of respite units is that inevitably they become blocked so that new people are unable to receive a service until a space is vacated by a regular user. An alternative solution is to offer respite in ordinary residential or nursing homes. This situation offers the benefit of a range of different venues, possibly in geographical areas closer to the individual's home. On the other hand, mixing people receiving respite with long-term residents can be intrusive, and such organisations are less likely to develop the expertise in managing respite needs that can be found in designated respite services. Similar problems exist where day care is offered in long-term residential facilities.

Turning now to home-based support, this obviously needs to be as flexible as unit-based respite and should be available on a 24-hour 7-day-a-week basis. Any home care service should provide the facility for waking night sitters, for people who need frequent care during the night, and sleeping night workers, where supervision rather than regular interventions is needed. The logistic difficulties of organising home care in a flexible way are similar to those of respite units and basically depend on the flexibility of the workforce. Sometimes problems occur because of traditional ways of working where workers are accustomed to providing a service between certain limited hours. In other situations, the demand for home care at peak periods, such as pension day, means a large number of workers are tied up at the same time, thereby decreasing flexibility. The increase in the use of independent sector services which are generally able to provide a more responsive service than local authority home care has seen a move towards developing flexibility within the latter.

Finally, day services which are limited to opening hours of nine to five, and operational hours of ten to three are clearly of little use for people needing respite to enable them to go to work. Centres which are open from 8 in the morning through to the evening are needed, as are social events organised at night. Day centres are primary sites for developing services for carers alongside those for the people they support, and could well include carer support groups, social events and related services. Carers' pressure groups can have a positive role in encouraging the development of these flexible services.

Benefit for users

Respite in residential or nursing homes or day facilities should have a number of key quality indicators. One of the most important quality issues is that any form of respite should also have a benefit for the service user. While in some occasions respite may be needed solely from the point of view of the carer, for instance, if they have had to go into hospital, best practice indicates that the service user should also benefit from what is provided. The ideal situation is where the respite service is of equal use to both parties, such as day care which provides a social environment with the chance for a session with a physiotherapist. Sometimes respite is looked on as a service which is accepted with reluctance by service users, but there is evidence to indicate that it can be an enjoyable experience. The following are a few of the comments made by people attending respite services. 'I enjoy the change in the environment.' 'I didn't particularly want to come into the nursing home, but I like the staff and there are people to talk to.' 'It helps to get a change of scene and someone else to talk to, but don't tell my wife.' 'I tell him about what is going on in the centre, and it gives us something new to talk about.' 'The day centre gave me a new lease of life.'

Carers may not be alone in feeling tied down within the caring relationship, and some service users clearly benefit from the opportunity to leave the home and make new contacts. On the other hand there are also negative comments about respite care: 'Its boring'; 'There's nothing to do'; 'I've nothing in common with those other people'. Although some of these comments may be made by people for whom organised activities have no appeal, they also reflect services which are clearly not meeting the needs of users or carers. While respite services are generally oversubscribed there also tends to be a surprisingly high level of refusal of take-up. While there might be a number of reasons for not accepting respite care, such as carers not being emotionally prepared to share the caring or feeling that if they stop they will not be able to start again, the most common explanation is because user or carer are not happy with the service.

Services are most often criticised by carers and service users because they do not provide adequate activities or stimulation for the people who attend. In particular, criticism is levelled at services which have an over-focus on respite to the exclusion of the needs of service users, such as day care within a residential home, or day hospitals where the individual may spend a whole day waiting for half an hour's speech therapy. A typical scenario is of a room where people sit around the walls while looped music plays constantly or the television is on unnoticed in the corner. Any organisation providing respite care must provide for the needs of the people using the service as well as the carer. In practical terms this means providing the sort of environment and activities which are meaningful and enjoyable for the user. While this may entail high-cost professional services such as nursing care or rehabilitation it could equally well involve informal social support organised by volunteers or users themselves.

Similar principles apply to sitting services in the home, where workers need to determine how best to use their sitting time in discussion with carers and service users. Depending on what people want, this might involve playing games, taking people on outings or simply spending time talking. What is not acceptable is for sitters to work with the ethos that they are there solely to look after physical needs and undertake supervision. Organisations providing respite care can benefit from undertaking an audit of the service they provide with reference to the wishes of users and carers. If the carer knows that the respite service will provide a friendly, stimulating environment with suitable activity there will be less chance that they will feel guilty about asking the person they care for to attend.

Sensitivity to carers

Furthermore, respite services need to be sensitive to the role and needs of the carer. Crossing the threshold into the strange environment of residential unit or day centre can be daunting for many people and a key way of addressing this is that staff should be welcoming and encouraging in attitude. Unfortunately, all too often the opposite effect is achieved and staff appear offhand and uninterested. In some situations this may simply be lack of empathy with the carer. Customer care training such as learning and using people's names, and being welcoming, courteous and helpful can resolve problems. Sometimes, however, there may be an institutionalised attitude to respite along the lines of 'we're taking over now – you have a break'. In extreme cases there may be antagonism towards carers, an attitude that suggests they are interfering with the smooth running of a service which knows what it is doing.

Example

A manager of a respite home described with exasperation the behaviour of the husband of a woman with Alzheimer's disease who was having respite care. The man, who himself suffered ill health, spent most of his day in the home with his wife, feeding her at mealtimes and going home late in the evening. The manager and her staff had done all they could to persuade him not to come to the home and to spend more time having a break. They could not understand the point of the carer having respite when he spent most of his time with his wife. There was also an undercurrent of resentment that the man was taking up a place which another carer could have used to more advantage.

In this situation the manager failed to see that the carer might be benefiting from the respite in a number of ways, for instance the break of being alone at night or being able to care for his wife without total responsibility. She was looking at things from her own perspective and failing to understand the attitude and feelings of the carer. The importance of providers of respite care being sensitive to the needs of carers and able to give support over emotional needs can not be over-emphasised. Two practical way of achieving this are either to have a designated carer support worker employed in respite facilities with the responsibility of picking up on the needs of carers, or to use the key worker system so that particular workers will relate to carers as well as service users. The need for carers to be reassured that their relative is being properly looked after should never be underestimated.

Of course, at the same time there will be situations where the relationship between carer and service user may be problematic and respite may be used as an opportunity to give the user a break from the carer. This scenario most often occurs where there are mental health issues on the part of the carer. In such situations a sensitive approach will need to be taken with the carer to establish parameters for their contact during the respite, based on the wishes of the service user.

Finally there are a number of practical reasons for establishing strong links between the respite facility and the carer. In relation to people who have mental confusion, or whose ability to communicate is severely impaired, carers have consistently pointed out that residential respite care can be detrimental to the individual's mental or physical condition. Their testimony is that people can return from respite care in a worse condition than when they entered it, involving considerably more work on the part of the carer (Twigg, Atkin and Perring 1990). Conditions include increased disorientation and agitation, reduced physical capabilities such as mobility and self-care, and health conditions such as constipation and infections. Carers who experience this often indicate that respite is more trouble than it is worth.

In order to address this, thorough preparation is needed from the respite unit. This involves: talking with the carer to understand the individual's condition and following their suggestions for how best to support them; getting the individual gradually used to the unit with visits, possibly involving the carer; and developing the environment so that it minimises disorientation. For people with advanced dementia, their condition may indicate that, however good the care, they will experience further confusion in an unfamiliar location. In these situations, care in the person's own home is indicated.

In the case of home-based respite, individual home care workers need to work on the basis that they are entering someone else's territory, therefore they should gather as much information about how carers/users like to see tasks carried out and, providing these do not contravene safety standards or agency policy, should endeavour to work to these requirements. Workers need to take care to fit in with the routines of the household. Timing of support and punctuality are also extremely important to carers. If a carer has arranged to meet friends to go shopping or on a theatre trip it is essential that the sitter or care worker arrives on time. Respite promised at a non-specific time during the day or even in the week is likely to be satisfactory to very few carers. The personal relationship between the home care worker and the carer should also not be underestimated. Many carers give witness to the personal support they receive through developing a positive relationship with such workers, usually through having someone to talk to who is sympathetic and who understands the situation.

Emergency care

Concern about what would happen to the person they care for, should they fall ill or have an accident, is a real concern for carers, especially those coping on their own, without back-up support from friends or relatives. With an ageing population of carers, illness and accidents are not uncommon events, and even relatively mild health problems such as flu can mean that a carer is simply unable to continue. Because of these concerns, carers require two main approaches to services. First, an emergency service so that care can be provided swiftly when needed, and second, to know that the care provided will be of a high quality so that they can have the peace of mind to concentrate on getting well themselves.

All agencies need an emergency social care service which operates outside office hours, is known to all relevant other emergency services such as the police and hospital casualty, and which offers access to practical support. A development from this which has proved particularly useful to carers is the Carers' Emergency Card, a card carried by carers which indicates that in the event of an emergency, there is a person who has been left alone who requires care. For instance, in the unfortunate event of a carer being knocked down and left unconscious, emergency services would find a large, distinctive card which gives a contact telephone number. To be effective, this system requires that there should always be someone on the other end of the telephone and that cards should be anonymous, in case they should fall into the hands of unscrupulous people. Such systems can be operated with any telephone alarm system such as Piper Lifeline. The central control office's would be the contact number on the card and would have names and numbers of people to contact in an emergency. Failing this they would alert the relevant statutory service. While such services are rarely used, they provide peace of mind for carers and in the exceptional circumstances when they are used, prove a vital service.

An emergency response service, specifically for carers, can also give great practical support and peace of mind in crisis situations. Such a service is again utilised if a carer is ill or has an accident, and provides very short-term intensive support to give the time for a more permanent solution to be provided. Rather than having to go into residential care, support can be immediately arranged within that person's home. Emergency response can either be a designated service for this purpose or, perhaps more economically, can be supplied as a component of an ordinary home care service. It is most helpfully used at weekends or during the night when access to personnel who can organise support packages is limited. However, with such schemes caution must be taken that expectations are not unrealistically raised. If alternative sources of informal care are not available it may be financially prohibitive for any agency to provide 24-hour care in an individual's home on a long-term basis.

A 24-hour helpline to give advice and support is also a service much requested by carers. Warner (1995) indicates that 20 per cent of local authorities already have such a service and suggests that this should be extended to cover all areas.

Specialist carers' services

That there should be one point of access to services is often a plea from carers, bemused by the variety of organisations which provide services and the different ways of accessing these. There are of course logistical difficulties in achieving this aim – carers form an extensive group with a variety of needs due to the different people they care for. Geography will also be a factor, with the dilemma between providing local access points which are convenient but may not serve a sufficient population and a central location which may be relatively inaccessible. Solutions to such problems include mechanisms such as having a carers' helpline number based in an organisation which has a thorough knowledge of issues relating to all groups of carers, where workers can give accurate information and refer carers on to appropriate services.

An extension of this is the carers' centre, of which there are over 50 in Britain (Carers Impact 1997). Carers' centres often prove a focus for generic services for carers, which might include: self-help groups, specialist carers' workers, training, counselling, information about services. Carers' centres often operate on both an informal, drop-in basis and with organised activities. They might have facilities for sitters to enable carers to attend the centre or may organise joint events. In one evaluation of a general carers' centre, it was found that the centre was appreciated by those who attended, who tended to be carers who had not reached the situation where they needed great input of services. It was, therefore, useful for targeting hidden carers at an early stage. However, it proved expensive to operate and had to negotiate conflicting demands from carer groups who wanted different things from the service (Department of Health 1991).

Some centres are more specialist, catering for groups such as people with mental health problems, people with dementia or children with disabilities. Depending on the scale of funding, these may be resource centres which include access to respite services such as respite beds or day care, outreach support, laundry services and specialist equipment. More modest developments will operate more on a self-help basis, perhaps a carers' organisation establishing a drop-in service for particular carers at the weekend.

Carers' support workers

Recent years have seen a great increase in the number of workers who specialise in working with carers. There are currently over 1000 carers' support workers throughout the country (Carers Impact 1997), generally working within voluntary agencies but with some placed within statutory services. Carers' support workers are likely to have a wide range of responsibilities which, depending on the focus of the post, may include: organising therapeutic or support groups, undertaking one-to-one support, giving information and advice, organising volunteers, taking part in development activities such as helping to develop services, and promoting carer involvement. Just as with carers' centres, many carers' support workers are generic, but some specialise in supporting particular groups of people. For instance, a mental health carers' worker might undertake the above duties, but in relation to mental health carers alone. In addition, a number of practitioners have specific responsibilities for carers as well as other work: for instance a social worker or social work team who have responsibility for older people *and* carers. Carers often express satisfaction with the services they receive from carers' support workers, because they are perceived as being specifically for *them*.

There are a number of advantages in having practitioners who specialise in work with carers. They will be able to develop considerable expertise in direct work with carers, generally undertaking interventions such as groupwork, individual support, and training. They will also be able to compile extensive information of relevance to carers. Their expertise is generally recognised by other workers who will use them as a resource for information and support, and in this way knowledge about carers is spread. Disadvantages include the danger that organisations, and other workers, can act as if all their responsibilities towards carers are discharged through the specialist worker. Carers' organisations generally agree that the most important aspect of support to carers are mainstream services which provide practical relief and that specialist support should be regarded as a useful adjunct to this.

The role of volunteers

Many organisations use volunteers to support carers and they provide excellent help in tasks such as taking people on outings, a sitting service and listening to carers. Twigg *et al.* (1990) indicate how volunteers who may find it unrewarding to work with 'unresponsive' service users such as people who have dementia, may gain satisfaction from establishing a relationship with their carer and perceiving how their help benefits them. However, it is extremely problematic to use volunteers to provide services which involve high levels of personal care or where services must be provided to eliminate risk. 'Volunteers can make a significant contribution…but the provision of regular respite and help with caring tasks that carers rely on can only be provided through a paid service (Department of Health 1991, p.60).

Services for carers from ethnic minorities

Carers from ethnic minority groups require access to the whole range of services appropriate for carers but often face the difficulty that the services on offer may not be appropriate. The white home-help entering a Chinese person's home may unwittingly cause offence. The Asian elder attending an English-speaking day centre to give their carer respite may sit alone and unhappy throughout the day. Specialist services for people from ethnic minorities will generally address such problems, but these are not widespread and many carers will need to access mainstream services about which they may have considerable anxiety. Here we consider the most commonly encountered concerns and some approaches to dealing with them.

Gender

People may be concerned that their relative may be given personal care by someone of the opposite sex, or that they may mix with people from the opposite sex. Where personal care is involved organisations need to ensure that a practitioner of the preferred sex is supplied.

Diet

Cultures with strong norms around food will need to have these respected. Most services such as meals on wheels, residential care and day care can now provide ethnically appropriate meals to at least the same standard as other meals which are supplied. Special meals can also be commissioned from local restaurants.

Language

Carers may be concerned that no one will be able to talk to their relative and that they will become withdrawn and isolated. Indeed this can be a problem even where there are specialist services. At a Chinese lunch club one woman who spoke Hakka was unable to communicate with the other members who spoke Cantonese. While there may be no ideal solution to such difficulties there are a number of measures which can be taken to improve the situation. Volunteers who speak the language may be recruited to support the person at the service, or, where unavailable, workers may be commissioned to take on this role. Interpreters should also be used on an ongoing basis, so far as resources permit, and should not be confined to the assessment stage of any care package. Practitioners can also be encouraged to pay particular attention to the needs of the individual; many in such situations learn some of the person's language in order to be able to communicate. Sometimes creative solutions can be sought. One man who was the only Asian person in a residential home was regularly visited by a college student who wished to learn some of his language and in return took him on outings.

Racism

Carers may fear that their relative may face racism either from staff or from other service users. Most established organisations now undertake staff training and have equal opportunities policies which preclude racist behaviour and remarks from staff or service users. Organisations need to continue to work to ensure that these policies are implemented effectively.

Religious/cultural practices

Carers may be concerned that these will not be respected. Any organisation which is commissioned to provide a service for someone from an ethnic minority has a responsibility to understand that person's religious and cultural needs and to try to meet these. Research, and good communication with the carer, service user and local communities therefore need to take place. At the same time an individual approach must be taken with work undertaken to match services, carer and service user appropriately. For instance, the assumption that people always prefer a home-help from their own culture may be confounded by a family who wish for a white home-help so as to keep a distance from their community.

One problem which is in evidence from the above concerns is that organisations are not adept at informing communities about what they can provide. There is little point in providing ethnic diets and then not informing people that you have done so, since they will undoubtedly operate on the assumption that you have not! Similarly, conforming to a policy which seeks to preclude racism may be second nature to people who work within social care, but black members of the public may have no knowledge that this policy exists. All organisations could benefit from a mechanism to inform black people about what they can expect from services. This could take the form of a list of service standards which would be translated into a number of relevant languages, publicised widely and given to any carer in receipt of services.

Direct support for carers

Perhaps one of the most difficult areas is in providing support for carers from ethnic minorities to enable them to talk through their experiences of caring and learn techniques for dealing with these more effectively. It is particularly difficult for people who are unable to communicate well in English to access services such as counselling or carers' groups. Where black people do speak English, many gain benefit from attending mainstream carers' groups – the experiences of being a carer in many ways transcend cultural differences.

Establishing specialist groups for carers from ethnic minorities will depend upon local circumstances. Wing Kwong and Kerrie (1992) describe a successful group run for Chinese carers of people with mental health problems, whereas Butt and Mirza (1996) indicate that a group for Asian carers was found not to be appropriate, instead individual home visits by a community worker took place. On the other hand, in research by Shah (1992), 98 per cent of Asian families indicated that they would like to meet other parents in similar situations. In order to develop such support the ideal solution is for organisations to employ a specialist bilingual carers' worker. Where such a person is not available, it is important for carers' workers and bilingual workers who may not be specialised in supporting carers to work closely together. Such co-working in carers' groups can prove very effective, combining expertise in language and culture with knowledge of working with carers.

The importance of support for service users

The services which have been discussed up to this point form components which can be combined to provide the basis of a strategy of service provision for carers. In organising services, however, it is useful to bear the following in mind as underpinning principles. Many carers point out that if service users received the level of services that they require in their own right there would be little need for specialist services for carers. Also that a small amount of the right type of service is of infinitely more use than a large amount of a service which is not really effective. For example there is little sense in someone attending a day centre all day in order to give a carer a break when what they really need is to be freed for two hours in the evening. All care should be organised in such a way that it is based on the individual needs of carers.

The point is also made that certain minority carer groups are at a distinct disadvantage in terms of service provision. These are carers who look after people with substantial and specialist needs, but where the numbers of people involved has been insufficient for agencies to provide the range and level of services that mainstream groups can access. These groups include carers of people with conditions such as autistic spectrum disorders, brain injuries and early-onset dementia. Many carers of these people find it difficult to obtain appropriate services for the people they care for, for instance carers of people who suffer from dementia in their forties will rarely find day care which is age-appropriate for their relative. Furthermore, a recent report by the Health Advisory Service (1996) indicates that poor co-ordination of services means that such carers are put under unnecessary stress. Obviously, specialist support for these service user groups should be well co-ordinated and as extensive as resources allow. It is also important that the needs of carers in such groups are not neglected and that they are informed about general carers' services.

A related issue which has been highlighted by the Social Service Inspectorate (1995c) is that of equity between services for different groups of people in need. Some services are common to all carers – home care, for instance, may equally well be delivered to the carer of someone with learning disabilities as to the carer of someone with dementia. Some services are carer group specific such as a resource centre for people with dementia. Resource allocation in relation to different carer groups may be totally different. The challenge for authorities is in finding ways of quantifying how much support is allocated to which service, in relation to priorities and level of need.

Checklist of considerations for services for carers

- Is there a multi-agency agreement on a definition of respite?
- Are there clear, available eligibility criteria for respite care?
- How many of the following types of respite are available: residential care, nursing home care, hospital respite, home-based day and night sitting, shared care, day care?
- How are mainstream services such as home care made carer-friendly?
- What measures are taken to ensure that respite is flexible?
- Are people able to book in advance and at short notice?
- What is the variation in lengths of respite available?
- What are the opening hours of day centres?
- What measures do day and residential units take to encourage carer involvement?
- Does unit-based respite have a full programme of meaningful activities?
- What specialist services for carers are available?
- What arrangements are in place for emergency care and how are these carer-friendly?
- Is there a 24-hour carer-friendly helpline?
- How does the organisation ensure that services between carer groups are equitable?

6

Direct Work with Carers
Preparation

'It's not just me! When I went to my first support group I just sat and listened. Practically everything anyone had said, done or felt also applied to me. I went home and felt so much better. The next session I went to, they could hardly shut me up. Even now the thought "it's not just me" gives me something to hold on to when things are really bad.' (A carer)

As we have seen, carers indicate that they have a variety of needs, some of which can be met by improving service provision while others require more personal support. In this chapter we examine what might be termed direct work with carers. This can be defined as interventions in which a carer has face-to-face contact with a worker or other carers, through which they are helped to develop personal strategies and skills to address all aspects of the caring role.

Direct work is a wide concept which can encompass a variety of aims. For instance, a group may be run to enable carers to learn skills better to support the person they care for, or alternatively the carer may desire individual space to examine their life with the possibility of withdrawing from caring tasks. Carers' needs are manifold and will change at different stages of the caring 'career', so there can be no one method of providing support which will be appropriate in all circumstances. However, work with carers in recent years has developed a number of approaches which have proven effective. Here we draw these approaches together to provide a clear framework for practitioners intending to undertake direct work with carers.

Key elements in direct work

In Chapter 3, the social care needs of carers were categorised under a number of headings: emotional support; information; improving communication and problem solving; stress management; training in caring skills. Almost every form of direct support for carers will involve at least one of these *key elements*. Even a carers' group focused on fund-raising and lobbying for services generally also provides some information and emotional support. In fact many groups cover all these topics, although they may not have distinguished them quite so clearly. By recognising these as distinct components, practitioners will have a model which they can use to plan and develop their work. In the following chapters the key elements will be presented in a modular form with the intention that they can be combined and customised to fulfil the needs of particular organisations and the carers they wish to support.

An example of a general course for carers of older people run by Cheshire Social Services included sessions on the following subjects: a perspective on ageing; handling medication; day care; health care; assessment; long and short-term care; safer handling; money matters; help in the home; coping with confusion; losing a loved one; emergency first aid; continence advice; making time for yourself. The programme had been designed following consultation with carers and based on experience of previous courses. As can be seen, it is a well-rounded course which encompasses many of the key elements. An alternative approach would be to focus on one particular area, such as an in-depth course on stress management.

However, before looking at the content of direct work, consideration needs to be given to the format for any intervention and the planning and preparation that needs to take place for it to be successful.

Choosing the format

Work with carers has generally taken place in the following formats: groupwork, individual sessions or sessions with the family. The key elements can be applied in any of these settings: for example, an individual session may be structured in such a way that the first half is spent listening to the carer and providing emotional support, while the rest of the time involves training in practical skills such as bathing; a series of sessions with a family may involve improving communication and problem solving, with an important component being that the family work on a stress management task, such as doing something enjoyable together. All three formats have particular merits and which of these is most appropriate for a given situation will depend upon the needs of the carer and the abilities and expertise of workers within the organisation. The following are considerations which need to be taken into account when choosing a format.

Groupwork and work with individuals

Groupwork with carers, in particular its subdivision, the self-help group, has proved particularly popular with practitioners and carers. It is significant because it is one of the few methods which focus almost exclusively on the needs of the carer rather than those of the service user (Twigg *et al.* 1990). Carers continually cite the most useful feature of a group as the chance to meet other people in the same situation as themselves and to gain support from feeling that they are not the only ones that are experiencing problems. In this they mirror feedback from a wide range of support groups, such as those for people experiencing depression, agoraphobia or redundancy, where, in evaluations, this factor is often cited as more important to members than the content of sessions or the role of the facilitator.

In addition to establishing mutual support, a group setting enables a skilled facilitator to draw upon the dynamics of group interactions. Members may be able to assist with problem solving or in giving suggestions as to how communication could be improved. Being in a group can be an extremely powerful experience for individuals, particularly in terms of the emotional effects of being truly listened to by a group of people. A further practical advantage of the group setting is that it provides value for money in terms of the ratio between a worker's time and the number of people seen. This combination of benefits has led to groupwork being a preferred intervention to support carers.

Individual work with carers is most appropriate for people who have a particular need for individual attention. There can be a number of reasons for this. Some people experience high levels of distress through coming to a crisis in caring. They may need the time and space to explore their options or may require the more intensive support involved in sessions with qualified counsellors. Alternatively they may have multi-faceted issues, complex situations where there are many factors to resolve, such as financial problems combined with a stressful relationship with the person they are caring for. Again, some people have very specific concerns such as complex benefits issues which can be resolved more easily in a way which focuses on detail and is less time-consuming than attending a general course on benefits. It can also be the case that someone presents as having problems due to their role as a carer, but on exploration it is found that their real issues may be around other life problems, such as marital relationships or previous childhood abuse.

There are a variety of ways in which individual sessions for carers can be organised. Workers in resource centres may have a brief to undertake individual work with new carers or those who are experiencing particular problems. Carers organisations may use workers or volunteers to give individual time to carers, either in a centre or within the person's own home. For carers needing more support than can be provided by someone with good listening skills, there could be a system of referring people to qualified counsellors who have an interest in working with carers.

Therefore, when assessing whether a person will most benefit from a group or individual time, consideration needs to be given to a number of factors. Generally, groupwork may not be appropriate for people who feel very nervous about being with other people and speaking in public. Being in a group not made up of family or friends is alien to many people and not everyone feels sufficiently confident to enter such an environment. Nor is this simply a matter of confidence; some people may mistrust a group setting from the point of view of confidentiality, while others may prefer the focused attention possible in an individual setting. Language may also be a barrier; if a person needs an interpreter, individual sessions may be more appropriate due to the additional time involved in interpreting which may interrupt the flow of the group.

Caution would also have to be used for those who have high levels of distress who may need more time than could be allocated within a group setting. Being part of a group involves a general requirement to share experiences and to value those of other people; if an individual is so involved in their own situation that they are unable to give sufficient attention to other people they will not benefit from a group. This also applies to people who may have problems which go beyond those which are generally experienced by carers. Someone struggling to come to terms with caring for a parent who previously sexually abused them may find it difficult to talk in a group where other members have no experience of this. Similarly, the rest of the group may find it difficult to engage with someone in these circumstances.

Finally, it can be useful to have a relationship between individual and groupwork interventions. Individual sessions can be used to introduce people to a group setting once they have established sufficient confidence. One method is to use a short number of individual sessions to allow people to feed into a group. This can be done if people are reluctant about joining a group but there are strong reasons for feeling that this will be of benefit to them. For instance, some carers have myths about how other people care, particularly that other people are coping better than they are, and may fear having 'inadequacies' exposed to others. In this situation it is exactly the format that the carers are afraid of which will almost certainly allay their fears.

Family work

With the exception of people with mental health problems, work with families involved in caring has not been prevalent in Britain. There appear to be a number of reasons for this. One of the most significant is that family work is seen as a highly specialist field. For instance, relationship counselling is viewed as requiring different, additional skills from individual counselling. This is even more the case with formal family therapy which is usually undertaken by qualified specialists working within a theoretical framework which may be professionally led, the opposite ethos to the carer-led approach. To some extent family work has also gained a reputation as a potentially harmful intervention. Work with families which has focused on analysing relationships has come to be regarded as counterproductive, inclining people to assign blame and scapegoat family members rather than work positively on solving problems. Also significant is the fact that much of the front-line involvement with carers falls in the field of work with older people, where practitioners are unlikely to have the experience to undertake family work.

Whatever the reasons for the lack of family work with carers, this is not because of absence of need. Relationship problems can make the caring relationship intolerable, if not breaking it down altogether, and even the most compatible relationships may encounter some problems. Appropriate family work can therefore be an extremely effective tool in working with carers. Most obviously, it can be used where there are problems and conflicts between family members. Problem solving and communications skills taught within the family environment can be more effective than in isolation. This can be compared with the well-known phenomenon of someone who attends assertiveness training, re-invents their style of social interaction and terrifies family and friends in the process! By all parties attending together, there will be mutual understanding of what they are trying to achieve. Of course, this assumes that there is at least a measure of openness and willingness to change in the people involved.

Family work is also useful as preparation for caring or as a preventative measure to avoid potential problems. To this end a family new to the role could meet together with a worker to plan how they will manage caring, and being cared for. Topics such as how to manage change, and relative roles and responsibilities, could all be covered, to enable family members to consider what might be involved in being carers. Problem-solving techniques can also be used in family groups and with couples. In the latter situation, relationship counselling may also be an effective intervention. Finally, where relationships within families have reached impasse and require the intervention of someone independent, workers can be involved in mediation.

The worker's skills

Direct work around the key elements can be approached by anyone who has basic training or experience in running groups or basic counselling skills; therefore it can be undertaken by paid workers, volunteers, carers themselves or with joint work between all three. There is certainly no sense in which people offering support to carers should only be highly qualified professionals. Carers who wish to take on the role of supporting other carers certainly have a valid role to play. At the same time there is a spectrum of skill involved in some elements. For instance, communication, covered as part of a course with the aim of increasing people's information about caring, will require the ability to facilitate a group; whereas teaching communication skills to family members where there is considerable friction will require greater levels of expertise.

Before starting any intervention, practitioners need to examine themselves, considering whether they have sufficient knowledge and experience to be effective in the work. In some areas, work with carers is undertaken by qualified health or social work care practitioners but in others, often because of resource issues, this is left to people who are not qualified or experienced. This can lead to a very real dilemma in that a need is perceived, but the only available people to address this lack expertise. In such situations a balance needs to be struck between doing nothing, and thereby depriving carers of a service, and protecting potentially vulnerable carers. Workers and organisations need to take on the responsibility of ensuring that the work they intend to undertake is within their level of skill. To this end it can be useful to consider the following questions.

Do I have the skills and experience to undertake this work?

Many skills are transferable: people who have experience in working in similar areas with other user groups will generally be able to call on these when working with carers; similarly, those who are accomplished in counselling individuals will be able to build on these skills to work with families. Other skills are comparable, in that they allow people to establish abilities in a particular area quickly. For instance, someone who has experience as a teacher, particularly if this has been with adults in a facilitating rather than a lecturing role, may quickly pick up groupwork skills. However, one fallacy which is often encountered is the belief that being or having been a carer means that an individual will automatically be able to help other carers. Having experienced any situation – caring, bereavement, mental health problems – may give empathy and understanding, but how effective such people are as practitioners depends on their ability to learn the necessary skills, and, most importantly, to be detached from their own personal issues.

Could I benefit from co-working?

A useful way of picking up skills is to be 'apprenticed' to another worker who has experience in the relevant area. This format is often used when a professionally facilitated carers' group develops into a self-help group. Members who wish to take on a facilitative role in the group might start by assisting the facilitator, thereby developing confidence and skills. It is often possible for less-experienced groups to ask for time-limited support from a qualified worker, especially if this is seen as a method of expanding expertise and increasing services. For instance, a social worker with particular responsibility for working with carers may be willing to provide initial support to day centre workers in running a carers' group. Furthermore, organisations with facilities for training may be willing to offer free places on internal training courses to enable people intending to work with carers to learn the relevant skills.

Is there anyone to support me when I do the work?

Working without support is generally acknowledged to be detrimental for both practitioners and service users. Supervision gives workers a chance to check out how the intervention is progressing, to consider options for improving their approach, and to address any personal issues which may have arisen. It is necessary for experienced practitioners, and essential for people who are less confident. There are a wide range of options for making sure that work is not carried out in an unsupported way. Professional supervision, line management and informal or peer consultation can all be used effectively.

Do I know where to refer to, if someone needs more support than I can give?

One of the main anxieties expressed by self-help groups is that they may be unable to cope if an individual becomes very distressed or unwell, or if a group member has mental health problems (Wilson 1988). Practitioners need a sound understanding of the options that are available for people who need further support. This ranges from immediate, emergency help to specialist workers or organisations to which the individual can be referred. Similarly, the practitioner needs to consider if they would know what to do if someone started crying, screaming, arguing, sleeping etc. If they do not, this indicates that they need to develop more experience or ask for support.

Defining needs, aims and objectives

Defining needs, aims and objectives are the foundation stones of any direct work with people in the field of social care and should be standard practice for all situations. Without going through the formal stage of considering these and, preferably, recording them, we run the risk of reverting to the type of intervention which was based on instinctive reaction to a good idea and was not thought through. Unless we achieve clarity about what we intend to undertake there will always be a tendency for our work to be vague, directionless, and unsuitable for evaluation. Thinking in terms of needs, aims and objectives can often become second nature, however even if this is the case it is always useful to go through the formal exercise of writing down our framework for action. This is especially pertinent if we are about to commit substantial resources, in terms of staff and carer time and energy to a project.

Posing the question 'what needs will be met with this intervention?' focuses us clearly on the reasons behind undertaking the work. Perhaps we have identified a problem of social isolation, or a particular individual is having trouble communicating with the person they care for. Once we have established the need, we can consider its extent. How many people are expressing feelings of isolation? If we have come across three people do we assume this is a trend and that others may wish to be involved in what we plan? Is the need within our remit or a priority for our organisation? Will our time best be spent by addressing it, or do we simply note it and carry on with work which is of a higher priority? When such questions have been considered we can then turn to aims and objectives.

Based on needs, aims and objectives outline what is intended to be achieved from the intervention. An aim is more general and indicates overall purpose, giving a clear answer to the question: what is the intervention for? Examples of aims include: to enable members of the group to feel that they have people they can contact if they feel in crisis; to help Stan to have some time off from caring for his wife. So long as they are not contradictory, an intervention can have a number of aims. Objectives are specific and measurable and indicate what can be achieved at particular stages. Relating to aims, they break down the overall purpose into realistic and achievable goals. Examples of objectives could include: the group will organise a visit to the theatre; Stan will ask his wife if she will accept a sitter so he can visit some friends.

Aims and objectives should be viewed as tools to enable the intervention to progress, rather than constraints that limit flexibility and response. It is not unusual in group settings, and in carers' groups in particular, to find that the focus of the group has to change due to the interests of members. This can be the case even when a considerable amount of research has been undertaken into what is needed. For instance, a group which is set up to look at training in practical skills may have more interest in disclosing feelings and generating group support. Alternatively, sessions to enable an individual to talk through personal problems may quickly run out of steam, and a need to address practical issues may emerge. In such circumstances we need to reformulate aims and objectives in light of newly assessed needs.

Another extremely important purpose of clear aims and objectives for an intervention is to use these to inform potential members about its nature and purpose. Carers are often on the periphery of any service and have an unclear idea of what might be involved in any organised sessions. The mistake of assuming that carers will know what to expect from a group by its title can easily be made and can lead to embarrassment, confusion and discontent in the first session. Good advance information about a group can enable people to choose whether it is, in fact, for them.

Carer consultation

Closely linked with the stage of evaluating need, the importance of consultation with carers cannot be overemphasised. Ensuring that their views are sought in relation to the form of intervention increases the likelihood that it will be relevant and useful. Without direct consultation there is a danger that what is planned will not meet people's needs. Even though a worker may have come across many people having problems with lifting a relative, this does not mean that they will be interested in attending a course to learn how to lift properly. Carers' groups are notoriously difficult to organise, since there are a number of reasons why they may prefer not to attend. For one thing there may be practical difficulties – if a sitting service is not provided they may be unable to leave the person they care for. Also, carers often indicate that their spare time is so precious the last thing they want is to spend this in a group talking about caring!

By gauging interest in the activity we can increase its potential for success. We will also avoid falling into the trap of assuming, from an 'expert' standpoint, what carers want. The process of consultation is undoubtedly easier if the setting is one which has a catchment of carers such as a day centre or a carers' organisation. In these cases there is often an established relationship with carers which helps communication. It becomes more difficult if carers need to be contacted through general advertisement or targeting locations such as hospitals or doctors' surgeries. However, the latter give the opportunity to reach a wider group of carers, and potentially those who have not previously had contact with services.

The information to be gathered from consultation needs to be as specific as possible. Questions such as 'would you find it helpful to have information on how to manage stress?' will give misleading information. People generally answer affirmatively to such questions since they agree in general that they are a good idea, but this by no means indicates that they would personally attend such a group. A recent carers' course covering such topics as assertiveness and welfare benefits fell through from complete lack of interest, even though a consultation exercise had been carried out and carers had indicated that these topics were what they wanted. If possible, questions need to be more specific to the point of asking whether individuals would be willing to attend and, if so, when they would be available.

It can also be helpful to use the first session to go through the aims and objectives to make sure that these are indeed relevant to participants. If necessary the agenda for further meetings can be changed in light of new information. Indeed, the process of consultation should be ongoing throughout any intervention, with the practitioner taking their direction from the members. All interventions should have a final evaluation in which those involved can give their perspective on what has been achieved, and what could have been improved.

While consultation is certainly not an infallible process, it certainly increases the chances of success. It is not unusual for carers' groups to fall through after a few sessions for the reasons already cited and others. Carers are often busy people with many commitments and unless they can perceive the benefits of what is happening they are unlikely to continue to give it their time. Even if they value and benefit from a group experience, carers often feel ambivalence about attending; perhaps through worry about leaving the person they care for or guilt about taking time for themselves. All this means that the drop-out rate from groups can be quite high and while it is important that workers evaluate what they have been doing, it is also useful not to be too sensitive about this and to recognise that they may have done nothing 'wrong'.

Practical considerations for running carers' groups

There is a wide range of general groupwork literature which gives guidance for planning and establishing a group (see for instance Brown 1989, Preston Shoot 1987). This section relates established groupwork theory to factors which are specifically pertinent to carers' groups. There is certainly no right or wrong way to plan a carers' group, and if we look around for examples we can find countless variations. Some are open groups where new carers are welcome at any time, while others are closed or have set times for new intakes. There are groups which are ongoing, operating on a weekly or monthly basis for as long as there are people willing to attend, and there are others which are strictly time-limited. Some may be large, up to 50 people attending at any one time, generally for information purposes, while others have less than ten members and tend to focus on personal issues. Basically, the group needs to be customised to fit the needs, aims and objectives of a particular situation.

Membership

In relation to membership of a carers' group, the facilitator needs to decide whether it is appropriate to include both people who have been carers for a number of years and those who are new to caring. There are often advantages to be gained from having such a mix within the group. Those who have been caring for longer may have valuable experience to share with the others. On the other hand there are dangers that long-term carers may be put into the role of 'expert' and thus not be able to have time for their own issues, or conversely may monopolise the group. Also, it may be apparent that people at different stages of caring have different needs which may be hard to reconcile within one group. This issue can be resolved by looking at the overall purpose of the group.

Another dilemma is whether the group should have a mix according to the needs of people that are being cared for. Many groups are organised on this basis – a group for the parents of children with learning disabilities, a group for carers of people who suffer from head injuries etc. Single-subject groups have the advantage of focusing on a particular area; experiences will be similar, information can be specific and expertise can be developed. Mixed groups may pose difficulties in that people cannot relate so easily to each other's problems or topics of interest. Information giving, especially, may need to be so wide that much will not be relevant to some members. On the other hand, a mixed group can prove very effective, with different perspectives contributing to a richness of experience, while single groups can become insular in approach. As a rule of thumb, a focus on information giving and practical support or training best lends itself to single-subject groups while those which focus on more general carers' issues can work with either style. A compromise position is for membership to include carers who fall into broader categories. For instance there could be groups for carers who are parents, for carers following an accident or for carers of older people. This type of arrangement can offer both the benefits of focus and a wider perspective, while avoiding potential problems of wholly mixed groups.

One approach to carers' groups which is less commonly used is that in which carers and the people they care for attend together. Before planning such a group the practitioner would need to consider the following factors. From a carer's point of view the clear disadvantage to this format is that the focus is no longer on their own needs. A support group may be the only place where the carer gets time to think about themselves and what they need. In that space they are able to stand back and reflect on the role of carer rather than simply carrying it out. Having the cared-for person present means that, almost inevitably, the carer will be fully back in role. Depending on circumstances they may be concerned about the person's physical comfort or behaviour. It can also be inhibiting; carers may find it impossible to be honest, or to say what they really think in such a situation. 'Don't deceive yourself that carers will be getting the support they need, if people who are cared for are also present' (A carer quoted in Wilson 1988, p.29).

In many ways it could be said that such joint groups are not strictly speaking carers' groups, although they may have a strong carers component in them. However in some situations this may be the preferred format. When carer and cared-for are working in partnership, attending a group together can reinforce this. For example, a group for people who have experienced strokes and their carers can be an opportunity for both to learn about the condition and ways of improving or managing it. Similarly, if both partners learn skills such as assertiveness or stress management they can help and reinforce each other. Joint groups can also be an opportunity to address problems which can beset the caring relationship in a non-threatening environment. Potential difficulties and conflicts can be introduced by the facilitator as general issues which many people encounter, and can therefore be discussed in a impersonal way.

A further advantage of joint groups is that they avoid any sense of divisiveness between carer and cared-for. Carers sometimes report that the people they are caring for resent them going to a group because they feel the carer will be talking about them and criticising them to other people. This attitude is most often found where the cared-for person does not also have the opportunity to speak with others about what it is like to have a carer! Facilitated sensitively, a joint group can be an opportunity to create open and equal relationships with good communication between those involved. It can also be preventative, in that those attending can consider the problematic issues that can arise from the carer relationship and agree to find methods to manage these. As such it can be particularly appropriate when people are new to the relationship, and can almost be regarded as preparation training, in a similar way to preparation for retirement courses.

In some situations joint groups will be organised in order to work on solving problems in relationships between carers and cared-for. While this has been most prevalent in the context of people experiencing mental health problems and their families, the model can be applied to any caring relationship. With this approach the aim of the group will be to enable families to explore together the difficulties they have been experiencing and to find ways of managing these. Nearly always a behavioural, problem-solving approach is emphasised and exploration of past events and causes of problems not encouraged. Group family work demands considerable expertise in the facilitator.

An important factor in deciding whether people might benefit from a joint group is the nature of the relationship between individuals. All must be willing at least to try to develop honest, supportive relationships and to work together to improve their lives. At a more basic level, if the person being cared for has some form of mental disability, such as advanced dementia, there will usually be little benefit in them attending a group with their carer.

Resources

Practical issues such as the time of meetings, venue and access to transport are important factors for the success of any group, but with carers we need to be especially careful about these issues because their responsibilities may prevent them from attending. Groups can literally stand or fall by whether arrangements are made appropriately. For carers who cannot freely leave the person they care for, alternative care will need to be provided. In some settings this is easily resolved – a resource centre may provide a group for carers at the same time as the service user attends the centre – however, for organisations without access to services or with limited finance this can prove difficult. Sitting services in a person's home may be freely available from some organisations, alternatively a system of reliable volunteers could be organised. An important point is that whatever care is provided the carer must feel both confident and comfortable with it. We can hardly expect people to sit easily through their first carers' group, which might be anxiety-provoking in itself, if they are worried that they have left their child for the first time with a strange carer. As a note of caution I would suggest that very careful enquiries be made as to whether people would actually use relief care. I suspect it is not an uncommon experience for organisers to provide an 'adult crèche' or sitting services only to find that, after all, people make their own arrangements.

The venue is also important. This needs to be comfortable and quiet with good access for people with disabilities. Ideally the location will be central to the catchment of participants and will be close to good public transport links. Sometimes members may require transport to get to the group, especially if groups are held in the evening or in areas where public transport is problematic. It is often possible to use the resources of group participants to organise transport, with people who have their own vehicles giving lifts to those who have not.

Endings

The majority of carers' groups which are organised by paid workers are time-limited. In such groups it is important that the ending is planned from the start of the group. Groups can become extremely significant for some carers, providing social and emotional outlets which they cannot experience elsewhere. It is important that such groups end on a positive note – the last session could be devoted to an evaluation of what people have learnt, to celebration, and to discussion about the future. Sometimes it is sufficient for group members to pursue informal friendships that have been made in the course of the group. If there is a genuine feeling in the group that there is still work to be done it is possible to extend it. Alternatively the group could develop into a self-help format.

It is important to realise that with carers' groups there will be both natural and unexpected endings. As we have seen, workers should not be surprised if the group fizzles out after a couple of weeks through poor attendance. In the case of an ongoing group, even if the group is thriving there is likely to come a time at which membership drops and there is not sufficient energy or will to revitalise it. An example of this is a group which became polarised in terms of the age of carers, with a faction of older carers looking after spouses and parents and a group of younger carers who were generally caring for disabled children. The aims and wishes of these two groups were so incompatible that the group experienced conflict then wound down, with a subgroup of younger carers forming a new group.

Another important feature of the end of a group is that, depending on its purpose, it may be appropriate to assess whether individuals could benefit from follow-up support of a different type. For instance, an individual carer experiencing problems at home might benefit from mediation or other family work.

Professionally led and self-help groups

The self-help group is run by and for its members. Its defining features are that it uses the experiences, skills and expertise of group members to help each other. Some groups adhere to the strictest form of self-help in which only members who are carers can be involved in the group. Sometimes former carers are expected to leave a group at a certain time after they have ceased to care for someone. Others have a looser format in which former carers, workers and experts in various fields can be invited to give information or assist members in some way. Groups can vary from highly structured – managed by elected committees – to informal – where members take on responsibility on an *ad hoc* basis. Generally, self-help groups tend to concentrate on information giving, emotional support, social support and campaigning. Self-help in relation to individual support is much less prevalent.

The relationship between professionally led and self-help groups varies across different areas. In some localities there is good communication with cross-referral between organisations. At the other extreme, relationships are poor, with carers' groups being set up in opposition to professional services and workers being excluded from these. Difficulties in relationships may arise through negative experiences that carers have had of paid workers or indeed, negative experiences workers have had of certain carers! They may also occur because of ideologies embraced by the respective organisations, with either carers or workers perceived as the true 'experts'.

Proponents of the two forms of groups have sometimes taken up mutually exclusive positions about their value, with carers' organisations seeing professionally led groups as disempowering and unresponsive to carers' needs, while paid workers view self-help groups as unprofessional with low standards on issues such as confidentiality. Not only is this polarisation an unhelpful stereotype, but the picture it presents is fundamentally skewed. In reality it is perfectly possible to find professional groups operating with poor professional standards while a carers' group may be dominated by one person and become the essence of autocracy. Furthermore, as services for carers develop, many carers' organisations employ their own paid workers who may often support self-help groups, while carers may be involved in co-working with paid practitioners in statutory organisations, thus blurring the distinction between professional and non-professional.

Obviously, where such divisions exist they can only be detrimental to the service carers receive. One way of breaking through this is to focus again on the needs of carers. If we examine what people generally want to achieve from any supportive intervention, there are a number of key factors that can be applied to carers. People attending a group generally want the facilitator to be skilled enough to manage the group so they can achieve their personal goals. They also want someone who is sympathetic and able to empathise with their problems.

They want an environment in which they are respected and in which they feel safe enough to express their views without any negative consequence. From this we can conclude that whether a group is led by a worker or is in self-help format may not be that relevant to its members. In many ways a group is as good as its facilitator – if he or she is skilful at their task then the group will be successful. To this end, facilitators have a responsibility to make sure they have the requisite skills. In particular, care professionals will need to make sure that they take their agenda from carers, while self-help facilitators need to develop groupwork skills.

Making the transition

An interesting link between professionally led and self-help groups is that many of the latter originate in the former. Probably the majority of practitioners who establish carers' groups have the intention that the group should develop into self-help when they withdraw. However, in many cases this vision does not transfer into reality – the self-help group fails to materialise or runs for a couple of sessions before attendance disintegrates. There are a number of reasons for this; sometimes the group has run its course or there is insufficient chemistry between members to make them want to stay together; alternatively the facilitator has not done sufficient preparation to help the group survive. In the worst scenario the worker will leave the group with an 'over to you' in the last meeting, leaving participants to sink or swim.

The following are elements of good practice to enable a group to make the transition from professionally led to self-help. The possibility for this should be raised by the facilitator at various stages in the group. However, it is important that this should be presented as a possibility rather than an expectation which might put pressure on members. If the group wishes to continue, the facilitator should set aside a number of further sessions to cover topics such as the aims and objectives of the group and members' responsibilities – a group may fail because of an argument about whose turn it is to make the tea! Preferably an agreement will be recorded in writing to form the basis of the group. It may also be useful for the facilitator to help the group plan their first few sessions, as a basis for future independent developments. Where groups are looking to become formally established, local voluntary organisations such as Councils for Voluntary Service can advise.

It can also be useful to organise training for group members in topics such as listening skills and facilitation so that they can develop the skills required to facilitate a self-help group. Finally the withdrawal of the current facilitator needs to be negotiated with sensitivity. There may be an emotional attachment between the worker and the group, so that both sides may find if difficult to detach. Sometimes this can lead to the worker being reluctant to leave the group, or alternatively withdrawing too soon because of concern about the group becoming dependent. The facilitator needs to have an open discussion with group members about these issues and work out a plan of withdrawal that is mutually acceptable. Useful guidelines on running self-help groups can be found in *Caring Together* (Wilson 1988).

Training

A point often made by carers is that they are expected to undertake tasks, which in other circumstances would be done by trained, qualified workers, with no training and little support. From this, it has been a short step to the idea that carers would benefit from training in relation to what they do. Providing training for carers is, however, a concept which is not without problems. There is a school of thought within the carers movement which views training as something which perpetuates the professional 'expert' attitude in which carers are the passive recipient of the knowledge a professional feels they should have, and in which their confidence is undermined. A contrasting approach views training as a way of legitimising the fact that carers undertake important work which should be recognised by society. In an article in *Community Care*, a carer from London suggests that training for carers could become NVQ-accredited (Clarke 1997). This would not only recognise the contribution carers make but would also provide a qualification should they be able to take on paid work.

Latterly, this approach has been translated into reality as a number of training agencies have become involved in offering qualifying courses for carers in which their everyday work can be assessed as proving evidence of competencies. While this approach includes a risk that carers might be stereotyped as potential paid care workers when this might be the last thing they have in mind, it certainly goes some way to highlighting the skills they have developed and gives an opportunity for education and training.

While many would not wish to go as far as qualifying courses, training is consistently requested by carers when they are asked what services they would find helpful. However, any worker who sets up a training course to meet a direct request from carers should beware of any over-optimism about the outcome. Even where trainers have covered every practical aspect of preparation, including providing a sitting service for service users, it is not uncommon for such courses to be extremely poorly attended. Just as with carers' groups, there appears to be a definite discrepancy between requests for training and attendance. To address this problem it has been suggested that it is more beneficial to target established carers' groups for training, rather than individual carers (Twigg *et al.* 1990). Such groups may have developed a confidence and identity which means they are more prepared to commit their time than other carers who may have anxieties about what is involved in 'training'. They may also be more prepared to focus on practical tasks.

Many of the requested subject areas of training courses are practical 'hands on' skills for carers who have to undertake nursing or personal care tasks. They include: lifting; turning in bed; toileting; washing; bathing; using wheelchairs and other mobility issues; transfer into vehicles; management of incontinence; first aid. Also useful are basic occupational therapy skills – how to manage the home environment so that it is safe and helpful to the person needing care; using equipment and adaptations appropriately; rehabilitative skills to help the user to help him or herself. Finally there could be training in the practical aspects of managing particular health conditions, such as how to change dressings. Often these skills are learnt under the supervision of an individual health practitioner, but they could also be covered in a group format. By learning such skills, carers will be better equipped to care and will avoid injury to themselves or the person being cared for. Needless to say, it is important that carers should receive training as soon as possible when they start caring so that they do not develop potentially harmful ways of caring. In addition, many training courses cover skills to enable carers to improve their ways of coping, such as assertiveness or stress management, topics which will be approached in the following chapters.

Checklist of considerations for direct work with carers

- Individual work: for specific personal needs, if the carer lacks confidence
- Groupwork: for general issues, if the carer is confident and able to listen to others
- Family work: for issues pertinent to the family, when members are willing to participate
- Is the worker sufficiently skilled for the intervention?
- Is co-working warranted?
- Is supervision available?
- Is the intervention based on need and consultation with carers?
- Are the aims and objectives clear and shared with carers?
- Are there mechanisms in place for evaluation and for ending an intervention?
- Have the following considerations for groupwork been taken into account: time, venue, transport, respite care, numbers, who should attend, open or closed, time-limited or ongoing, carers or carers and dependants, mix of carers or focused groups, professional or self-help?
- Are training opportunities available for carers?

7

Improving Communication

'My mother never shuts up, its natter, nattei, natter the whole time. My husband never opens his mouth. Sometimes between the two of them I think I'm going to scream.' (A carer)

Learning to improve the way we communicate would undoubtedly be beneficial for most of us in order to improve our relationships with other people. Because of the added stress of the caring relationship, carers and the people they support may often benefit from reassessing how they communicate with one another, and when caring is breaking down or becomes highly stressful this becomes essential. By learning methods of clear and constructive communication, carers and the people they support will be able to resolve problems such as misinterpretation, poor listening and failure to disclose true feelings that often cause difficulties in relationships.

This chapter examines a number of practical methods for training people in communication skills and problem solving. The emphasis is on teaching people skills which they can then go on to use independently. In some situations, however, this will not be possible and individuals will need further support to find solutions. The final part of the chapter considers the technique of mediation, in which practitioners take on the role of mediator to help people resolve problems.

Communication skills training

Theories of how to improve communications skills have developed within a number of therapeutic approaches, including counselling, assertiveness and psychotherapy. Here, an eclectic approach is taken to highlight skills which will be of use in situations involving carers. When teaching communication skills it is important that the methods used should be as close as possible to the way in which people naturally interact with each other. Complicated or technical approaches will make people feel self-conscious and they are unlikely to build these into their everyday lives. It is not the intention to enable people to be therapists or to gain great insights into their behaviour, rather to equip them with basic, practical ways of dealing with problems.

The level of skill of practitioners involved in enabling people to improve their communication skills should be high. As a minimum they should be competent in therapeutic work or in facilitating groups in related areas involving interpersonal relationships. In order to teach the skills they should be familiar with techniques such as modelling, rehearsing, role play, and coaching. Ideally, they will be familiar with communication approaches such as assertiveness training. The techniques outlined should not need a great deal of time input from practitioners and it is likely that between two and five sessions should be enough to teach the basic skills.

The nature of communication means that it is usually best taught in a group or family setting. In a group, members can practise skills together and can learn from each other's experiences. At the same time there can be dangers if it is the carer alone who learns skills which may change the way they relate to others. The person being cared for, who has not had this opportunity and does not understand the context, may feel confused, threatened or annoyed to find that the carer has changed. Sometimes, then, it can be useful for communication to be taught in a family setting so that people can learn and develop together, and can address issues which are of immediate concern to themselves. Where group or family settings are not possible, it may be appropriate to cover communication in individual work with a carer, in which case the practitioner would be involved in modelling and role play.

The following approaches cover basic skills in communication. While these may also be of use in everyday conversation, they are introduced here mainly to be used in situations where communication may be breaking down, in times of crisis, conflict or confusion when people need to sit down with one another and talk things through.

Listening to each other

People can be surprised to find that listening skills are the basis of good communication, since they often have the preconception that improving communication means learning how to put across what they themselves want to say. It can be a useful exercise to establish whether carers feel that anyone really listens to them and extend this to encourage them to examine whether they listen to other people. This is particularly appropriate for carers who might experience a confined relationship in which there is a lot of talking but very little listening.

Effective listening can be described in the following way. The person who is listening is genuinely interested in what the person has to say. They are concentrating on what they are hearing, their mind is not wandering and their attention is *out with* the person, rather than *in with* their own concerns. The usual form of mental activity that goes on when we are listening to others – judging, analysing, criticising, comparing – is kept to an absolute minimum because this inner dialogue is about the self rather than the other person. It can be seen that this is a form of pure attention, very different from that which we normally practise. It is also an extremely simple method of communicating, but so different from how we usually conduct ourselves that people can find it extremely hard to practise.

Much of the time spent listening is done in silence, and silent listening in which the individual says nothing, but expresses interest through body language and expression is an extremely valuable exercise. However, people are often more comfortable if they get definite encouragement from their listener. Offering the right form of encouragement is crucial for effective listening, since people are often accustomed to use interventions to throw people off track and divert the conversation to something which is more interesting for them. The aim of encouragement is to enable the person to explore their topic fully and when they have done this, to bring it to a natural conclusion. Techniques include simple words such as 'mmm…really?… I see' and occasional, open questions such as 'What would you like to do?' The intention behind the questions should be for the other person, not for the listener. It is easy to be diverted by a particular thing someone has said and try to focus on that, when it is entirely peripheral to what the person is trying to express.

There is a natural rhythm in most people's communication and listeners need to be able to perceive when the person who is talking is winding down. Signs for this are pauses, a lessening of animation, and shifting position. This could be the cue to check out that the person does not have unfinished business by using questions such as 'did anything else happen?' or 'how do you feel now?'.

While listening techniques can be used in all interactions with others, they are crucial when someone has something to say which is significant to them. Cues to these situations include: the person becomes animated, they express emotion, they are making plans, they are talking about themselves, the topic is something they feel strongly about. Not listening when people are talking about something which has meaning to them can be received as a powerful 'I don't care' message.

There are a number of issues regarding listening skills which may be particularly pertinent for some carers. When people are living in close proximity in a relationship involving dependency, personal space can become an area of contention. Often this involves not physical but mental space and focuses on such issues as lack of emotional privacy and expressions of over-concern. If either the carer or cared-for person feels invaded by the other, then these feelings may be triggered by that person developing listening skills, which might initially be seen as making them even more intrusive. A related situation is where the balance between the amount of time people spend listening and talking is skewed. In relationships, we usually achieve an acceptable ratio between how much time we spend listening and how much time we spend talking. However, if one person takes over as the talker, with the other in the reluctant role of listener, this can cause strong resentment. There can be a genuine fear that if the listener improves their skills this would make the person who monopolises the conversation unstoppable. In both these situations it would be preferable if the family was involved in learning techniques together so that such problem areas could be addressed. It may be also that if the person who is an incessant talker finds that someone really listens to them, they may feel less need to talk. However if this remains a problem it may need to be addressed by problem-solving techniques within the family.

EXERCISES

In pairs:

- Practise silent listening. Each individual has equal time which is kept by the facilitator. Pairs give feedback on how 'listened to' they felt.

- Practise asking open questions.

- Practise ways of helping people to explore topics by giving appropriate encouragement.

Individually:

- List the cues which their family members use when they have something significant to talk about; then discuss in group.

Home exercises:

- Observe a conversation between people – perhaps family members, people at work or (with caution!) strangers on a bus – and evaluate the listening skills that are being used.

Body language

Learning basic principles of body language can improve people's ability to communicate, be it as talker or listener. Effective body language should show that someone is:

- Relaxed – avoiding signs of tension such as hunched shoulders or fidgeting

- Open – arms relaxed rather than crossed and protecting the body, posture neither straining forward or collapsed back

and should use:

- Eye contact – looking at the person, making contact with their gaze but without fixed staring

- Tone – calm, even and clear.

Adopting the above signals that an individual is alert and interested in the conversation. Tense or aggressive body language can indicate a variety of messages such as: 'I'm not interested,' 'You're talking rubbish' or 'That's too hurtful, don't tell me'.

EXERCISES

- The facilitator models body language which can both help and detract from communication.

In pairs:

- Participants practise appropriate body language in the role of listener and talker.

Keeping calm

One of the biggest difficulties for effective communication can be when people's emotions become engaged in a subject. When this happens, people generally get caught up in their own agenda and any pretence about listening to the other person disappears. Similarly, their ability to speak clearly and put their point across often decreases when they are emotionally involved. With neither side listening or talking clearly, communication is clearly under threat! There are a number of techniques that can be adopted in such situations. Relaxation methods can be employed by individuals to avoid being sucked into the emotional level of a situation. Some people who know they easily become emotionally involved, perhaps getting angry or upset, find it beneficial to adopt an inner message to break through this automatic process and give themselves time to consciously decide what is going on. For instance, one woman uses her name and says to herself 'Diane, what's going on?', another person tells himself to 'watch it!'.

Time out is another effective method, provided that this is agreed between the people involved. For instance it could be useful to have an agreement that if any discussion gets heated they will stop the talk at that stage and spend some time apart. If this is not mutually accepted there is a danger that the person who wants time out may be viewed as backing out or evading their responsibilities. Temporarily changing to a less controversial subject or consciously diverting onto another enjoyable task are also possible methods and again are best used when they are an acknowledged strategy and there is agreement to return to the original topic at a given time when emotions have cooled: 'We seem to be getting upset. Let's get some fresh air for half an hour and talk about this tonight'.

Checking things out is a further means of avoiding emotional heat in any situation. Many communication problems arise from misunderstanding and misinterpretation of what people have said. Sometimes wholly unintentional remarks can result in unnecessary tension. By checking things out – 'I'm feeling a bit confused. Could you explain what you meant when you said you didn't want me to do the shopping tonight?' – we can clarify the situation, which is eminently preferable to an argument or silent hurt. By doing this we are really giving people the benefit of the doubt that they were not intentionally being aggressive or hurtful. Of course, care must be taken not to check things out in a way which is threatening – 'What did you mean by that?!' – otherwise exactly the opposite effect will result.

EXERCISES

In the group:

- Discuss techniques which have been effective in defusing emotional situations.

In pairs:

- Individuals decide on a way to prompt themselves not to get emotionally involved
- Role play asking for time out
- Participants choose a situation which they find personally stressful, and describe it while rehearsing staying calm.

Verbal communication

In terms of direct verbal communication, some of the principles of assertiveness training are extremely useful for improving how we interact. Carers often find that their everyday communication skills are insufficient, especially in significant situations such as negotiating with professionals. Problems we may all experience at some time include rambling, hesitating, repeating ourselves, losing track of what we want to say and drying up. Assertiveness advises us to be specific about what we want to say and to stick to the point. One of the main purposes of communication is so that the person we are talking to will understand what we are saying. By keeping what we want to say simple and brief, our message should be clear and unambiguous.

Another useful verbal technique is the appropriate use of 'I' statements. While a minority of people over-use 'I' by peppering every sentence with what they think and how they feel, most people tend to avoid this use. Not using 'I' indicates that we are not owning thoughts and feelings, and are not taking responsibility for ourselves. Simple observation of how people talk will show how many people say 'you' when they mean 'I' – 'you feel awkward when you're talking about personal problems.' Rephrased, 'I feel awkward when I talk about personal problems', the increase in power of this statement is obvious. Disclosure of feelings is another assertiveness technique which can improve communication.

Statements such as 'I feel afraid' bring an immediate honesty into a situation, relieve anxiety for the person who is talking and make the listener clear about what is happening. In relation to both these points, a construction to be avoided is 'You make me feel…angry, sad, confused…' While this is a disclosure of feeling, this is not owned but attributed to another person in a way which is likely to reflect blame.

EXERCISES

In pairs:

- Rehearse saying what you want to say in a concise, clear manner
- Practise 'I' statements
- Practise disclosure of feelings.

Patterns to avoid

In addition to learning positive communication skills there are a number of common communication patterns that most of us use at some time which can sabotage how we interact with others. Some of these are obvious to all concerned – the aggressive patterns of sarcasm, abuse or threat make no pretence at being constructive. Other forms may be almost as destructive and at the same time will be much more difficult to detect. These are the indirectly aggressive or manipulative ways of communicating, which may be done either consciously or inadvertently. Particularly relevant in terms of the carer–cared-for relationship are the following.

TAKING OVER

One individual will monopolise the conversation, will not allow the other person to speak and will speak for them in company. This can be particularly prevalent when the person being cared for has a speech problem, such as that which is caused by a stroke, which inhibits how quickly or fluently they can speak.

BEING AN EXPERT

This may often accompany the situation above. Here an individual has taken on the role of knowing best. Verbal communication often involves 'should' statements: 'You should keep the brass polished'; 'You should make more of an effort to get dressed yourself'. Also common are 'I would have' statements: 'I would have told him where to get off'; 'If I'd been there this wouldn't have happened'. In terms of behaviour, the person in the expert role may take on the decision-making role, while the other person becomes passive and/or resentful.

CRITICISING THE OTHER PERSON

It is easy for criticism to become habitual in a close relationship, so that people become accustomed to giving and receiving it. As above, the effects can be a grinding down of morale and simmering resentment at never being thought good enough. Criticism may be directed from carer to person cared for or vice versa and, when the latter, can be a very significant factor in demoralising the carer.

FOCUSING ON THE NEGATIVE

Another habit which can be detrimental to the relationship is where individuals constantly focus on the negative of any situation. There are a number of ways in which this tendency can manifest itself, some of which include:

- Catastrophising – people imagine that the worst will always happen; a dose of flu becomes life threatening, going out alone involves a mugger or a car accident.

- Suspicion – negative motives are attributed to other people; the neighbour has only offered help because they want to know the family's business, the relative is only friendly because they think they are mentioned in the will.

- Half-full – any situation is looked at from a pessimistic point of view; the box of chocolates are a kind thought but they aren't Belgian, it's too cold to go on that theatre trip in March.

Focusing on the negative reveals fear in the individual who communicates in this way and promotes anxiety and exasperation in the person who is on the receiving end.

MANIPULATION

Manipulation is used in any consciously insincere communication which seeks to influence another person's behaviour and get them to act in a way which the individual wants. This can involve compliments –'You're so good to me, would you just…'; comparisons – '*Elsie's* daughter takes her to the chiropodist'; and feigning helplessness – 'I'm not very bright with figures, perhaps you could look at the accounts'.

AVOIDANCE

While a number of methods have been discussed which defuse potential conflict situations, these can also be used to negative effect to prevent people expressing their emotional needs. Powell (1992) lists a number of ways in which people try to avoid talking on an emotional level. These include:

- Diverting – taking an individual's attention away from something you do not want them to focus on, perhaps by starting an argument or offering a treat
- Being logical – failing to empathise with someone in emotional distress and insisting on a logical or practical approach
- Reassuring – trying to tell someone there is nothing wrong, so failing to acknowledge the legitimacy of their concerns.

Of course it is not always appropriate for people to express how they are feeling. If, for example, someone is crying regularly every day for a long period of time it is evident that they need professional support rather than just sympathy. However if people neglect the emotional dimension to relationships they may be storing resentment for the future.

There are two main ways of approaching such communication problems. In an ideal situation the individual whose patterns they are will recognise them and will agree to work on changing how they interact with others. If this is not feasible, then there are a number of strategies which can be adopted, mainly based on assertiveness training, which helps people to develop the self-confidence not to get drawn in to other people's negativity. For instance, there are methods of approaching criticism. If the criticism is justified then own it and, if appropriate, apologise, without becoming filled with guilt. If it is not clear whether the point is justified or not then more information is needed: 'You say I am thoughtless, can you give me examples of this?'; and if the criticism is not true then convey this clearly: 'I don't accept what you are saying'. But not 'You're wrong!' which is a counter criticism.

EXERCISES

In the group:

- Discuss patterns of poor communication that exist within participants' families
- Discuss methods of managing these.

In pairs:

- Role play one of these methods based on an actual situation.

Emotional triggers

In this context, triggers are ways of communicating which lead to high levels of negative feeling in relationships. Triggers focus on particular areas and build up over time, usually within the family environment, where they become significant stressors. Triggers often involve the sabotaging techniques discussed above, but with a content which is specific to the particular situation. Often the communication which falls within these areas can appear entirely innocent to an outsider who may be baffled by the reactions it causes. Examples of common trigger areas include:

- Concern about health: 'You look tired; are you getting enough sleep?'.

- Focusing on food: 'I'm sure you're not eating properly... Are you getting enough vitamin C?'

- Insisting on emotional disclosure: 'Tell me about it; I won't get upset' – then getting upset.

- Trying not to be a nuisance: 'I didn't want to bother you, so I just tried to reach that jar on the top shelf' – from their hospital bed – when by not bothering someone they end up causing much more inconvenience.

Triggers also extend beyond communication to behaviour patterns. Irritating habits are classic examples of these and often become an issue of personal space with people defending their right to carry on with behaviour which annoys their family. The list of potential triggers is endless, and almost entirely dependent on family circumstance. Again, the optimum way of addressing these is that the individual acknowledges their existence and is prepared to work to change the way they communicate. Alternatively, if the situation necessitates action, a solution could be found through the problem-solving mechanisms below.

Problem solving

Many of the problems that we encounter in relationships are based on communication difficulties and can be improved by applying the approaches outlined above. Problem solving, however, is a technique in its own right which can be used to address issues that families find particularly difficult to solve, especially those which are contentious or involve conflict of opinion. The technique is based on the ways people solve problems naturally, but has taken these unconscious processes and formalised them into stages which unite into a whole process. The purpose of this is to make problem solving effective; without it we might miss out crucial stages such as failing to prioritise the action we wish to work on or trying to solve everything at once. There are many different models of problem solving, but most involve variations of the stages outlined below. See, for instance, Priestly *et al.* 1978 and Atkinson 1986.

Problem solving is most appropriately taught in a group or family setting. A particularly effective method is to teach the problem-solving stages using case examples and then to follow this with examples from people's own experience. A checklist can be given to participants for use at home. However, it should be emphasised that people generally customise the approach and make it simpler once they are familiar with it. Problem solving is most effective in conjunction with communication training, which provides a sound basis for generating effective solutions and also makes it less likely that individual will unconsciously 'sabotage' the process. Finally, in the main, problem solving can only be used effectively by people who are committed to finding a solution and enjoy reasonably supportive relationships with each other.

Preparation

Some planning is necessary for effective problem solving. All the people involved need to get together at a time and a place which will give sufficient uninterrupted space for them to complete the process. It can be useful if one person takes on the role of facilitator – making sure everyone has their say, moving things on, ensuring that people keep to the topic. Using pen and paper for recording means that the process is likely to be thorough and clear. Two concepts which are intrinsic to this process are negotiation and compromise, and it is important that participants are clear about these. Family conflict can often become a power struggle with a win or lose scenario. In contrast, this approach stresses that participants should seek a fair solution, and should strive to see the other person's point of view. They should also be willing to negotiate away from their ideal solution to a compromise which is more acceptable to all concerned. In teaching problem-solving skills, facilitators should cover techniques such as:

- Putting yourself into the other person's position and trying to understand their perspective

- Encouraging the other person to describe their position by asking appropriate questions like 'What are your thoughts on this situation? Can you describe how this would make you feel?'.

Inevitably, there are certain behaviours which can sabotage problem solving, particularly in the initial, unstructured discussions of Stage One. It can be useful for these to be flagged up and agreed beforehand as approaches which should not form part of the process. Common examples include:

- Historicising – we can learn from the past, but if we dwell in it while problem solving we are unlikely to find a solution

- Analysis – we can also learn from analysing situations and gaining insight into why people behave the way they do, but this alone is unlikely to effect any practical change

- Blame and guilt – in any discussion it may be tempting for some people to apportion blame while others take on guilt. Blame and guilt will only serve to make problem solving uncomfortable and ineffective.

Example

The following example will be used to illustrate the problem solving process.

> Evelyn is 76 and suffered a stroke four years ago. Evelyn can walk inside slowly with a zimmer and has the use of one arm. She is confined to the ground floor of the house and requires a wheelchair outside. She needs help with some personal care tasks, such as dressing and cutting up food. Her speech has been affected by the stroke and now she is only able to say 'yes' or 'no', sometimes inappropriately. Evelyn has full comprehension and can read, although she can only write with difficulty. Following the stroke she went to live with her daughter, Jean, son-in-law Martin and their children aged six and eight.
>
> There is generally a good relationship between all members of the family. Lately a problem has arisen because Evelyn offered to take over the role of baby-sitter when Jean and Martin go out, since the children are now older and do not need physical care. Jean has refused this and says that they need to have a baby-sitter. A great deal of bad feeling has developed in the family and Evelyn is now considering moving out into her own accommodation. Kate, a worker at the day centre that Evelyn attends who is well known to all the family, has agreed to speak on Evelyn's behalf. She has previously spent time with her to ascertain her views. Martin has agreed to facilitate the problem solving.

STAGE 1: DEFINING THE PROBLEM

Sometimes the problem to be tackled is clear and defined, but more often there is a general situation in which problems and issues are interlinked. It can be useful to discuss all aspects of the situation because, particularly where complicated issues are involved, the presenting problem may be different from the real issue. Following open discussion, a useful exercise can be to compile a list of all the participants' points of view on the problem. This could be done in a quick brainstorming fashion, not looking at priorities but compiling all relevant information without analysis. This should be done in such a way that everyone involved feels their point of view has been taken into account. Points of view from the above example include:

> Evelyn indicated that she felt extremely angry that she was not trusted to look after the children. She had brought up four of her own and was quite capable of looking after two. Did Jean think she needed a baby-sitter herself? She did not particularly want to move out, but she wasn't going to stay where her own daughter treated her like a child.
>
> Jean acknowledged that she did not feel Evelyn was able to look after the children. She was worried that they would not behave themselves for her and even if they did, what if one of them was ill or Evelyn had a fall.
>
> Martin said that he felt Evelyn could manage the children. He had noticed that they were able to communicate with her better than the adults and that

they stayed safely with her for long periods of time when Jean popped into a neighbour's. There was a sub-discussion about this – Jean was upset that her mother was angry, but was also annoyed that Martin was not supporting her.

Where a situation proves to be complicated it is useful now to prioritise to discover what is the most important issue. This may involve examining the problem again and defining it in some depth. Most importantly it also involves negotiating an agreement about what the priorities are.

> The priority agreed from the above example was to decide whether Evelyn was able to manage the children safely.

STAGE 2: DISCUSSING SOLUTIONS

With the problem well clarified, the next stage is to look for solutions. Again, it is often useful to start this stage with listing any and all solutions which are suggested, then, once people have run out of ideas, examining these in more depth. Where there are a number of possible solutions one way of deciding between them is to consider the relative advantages and disadvantages of each. There are a number of sophisticated methods of achieving this, generally adopted from management theories, but a simple way is to divide a page into two parts – advantages and disadvantages or for and against. The solutions outlined for this example include:

1. The family continue to use a baby-sitter.

2. Evelyn undertakes the baby-sitting, if measures can be put in place to put Jean's mind at rest.

Jean agreed to explore the second solution.

STAGE 3: PLANNING HOW TO IMPLEMENT THE SOLUTION

In Stage Three the family looks at the practical issues of what they need to do to put their solution into action. This involves the usual elements of planning – what needs to be done, who is doing what, when they are doing it and when they are reporting back. This stage can also be a double check that the solution is achievable – if it is not then the plans are likely to be difficult to implement.

> It was agreed that initially Evelyn would only baby-sit for short periods of time, such as for an evening out. The family agreed to invest in electronic alarm equipment which would mean they could be instantly alerted if there was a problem. It was felt that this could also be useful if Evelyn was left alone in the house and had a fall. Also, the eldest child asserted that he was able to use the telephone, which proved to be the case.

STAGE 4: REVIEWING WHAT HAS BEEN DONE

Monitoring and reviewing the results of problem solving can be helpful in situations where the plans are long-term and need to be revisited or renegotiated. It can also be useful when things go wrong, if only to show that what happened was based on a fair decision made by the group! Reviewing should always be carried out in an atmosphere of non-recrimination. However, practitioners often find it difficult to allocate time for review and it would be unrealistic to expect families to go through a formal process. In the given example, if the baby-sitting is successful, the family are unlikely to review their problem-solving exercise, though hopefully they would be more confident in using it in the future.

Mediation

While the aim of teaching problem-solving skills is to enable individual families or groups to address problems independently, there will be many situations where this is not possible. This can be because the family do not have the necessary skills or sufficient goodwill and trust to work together. Sometimes the problem may be particularly contentious, involving emotional issues or conflict between individuals. In these situations, a practitioner who is skilled in mediation — working with two or more people to come to an agreed solution — can be used to great effect.

The role of the mediator is to facilitate the process — keeping on the topic, ensuring that everyone has an opportunity to say what they want and keeping time, much in the same way as the facilitative family member discussed with problem solving. However, the mediator holds a clear objective standpoint and has the skills to address issues of conflict which may come up in the course of the session. Most crucially, they will have the ability to manage differences of perspective while keeping the discussion on track for a positive outcome. It is important that mediation is done in as informal and low key a manner as possible so that all participants can feel relaxed and comfortable, in what is generally an unusual situation for people to experience.

Mediation could be offered by carers' organisations, and workers within health or day centre settings. It could be a cost-effective method for social workers working with a conflict situation which looks like resulting in a breakdown of care. As presented here, the process is based on principles of problem solving and involves short-term work — possibly one to five sessions — always focusing on specific problems. It should be contrasted with family work which may involve working to improve relationships on a more long-term basis.

Preparation for mediation

Because one of the most important features about the mediator is that they should be seen as independent, all members involved in the discussion should be in agreement about who should take on this role. The timing and location of the session should be arranged with care to ensure that all parties can be present. Sometimes work will need to be undertaken with individuals before the sessions, particularly to enable people who have communication difficulties to work through what they want to say. In such cases it may be helpful if a worker, not the mediator, spends time with the individual, perhaps writing down the key points or rehearsing what they want to say. Having an advocate to speak on someone's behalf is one option when an individual feels unable to represent themselves, however the more people that are present, the more formal the situation will feel. Finally, it is essential that all parties should be aware of what to expect from the process of mediation and clear explanations should be given well in advance of the first session. This should include ground-rules such as confidentiality and good listening and should define behaviour which would not be acceptable, such as verbal attacks.

STAGE 1

The first stage of this process involves each person individually stating their position on the problem. This should include how they see things and how they are feeling. The mediator ensures that each person has time to say what they want to say, if necessary arranging for equal time and making sure that the others are listening and do not attempt to interrupt. At the end of each person's narrative, the mediator could summarise the main points they have made, taking care to check this out with the individual. It can also be useful to make sure that everyone understands what the person has said, even if they do not agree with it.

When everyone has spoken, the mediator can summarise the situation. A discussion can then follow in which people are able to ask for clarification on what other people have said and can put further comments. The mediator may need to control this process to keep it within the ground-rules. Finally the mediator would assist the participants to define the problem and clearly highlight areas of difference.

In addition, the following techniques could be used, particularly if the discussion is reaching an impasse.

- One of the participants is asked to summarise what another has said and vice versa

- One of the participants is asked to put him or herself in the other's place. For instance, 'If you were in your wife's situation how would you feel?'

STAGE 2

With the problem defined, the next task is to look for solutions. If it appears that people need time to reflect, the mediator could suggest taking ten minutes or so to think of solutions. The mediator would then compile the list of solutions, with advantages and disadvantages, ensuring that all parties are involved. Mediators can also suggest possible solutions, checking out how people feel about these. Finally they would try to gain consensus on what is felt to be the most appropriate solution.

STAGE 3

This is the planning stage of mediated problem-solving, in which the action and relative responsibilities are agreed. A technique which can be used in situations which are particularly problematic and in which there is doubt whether people will abide by their agreements is to design a contract which is signed by all parties. The purpose of contracts is to signify clear outcomes of a situation, in terms of what is expected of people involved, and to formalise their commitment. Although psychological rather than legal in function they should be used sparingly, since they introduce an official, even alien element into families. However, they can be useful as a means of encouraging people to stick to agreements, and should be considered if it is felt that reinforcement is needed. Contracts need to be simple in language, specific as to who is doing what and for how long, signed and dated (Coulshed 1991).

STAGE 4

Monitoring and review are particularly important when problems have been solved through mediation. As these are likely to be problematic situations, time-limited contact with a mediator, once a week, fortnight or month depending on the circumstances, may be useful to keep the family on target, and to pick up issues which need further resolution. The final review of the action will reinforce what has been learnt from the experience and what the family would need to do in order to problem solve independently in the future.

Checklist of considerations for improving communication

What measures are in place to help carers and their families:

- improve the way the communicate?
- learn to problem solve?

Is a mediation service available to carers?

8

Emotional Support

'I hadn't realised until Mark had his accident how vulnerable I was. Suddenly everything I had to hold on to had gone.' (A carer)

As we have seen, some carers experience emotional distress from their caring role, which may be compounded by their social isolation. The long-term effects of this can include depression, anxiety and even serious mental or physical health problems. Here we examine a number of approaches that have proved effective in enabling carers to examine the emotional impact of caring and to design strategies to improve the way they cope. The specific areas covered include methods of helping people to talk about their problems and release distress; techniques to build up social networks and improve relationships; and stress management approaches which are particularly appropriate to the needs of carers.

Carers' support groups

There are a variety of methods of providing emotional support for carers, including individual counselling or therapy, both of which can be extremely useful for carers needing extensive or individual support. But here we consider an approach which has proved enduringly popular – the carers' support group. When such groups are running effectively they provide an excellent means of allowing carers to express how they feel in a supportive environment. However, as was noted in Chapter 6, one of the problems of this approach is that when groups are run by volunteers, carers or workers without a background in therapeutic work, it is the area of emotional expression which can be the most difficult to deal with.

This means that the level of emotional support provided by groups may be variable. Often people may be encouraged to talk, but then the facilitator is unable to cope if they become emotional. For instance, the facilitator or other members may try to discourage someone from crying through comforting them, rather than allowing them to release their emotions. Sometimes support groups may not address people's emotional needs at all, because the ethos of the group is to keep things on a practical or discursive level so as not to 'upset' people. Unfortunately, such an approach underestimates the power of a group to move an individual who may have had little previous experience of people listening to them sympathetically. Even where groups are determinedly practical it is quite usual for some people to become emotional when they first attend and the facilitator needs to know how to handle this appropriately. It also fails to address some important needs – the opportunity to express their feelings in a safe, non-judgmental and understanding environment may be an essential stage for carers who may have been socially isolated, or have not had the sort of relationships in which discussing emotional issues was acceptable.

One model which can be effectively used as a basis for an emotional support group has its theoretical base in a number of sources, including the theories of re-evaluation counselling and the work of women's self-help organisations (Ernst and Goodison 1981, Chapter 2). This model can be used safely and effectively in both professionally led and self-help support groups. The aim of this form of group is to give people the opportunity to talk about what they think and feel in an environment where other people give them total attention and encouragement. The approach is based on the important principle that releasing distress by crying, shaking, laughing or shouting is an important process which should be encouraged rather than repressed. By expressing feeling in this way we are releasing negative energy which we have bottled up and which may be keeping us afraid, angry, depressed and so forth. Often when people talk they re-run old patterns of mental dialogue which appear lifeless and tired. While this process may be useful in the short term in terms of getting people talking, if we do not get beyond it we are tied to these old programmes and cannot move on.

In helping people to discharge emotions there is a release of tension which can be an important forerunner to problem solving. Practitioners will have observed how people who are blocked with feelings may find it next to impossible to consider a situation realistically. In some cases there may be a solution to their problems which is obvious to other people but they are unable to see this because they are stuck in their own mind-set. Through emotional release most people appear more real and alive. People listening may have a sense of seeing the 'true' person behind their role or superficial personality traits. For people who are stuck it can be a way of moving forward and viewing things more rationally. For example, Mary had been becoming increasingly irritated with her mother who suffered from advanced dementia. Although she knew rationally that her mother was not doing this on purpose, on an emotional level Mary felt angry towards her, as if she was being deliberately perverse. By attending a support group and expressing how she felt, she experienced an immediate sense of release and sympathy towards her mother. She realised that she had started to blame her mother, rather than her mother's condition, for her disruptive behaviour.

Process

The process by which the aims of the group are achieved is extremely simple. The group forms a circle and each person in turn has a chance to talk about what is uppermost for them. Rather than a free-for-all in which the people with the loudest voices get the most time, each person has individual time to talk and the facilitator keeps the time approximately equal between each member. Obviously sometimes people do not wish to speak, while others have particularly pressing issues they wish to discuss and these variations can be accommodated by some flexibility in regard to time. Generally, people in the group will decide on the order in which they speak, although the facilitator may wish to ask individuals such as new members, or people who appear in distress, whether they would like to speak towards the start or the end of the session.

It can be useful to start and end each group with an exercise to enable members to focus on something positive. For instance, the exercise at the start of the group may be to say one enjoyable thing that has happened during their week, however small. The final exercise may be something they are looking forward to. There are a wide range of topics for such exercises – an animal you would like to be; your favourite item of clothing, TV programme, sport, etc.; your ideal holiday, night out, way of relaxing, pet etc. The purpose of these exercises at the start of a group is to act as ice-breakers to encourage people to talk, and at the end to be a lighter note so that people can return to a more everyday consciousness.

In such a group, members are not passive observers, but are responsible for actively and silently listening to the person who is speaking, following the principles of good listening described in the previous chapter. They will not intervene when it is another person's turn, either to reveal their own problems or to comfort that person, unless requested by the facilitator. One problem in support groups is often that people are very caught up in their own issues and find it difficult to get their attention out with another person. An alternative difficulty and one which, anecdotally, may particularly apply to some carers, is that people may also hate to see anyone in distress and may act to 'make it better', by rushing to get them a coffee or trying to divert them onto a more 'cheerful' subject. The facilitator would need to be mindful of these tendencies and keep the group on track; it is essential for facilitators to establish the principles of the group with the members so that everyone is aware of its nature and purpose.

Facilitation

In a support group, it is important that facilitators do not use complicated therapy skills which introduce a power imbalance between facilitator and members. The aim should be that once accustomed to the group, members can take on the role of facilitator if they wish, thus becoming a true self-help group. Co-facilitation – two people taking on the facilitative role together – can be particularly useful, since it enables one of these to take part in the group, if they wish. In order to lead such a group, facilitators would need basic counselling and groupwork skills; they would also benefit from attending co-counselling training. Co-counselling originated in North America in the work of Harvey Jackins.(1965) and is a community-based approach to counselling in which individuals learn to be both counsellor and client. Having completed the basic training, which emphasises the importance of discharging emotion, people would be able to organise a co-counselling session in which they counselled someone for the first half, then swapped over and became client for the second. Thus an egalitarian, self-help approach is paramount, which can be used either in pairs or in a group situation.

Format

I have experienced the positive effects of such groups for carers and for people with a wide range of emotional needs on many occasions; there are, however, some issues that need to be considered. It is important to explain to prospective members the nature of the group so that they can make an informed choice about attending. Some people, perhaps men in particular, are not comfortable with talking about their feelings. On the other hand, it can be useful to encourage people to give it a try; since sometimes it is the people who are most dubious who get most out of the experience.

The format for the group will also need to be considered. Such groups can work on a time-limited or ongoing basis, since the approach is extremely flexible and can be adapted to the needs of the members. For instance, after a period of time a group may feel that it is 'talked out' and wants to extend its activities to include education or campaigning. Therefore it may decide to spend the first hour of a session on emotional support, while the second may be a talk or information session. Alternatively, in a fortnightly group, the focus of the group could be emotional support in one meeting and campaigning or training the next. One factor which has been stressed as important by people who attend support groups is that it is a comfort to know that there is always somewhere they can go to be truly listened to and supported, even if they do not attend every session.

Topics for emotional support

This approach can also be useful to enable carers to examine specific topics such as dealing with loss and anger. For instance, within a support group, one or more sessions could be focused on exploring loss and could cover such areas as: what loss means to carers, bereavement, losing freedom, and losing the caring role. People could be encouraged to discuss their feelings of loss either in the group or in pairs. The session could end with practical techniques for coping with loss, such as recognising the stages of loss, talking things through, using support networks, allowing oneself time, making plans.

Similarly, sessions about anger might cover such topics as: understanding the causes of anger, the importance of not repressing feelings, worries about expressing anger – fear of being rejected by or hurting others, constructive ways of expressing anger such as physical activity, and ways of expressing feelings assertively rather than with aggression.

Support outside the group

While being able to attend a regular group can be an effective support for some carers, others will benefit more from one-to-one contact outside a group setting. Some groups develop networks in which carers provide emotional support for each other. There are a variety of ways in which these can be organised. One which works particularly well is if a number of carers or former carers are willing to be telephoned at home. Alternatively, group members could form themselves into pairs or sub-groups and offer mutual support. Whichever system is used, it is important that clear parameters are set. Such support networks are rarely abused, but if they are this can be extremely distressing for the people involved. Issues which need to be clarified in advance include the times when phone calls are acceptable, whether phone calls from people outside a group of named individuals are allowed, and whether face-to-face contact can take place.

Developing support networks

The therapeutic approach of creating and improving individual's support networks developed from work with people with mental health problems and learning disabilities, in which it was recognised that their networks for support were much more limited than those of other people in the community. For instance, it might be found that the most significant other person in the life of someone with mental health problems is their key worker at the day centre. Developing social networks is a method of enabling people to live more 'normally' and to improve their quality of life. It also has strong connections with stress management techniques, since having significant people in our lives can be an important way of reducing stress. If we have no one to talk to or to enjoy things with we may bottle up worries, anxiety and even our happiness. The theory is that we need a number of people within our social network who fill particular roles in our lives, just as we do for them. If our circle is insufficient, then we are missing out on support or stimulation which will impoverish our lives and diminish our ability to cope with life events.

Carers may benefit from improving their social networks for a number of reasons. Because of the social isolation of their caring tasks many carers may have a distinct lack of other people in their lives. Again, because of their role they may have a greater need for a good support network than other people who have less stressful commitments. If carers are helped to consciously address the issue of their networks and to work on improving these, they are likely to experience significant improvements in their lives.

Methods of developing networks involve two main stages. In the first there is an audit or mapping exercise of the person's existing networks, followed by a discussion about what has been revealed. Then the carer will be taken through options of how to develop their network either from within existing contacts or by making new friends. Networking discussions can be undertaken with individuals, in groups or with families. An individual setting is useful to make sure that the carer has sufficient time to cover all their issues and for carers whose lives may be unusually isolated. This exercise can bring home to people the loneliness of their situation and needs to be handled with sensitivity, making sure that the carer feels that something positive can be achieved. A group setting offers the opportunity to see that others may be in similar positions, and can also offer the potential for group solutions. However, facilitators should be wary of impromptu suggestions of support from group members such as 'Let's meet for coffee on Thursday'. Such unplanned ideas often fall through, leaving vulnerable people feeling even more unsupported.

Stage 1: Mapping the current situation

Rather than simply talking about their current situation, it is helpful to use an aid to trigger people's thoughts and to demonstrate their network clearly. One useful tool is to design a question sheet which the carer spends some time filling in on their own. Effective questions may include:

- Who can I have fun with?
- Who can I talk to about the issues of being a carer?
- Who can I talk with about how I feel?
- Who can I share with when something good happens?
- Who can I go on outings or holidays with?
- Who can I contact in an emergency?
- Who can I ask to give me practical support?
- Who do I feel comfortable with?
- Who can I have a stimulating conversation with?
- Who shares my ideas and hopes for the future?

People should be encouraged to list as many names as possible under each of these categories. Some carers may also have their own ideas about what is important in their lives and may wish to look at additional areas. It might also be useful to break down the most significant categories into more detail. For instance, an area which may be particularly important is that of practical support for the carer. This question could be looked at in more detail to determine exactly who is prepared to offer what support and to what level.

An alternative approach is for the carer to represent the people in their lives diagramatically, which can be useful to enable people to gain an overview of their networks and how they link in with each other. One way of doing this would be to divide a circle into cake segments representing the above questions and put the individuals within relevant sections. The carer would be in the centre of the circle. Bands could also be introduced to show to what extent a person is supportive – for instance, those closest to the centre of the circle would be closest to the carer, with those further out towards the rim being less significant. Alternatively an ecomap can be adapted for this purpose, with symbols representing individuals and lines linking them indicating the type of support offered and how strong or weak this is.

Whether in verbal or diagrammatic form, the questions are used to stimulate discussion and enable the carer to explore things in more depth. Topics which may be useful to examine further include:

- Are there a spread of names or are most of the functions concentrated in one or two individuals?
- What is the quality of the relationship? Someone may be available to talk to, but how satisfactory does this feel? For instance, does the carer really trust that person?
- Is the relationship reciprocal – what does the carer offer in return?
- Where does the person receiving care stand in relation to these relationships?

Stage 2: Developing networks

An important principle of developing a strong social network is that we should have a number of people in our lives, rather than focusing everything on one or two people only. We also need to feel satisfied with the relationships that we have and, if they are not truly meeting our needs, take measures to address this. When a clear picture has been formed, and if this reveals gaps in the social network, the next stage is to look at ways of improving this. Within this, the first approach is generally to help the individual to examine existing networks and whether there are any ways in which these can be developed.

Initially, this could involve asking the carer to consider whether the people on their list could be involved in other areas of their lives, or whether they might increase the quality of their involvement. If there is insufficient room for development within existing relationships, the carer can be helped to build up new contacts. However it is important to bear in mind that strong bonds of friendship cannot be built overnight and the only areas in which it is practical to look at developing in the short-term are social contacts. For some carers, who have access to organised respite or support from others, it may be sufficient to realise that they have been neglecting their own needs and to decide to pursue a hobby or interest without feeling guilty about this. But some carers will have a need for a deeper level of support than can be afforded by social relationships. Therefore workers involved in exploring social networks with carers require access to strong systems of carer support, such as self-help groups, social clubs with organised respite, and individual counselling opportunities, so that they can enable the carer to develop their network quickly and easily.

Improving family relationships

As we have seen, caring may induce an added dimension of strain in relationships. In order to address this there are a number of strategies for improving how families interact. Many of these are things that we might do more or less instinctively in our everyday lives as an expression of affection for our friends and families. However, they can also be learnt and applied in a conscious way, when spontaneity and love may have become submerged under caring responsibilities.

The following techniques can be taught as the main subject of sessions within a carers' group. They can also be used as ice-breakers or homework exercises throughout a series of sessions. Similarly, they could be used in work with families or individuals, although the reciprocal nature of the techniques means they are better employed when both carer and person receiving care are involved. Some of the following methods, such as 'paying positive attention', may involve changes in attitude and behaviour which would apply to all the interactions within the family. Others, like 'putting the other person first', could be specifically planned events. While most appropriate for people who have a reasonable level of understanding, some of the techniques are suitable for use with people with learning disabilities or dementia. This list is by no means exhaustive and people should be asked for their own suggestions on practical techniques to improve relationships. Some of the following techniques have been adapted to fit the needs of carers from suggestions in Powell (1992).

Paying positive attention

This has much in common with the listening skills discussed in the previous chapter. Using these skills as a basis, there are particular methods of improving relationships which include: remembering to show affection and appreciation; never criticising in public; being courteous and polite; and encouraging the other person to talk about their worries, hopes and successes. The implication of this approach is to improve the quality of the relationship, making it more conscious, so that family members are aware of each other and how what they do affects the family as a whole.

Avoiding conflict situations

Families often have particular events or times in which the probability of conflict is high. Classic examples are major events such as weddings or holidays, but minor, everyday events like mealtimes or travelling can be equally problematic. For instance, if the children find it particularly difficult to go through mealtimes with a relative with dementia, then, rather than insisting on meals together as a principle of family life, it may be better to allow them to eat separately. This technique involves the family identifying which situations tend to end in conflict and finding methods for avoiding this.

Spending enjoyable time together

This can involve deciding to do something together as a family that all members would enjoy. It can vary from the elaborate and expensive – organising a holiday abroad – to the simple and cheap – going for a walk on a spring day, or ordering a takeaway to avoid having to cook. An alternative approach would be to plan something new to do together. It is important to build such 'treats' regularly into everyday lives, possibly planning one per week or more. If experience has shown that treats can also be situations which trigger conflict then these would have to be chosen very carefully.

Spending enjoyable time apart

Spending time apart does not mean getting out of each other's way; rather individuals do something they enjoy and then share this with the rest of the family. An important factor in this is that the rest of the family should listen to, and appreciate, what the other member has been doing. This approach can be useful if the carer and person receiving care have very few social interests in common; for example, the carer may balk at the idea of spending time watching motor racing but may be quite prepared to listen to an account of it. It can be particularly important when the person requiring care is very dependent on the carer and is limited in their ability to do things independently. Undertaking activities supported by friends or volunteers can be a way of developing more independence.

Talking about important things

Putting time aside to talk about things of significance can be useful to bring more meaning to relationships which can become preoccupied with everyday problems of caring. Depending on the interests of individual families this may involve discussing death, money, sex, the future, whether there is life on other planets, which team will win the cup... On one level this is a technique to improve relationships through talking and sharing. However, in the context of caring it can also involve discussing topics which are of vital significance to the family, such as what caring or disability means to individuals, and what the future holds. For instance, the person who refuses to discuss the implications of their death with the person they care for may be just as damaging as one who brings it into every conversation.

Putting the other person first

In this, there is an agreement to take turns to spoil the other person and treat them as special, perhaps acting as if a day and/or evening is their birthday, and making sure that they are treated with extra consideration. Unlike birthdays which happen once a year, this approach could be taken as often as the people involved wish, so long as this is a reciprocal arrangement.

Stress management

Stress management techniques are wide ranging and well-documented, and it goes beyond the scope of this book to consider these in detail. However, stress is an extremely significant problem for carers and we will, therefore, examine some of the areas which are repeatedly indicated as of concern specifically in relation to carers. Again, these techniques are best taught in a group setting which can provide reinforcement and encouragement. Stress management techniques are futile unless built into people's everyday lives, yet for most of us the temptation is to go for quick-fix relaxation such as a glass of wine or a TV programme, instead of something which will really do us good. Carers are no different and the more they are supported by a group the more likely it is that they will be able to adopt good methods of stress management.

Stress assessment

The first stage of any stress management process is to find out whether there is a problem. There are a number of simple and non-threatening stress assessments which can be used for this (see for instance Heron 1996). Stress assessments used outside medical or clinical settings generally take the form of a number of questions which will be answered by the individual. Questions are designed to discover whether individuals are experiencing physical, mental or emotional stress. Examples of questions include:

How often and in what situations do you experience any of the following?

- Muscle tension
- Breathing problems
- Headaches
- Disturbed appetite
- Poor sleep patterns
- Feeling overwhelmed
- Forgetfulness
- Nagging worries
- Feeling trapped
- Panic attacks.

Scoring systems in stress assessments should be viewed with caution since they can make the process seem mechanical and can make people with high scores feel even more stressed! They may also be inaccurate; when using scoring I encountered a carer of a child with disabilities who also had a full-time job, who got five points out of 100 and denied he was under stress. Later in the session he acknowledged that he rarely got any sleep at night because his mind would not cut off and that he was unable to lie down to relax because it made him feel agitated! Instead, the topics should be used as pointers for discussion about how a person is affected by stress and what solutions should be sought. Obviously the more factors a carer has in the 'often' column, the more serious the problem and the more the worker should consider taking immediate action, such as arranging respite care.

Stress management techniques for carers
EATING HEALTHILY

Failure to eat appropriately can exacerbate stress and lead to illness. Because of the nature of their tasks, some carers may be inclined to skip meals or build their meals around the erratic behaviour of the person they are caring for, or may find it difficult to afford food. Sessions on healthy eating, covering nutrition and cooking easy and inexpensive meals, can be extremely useful to some carers. Even where carers already have a high level of skill in cooking, such sessions can be helpful to reinforce existing abilities.

TAKING EXERCISE

Some carers may have a problem with not achieving a sufficient amount of the right sort of exercise. At the same time they may experience too much of the wrong sort, such as strain through repetitive lifting or bending. Sessions on correct exercise, including stretching, cardiovascular exercise and muscle strengthening, and good posture will be useful.

RELAXATION TECHNIQUES

All of us can benefit from building relaxation into our everyday lives, particularly when these are stressful. There are a variety of relaxation techniques, such as progressive relaxation (relaxing the muscular and skeletal systems), mental visualisation, breathing techniques, physical methods such as yoga or tai chi, and meditation. Different types of relaxation will be suited to particular individuals and, if possible, people should be taught the range of techniques so they can choose which is most appropriate for them. A comprehensive range of relaxation techniques for workers wishing to teach relaxation is covered in Heron (1996).

TIME MANAGEMENT

Some carers often feel that there are not enough hours in the day to do everything they need to accomplish. They become exhausted from rushing from one task to another. Learning time management techniques can help them to distinguish whether, indeed, they have too much to do or whether they could use the techniques to make more time for themselves. While people may often state vehemently that the former is the case, on analysis it is often found that people lose time through activities such as starting one thing before finishing another, allowing themselves to be distracted, doing things of a low priority, or basic lack of planning. Even if a carer is truly overloaded, time management is an objective way of demonstrating this, to form the basis for obtaining more support.

TAKING A BREAK

The importance of taking a break from caring in order to relax, have fun and recharge the batteries has been covered on a number of occasions. A session on how to build this into carers' routines, along with discussion of strategies to overcome difficulties in this, can be a useful topic in any carers group. It is important to stress the point that taking a break does not need to be expensive, or even involve leaving the house so long as it is enjoyable. For example, one carer gained some benefit from deciding to have a bath with the bathroom door locked and leaving her mother who had dementia to her own devices for a short period of time.

CONFIDENCE BUILDING

Some carers suffer from a lack of self-esteem through the limiting nature of their role and can benefit from confidence-building exercises to increase their sense of self-worth. Sessions would include discussion on what is meant by self-confidence and would explore the fact that people often have an unrealistically low view of their own abilities. They would also involve exercises such as making lists of 'Things I do well', 'Five things (or more) I like about myself' and 'Things other people like about me'. Sessions could also include affirmation exercises in which people design their own affirmation, such as 'I am a strong and capable person'.

However, facilitators need to be aware that confidence building can be very threatening to people who have extremely low self-esteem, such as some people who have been sexually abused in childhood, or people who feel high levels of guilt about their actions. While one would not necessarily expect to encounter people with such deep-seated problems in a carers' group, facilitators need to be aware of this possibility and exercise sensitivity in how the session is handled.

MANAGING SLEEP PROBLEMS

Many carers suffer from disturbed sleep patterns such as inability to get to sleep, interrupted sleep through the night or waking very early in the morning. Sometimes this will be as a result of the needs or behaviour of the person they are caring for, such as a person with dementia who wanders in the night or someone who is bedridden and needs to be regularly turned. In these situations, any practical solutions to help the carer improve their rest should be considered. In other situations however, sleep disturbance is due to stress or overwork and carers can benefit from examining personal strategies to address these problems. These could include information on sleep, techniques for getting to sleep and individual action plans for improving sleep patterns. For more information see, for instance, Simmons and Daw (1994).

MANAGING CRISIS

A crisis is a situation which challenges an individual's ability to cope with events. Initial work into crisis theory was undertaken by Caplan, Parad and Rapoport in the 1960s. In this, a crisis was viewed as a time-limited event, usually of four to six weeks' duration in which participants experience a number of reactions, such as fear, anxiety, and excitement (Caplan 1964). Crises have a strongly subjective component – the same event may be a major crisis to one person but virtually unnoticed by another. The progress of a crisis can be portrayed in graph form as a curve which ascends steeply, peaks and then descends, representing the energy that individuals put into trying to manage the crisis. Individuals either learn to manage a crisis situation or to avoid it, perhaps by denial. Depending on how they manage the crisis, people can emerge strengthened or weakened from their experience. A well-handled crisis will give confidence, while one which is not managed well will result in anxiety about handling problems in the future. Coulshed (1991) emphasises that crises can be a positive learning experience for those involved.

Crises are likely to figure significantly in the lives of carers, often at the transitional stages of caring such as starting to care, finishing care and disruptive life events. Therefore it can be extremely helpful for carers to understand the mechanisms of crisis and ways of managing these effectively. For instance, 'managing crises' can be the subject of a session in a carers group. The keys to effective crisis management can be described as follows:

- Avoid hasty decisions – ill-planned and ill-thought-out actions during a crisis are often regretted once this is over. A classic example of this is of someone who needs care selling their own home to move in with their family and then regretting the loss of their independence. Often it can be more appropriate to take no action, instead assessing the situation over time to decide on the best course to take. Professionals need to take note of this too!

- Utilise support networks – crises can bring out a tendency in some people to try and go it alone with an accompanying belief that they do not need any help. Instead of this approach it is generally more useful to involve other people, especially to gain emotional support and to talk things through with someone who may be able to give a more objective viewpoint.

- View a crisis as a learning experience – adopting a positive attitude towards crisis is rarely easy, but it may certainly enable people to achieve a positive outcome. Negative attitudes such as catastrophising or self-pity are likely to make it more difficult for people to summon the resources to cope effectively.

Checklist of considerations for providing emotional support

What mechanisms are in place to enable carers to:

- express how they feel?
- build up social networks?
- reduce stress and improve their lifestyle?
- manage crisis situations?

9

Information and Involvement

'If I knew then what I know now... I know its a cliché, but it's how I feel. In heaven's name why did I have to struggle on for five years before finding out about the community respite service?' (A carer)

Information and involvement are two key factors in ensuring that there is an appropriate balance of power between carers and service providers. Without information, carers are severely impeded from accessing support. The effects of poor involvement may be less immediately obvious to carers, but may ultimately result in services which are focused on the needs of organisations or service users without reference to carers. This chapter considers practical methods for organisations to inform carers about what they do and to involve them in the planning and delivery of services.

An information strategy for carers

At the point they begin caring, the majority of carers will need information about the condition of the person they are caring for and the support which is available to help that person or themselves. Carers often require specialist services which they may not even know exist, let alone know how to access. For instance, there is a confusion in many people's minds about the distinction between the Department of Social Security and social services departments. Fewer people again will understand the distinction between statutory and independent sector services. It can be argued that carers do not care where the services come from, only that they do receive them and that they are appropriate. But, unfortunately, without this knowledge it is difficult to access and get the best out of services.

There is a suspicion amongst some carers and their organisations that information is kept deliberately vague or even non-existent because agencies are not able to cope with the demand that would be generated if carers knew what was available for them. While there may be some truth in this belief, in recent years a considerable amount of effort has been put into developing appropriate ways of informing carers and a great deal of information is available on both a national and local basis. However, although much good work is being carried out, it is important that this is done as part of the strategic planning process within local areas. Without this level of planning there can be a tendency for positive but unconnected ideas which may fail to reach the maximum number of carers or which ultimately fall through as workers or agencies change. In this section we examine the fundamental requirements of a successful information strategy for carers.

The stages of an information strategy

In order to be effective, any information strategy requires the following stages to take place:

1. Deciding what information is needed, when and who is responsible for it.

2. Designing and planning the information.

3. Distributing the information.

4. Monitoring its uptake and effectiveness.

5. Keeping it up to date.

The sections below examine these factors in more detail, examining such issues as consulting with carers, assigning responsibility, and design and distribution of material.

Multi-disciplinary co-ordination

The most essential feature of any information strategy for carers is that it should be owned and managed by all the organisations, agencies and groups which have an interest in providing information for carers. One method for achieving this is that interested groups could form a steering committee, which would meet to plan the strategy and agree who has responsibility for implementing its various stages. Without the involvement of key organisations there are many opportunities for waste of effort, duplication of services and failure to target information at those who need it.

Take, for instance, the voluntary organisation with a marginal role in relation to carers which gained funding from a national company to establish a local carers' information helpline. This multi-phone helpline was advertised with a splash of publicity in the local press, much to the surprise of other organisations with a remit to support carers, especially the agency which already ran a long-established carers' helpline! The problems in this situation were manifest. The 'new' helpline clearly did not have sufficient information about other local services and its value for carers was questionable. Furthermore, it emerged that the service was a temporary one, funded for three months as part of a sponsorship deal. The sponsor, no doubt, felt they had excellent value for money when they learnt about the number of people who had contacted the line. They would be less aware of the poor quality information available to carers and the expectations which might have been raised.

There should be no place for carers' organisations to operate in this uncoordinated fashion. Although voluntary organisations often feel as if they are competing for limited funding and therefore need to keep a step ahead of their 'rivals', this should never take precedence over the need to work together. In such situations it can often be useful if a commissioning agency takes overall responsibility for co-ordinating the information strategy. It is also essential that any information steering group regularly advertises its existence and invites relevant agencies to join its ranks. An information group that no one knows about is unlikely to be performing effectively.

Once the information strategy is in place, the steering group would be responsible for ensuring that its components were effective. There is no point in a series of carer information days which are poorly attended, or expensive leaflets which go out of date in a month. Additionally, it is essential that information leaflets and such like are kept in stock and supplied to distribution points.

Assigning responsibility to a named individual in each agency

Named individuals with an identified responsibility for information on carers' issues are a vital element of any information strategy. They are useful because of the clarity which this gives to people outside the organisation who will know whom to approach for information; also because the 'pressure' of being a named person means that there is an added incentive to do the job effectively. Each organisation should be encouraged to have an information officer who can act as contact person and who will have responsibility for disseminating information to the carers with whom they work. Needless to say, this role also needs to be widely and regularly advertised to ensure people are aware of it.

Basing a strategy on carers' views

The most appropriate information strategies will be based on the information that carers indicate will be useful to them. Consideration also needs to be given to when they would like the information and in what form. While workers who have regular contact with carers will have a good idea about what carers want, before any major initiative it is always useful to double check this. In 1996, a survey was conducted in Wirral to establish what types of information carers wished to see included in a pack for carers. Two hundred questionnaires were sent out and 93 were returned. At almost 50 per cent this was a high rate of return indicating the interest carers have in this topic. A number of suggestions were made for what could be included in the pack, and a space was left for people to make additional suggestions or comments. The areas for inclusion which proved most popular were: respite care, social services/health support, carers' helplines, benefits advice, carers' rights, crisis support, equipment, carers' emergency card, day care services, support groups and assessment. The small number of additional suggestions which carers made were not repeated by other carers and therefore were not taken to be trends. In addition the survey indicated that carers wished to receive information at the earliest possible opportunity (Morris 1996).

The components of an information strategy
LANGUAGE

The importance of providing jargon-free information without the use of technical terms is continually stressed. In relation to carers there are a number of words which are not yet in general use which are best avoided especially when trying to contact new or hidden carers. The word 'carer' itself may fail to attract people when used as a main title, since they may not view themselves as a carer. Moffat (1997) suggests alternatives such as 'Are you looking after someone?' or 'Does someone depend on you?'. The term 'respite' may also mean very little to carers until it is explained fully and is generally rephrased along the lines of 'help which gives you a break from caring'.

FORMAT

Information for carers needs to be produced in a variety of formats, such as large print, braille, tape and pictorial, for people with special needs. Research needs to be undertaken before producing special formats to ensure that these will actually be used, particularly if substantial resources are to be involved in their production.

FACT SHEETS AND LEAFLETS

Fact sheets and leaflets are quick and easy ways of providing summaries of information about a variety of topics relevant to carers. They should be concise, clear and freely available and have contact names and numbers for further information. Ideally they will form part of a series, and information about other leaflets in the series should be included on each sheet so that they can be requested if not immediately available. Leaflets are ideal to accompany face-to-face sessions with workers. For example, since it can be notoriously difficult to take in all that is said when a serious condition is diagnosed, leaflets can be supplied by a doctor for the family to read in their own time. Needless to say, written information should never be used as an alternative to a sensitive verbal explanation.

CARERS' PACKS

Carers' packs aim to compile as much information as possible which is of use to carers. Packs can be basic and inexpensive, perhaps in the form of a series of monochrome printed fact sheets stapled together. They may also be elaborate – a pack I obtained from Australia contained a number of full colour, glossy booklets plus an audio tape on how to reduce stress (Commonwealth Department of Health, Housing and Community Services 1993). Whatever their degree of sophistication, packs tend to include similar information. The problem in compiling packs is to make the decision on what should be a priority and what left out. It may be relatively easy to determine general areas in which most carers have an interest, but there are endless specialist areas which will only be of interest to a few people. Including all these can make the pack bulky, costly and so lengthy that it can be off-putting. Some packs are customised for individual carer's needs; they include basic information relevant to all carers with additional sheets for carers with specific needs, for instance information on dementia or mental health. This approach, of course, requires a system in which packs can be compiled for individual carers.

BROCHURES AND SERVICE LEAFLETS

Brochures and information leaflets about services are extremely important as part of good practice and customer care. Every service should have some form of information leaflet which includes the following areas: details about the service such as opening times; activities or support it offers; a profile of the staff, their training and qualifications; contact names; who is eligible for the service; how to access the service; costs involved; and finally, standards to which the service promises to operate so that service users will know how to assess the service. A general, multi-agency leaflet on services for carers is essential for every local area.

The impetus to provide information about services has been very much fuelled in Britain by private sector residential and nursing homes which developed brochures as a method of advertising their services. This has provoked emulation in local authority services, but also a reluctance by some to go down this road. Some managers believe that information leaflets will stimulate a demand which could not be met. This is based on a misapprehension that leaflets have only an advertising function. In fact a leaflet which sets out eligibility criteria will clearly inform individuals about whether they are likely to be eligible for support and can operate as a filtering mechanism. Having produced regular leaflets for day services I can attest to the usefulness of up-to-date information leaflets for referrers, service users and carers. Such leaflets are also important to provide a link between carers and services – while carers may not visit the service they will still have good information about what it provides.

NEWSLETTERS

A newsletter is an excellent means of providing current information of interest to carers in local areas. Newsletters produced monthly have the advantage of keeping people in touch with one another and promoting a sense of community amongst carers, which can be vital in reducing their sense of isolation. Newsletters have the space to consider issues in more depth than leaflets or fact sheets and can give up-to-date information. They may cover analyses of legislation, benefits changes, advances in medical research into illness, interviews with key people, practical tips on how to manage problems when caring, information about how to tap into services, agony pages, pen-pals...the list is endless. Most importantly they can include articles *by* carers *for* carers and humour, which has been highlighted as particularly important by carers, who do not want a read of 'doom and gloom'. Comments which have been made about carers' newsletters include: 'I feel as if it is written especially for me', 'Helps me feel in touch', 'Invaluable information'.

NATIONAL INFORMATION

Information produced nationally is often an excellent source of information for carers and should not be neglected by local groups. It can be particularly useful in terms of general information about medical conditions, benefits changes and updates on legislation. There is no point in producing a local, possibly inferior leaflet about a particular illness when a national organisation has already done this work and will supply these at very little, if any, cost. It is possible to customise some national leaflets with stickers or stamps to provide local names and contact addresses so that interested carers can request further, local information.

THE INTERNET

The internet is not short of information on carers, which varies from extremely useful to obscure. Use of the internet will become increasingly important and carers' organisations should consider tapping into this resource. Many national organisations have web sites and local organisations could benefit from developing a home page for local carers' issues. This site could include all the information of a carers' pack. While it will take some time before the internet is of use to the majority of carers, it should not be forgotten that it is a particularly useful way of communicating with people, allowing both instant access and easily updated information.

Advertising and distributing information

Producing information is often the simple part of an information strategy; disseminating it can prove much more problematic. The twin nightmares of anyone involved in this process are to see the entire production disappear within days or to have stacks of unopened boxes lurking embarrassingly in the back of a cupboard. Therefore a plan for distribution, and someone to implement this, are essential!

The key to distribution involves ensuring that the right information goes to the people who need it as quickly as possible. A choice will often have to be made between leaving information in public places like libraries or GPs' surgeries and directing it through specialist resources such as carer helplines or lists of interested carers. The wider the range of sources of information the more difficult it is to keep it up-to-date, complete and available. Also the information may be taken by people who have only a casual interest in it. At the same time, however, it is likely to be accessible to the widest range of carers. Information through specialist sources is easily maintained and can be customised for individuals but may reach less people. A compromise position may have to be reached, with as much material as possible available through locations which carers are likely to visit and more specific information available in agreed central locations. Named workers in a variety of locations are essential for good distribution.

Timing of information is particularly important. Carers have indicated that they would find information useful at the start of caring, some time later when they have a better idea of what is involved and during crisis situations (Social Services Inspectorate 1995b).

Reaching 'hidden' carers

It is often remarked that once carers get known to 'the system' their access to information immediately improves, thus enabling them to get the best out of services which are available. In contrast, concern is often expressed for hidden carers, those who are caring in isolation, unknown to services providers. The techniques for reaching hidden carers involve wide use of different types of publicity.

- Poster campaigns in locations such as health or social services buildings, post offices, local shops and supermarkets can be effective.

- Advertising in newspapers and on radio and TV will involve varying levels of expense, but is a sure method of reaching a wide range of carers. It can be possible to get newspaper and radio space and even time on TV at no cost, in programmes or articles devoted to discussing welfare issues or promoting local services. Special events, such as roadshows or fund-raisers, are often a way of attracting local media coverage. However, it is important to realise that organisers will have no control over free publicity, which may not always take the form that they wish to see. The Carers National Association will give advice on working with the media.

- There are a number of special events which can help contact hidden carers. Roadshows can take place in hospital foyers or shopping centres and provide an intensive information session, with posters, leaflets and displays. These are generally staffed by workers or carers who can answer individual enquiries. I was recently part of a group, promoting services for carers in a shopping precinct on pension day, which was able to contact a small but significant number of 'hidden' carers by approaching people who were pushing people in wheelchairs and older men carrying shopping bags! A more elaborate event would be a carer fair in which representatives from the range of local agencies which provide services for carers could have stalls and displays indicating what they do.

• If resources permit, a mobile information unit which can travel around the locality and park in areas such as markets can be an excellent source of information both for hidden carers and, if its time-table is advertised in advance, for carers who can plan their visit. A mobile unit can be particularly appropriate in rural areas.

• There are many advantages in a one-stop shop (one location at which all information can be obtained) for carers. Carers' centres or helplines, if well advertised, may attract hidden carers. At the same time, since people may not think of themselves as a 'carer', it can also be useful to have regular advice points at places which carers are likely to attend, such as hospitals or health centres, where face-to-face explanations can be given.

• GPs are consistently shown to be of great significance in targeting carers but the problems of engaging with them for this purpose are equally well known. Some areas have established excellent relationships between individual practices and carers' workers through mechanisms such as running advice points in surgeries. Such developments require significant human resources and, unfortunately, remain locality-based rather than widespread.

Information for carers from ethnic minorities

While most carers experience difficulties in receiving appropriate information, the situation for carers from ethnic minority groups is likely to be even more difficult, and requires a specific approach in order to address their needs. An information strategy for carers from ethnic minorities should involve both written information and personal support to enable people to use the information to the best effect.

Before producing written information it is useful to estimate the numbers of people who are likely to benefit from it, in order to balance the level of need and the cost of translating material. Most areas have had to make decisions about what information will be translated, based upon the size of ethnic populations. For instance, if an area has a large Chinese population it is clearly appropriate to have documents translated into Chinese. However, most areas have a mix of ethnic minority groups varying in size from many thousands to under one hundred individuals. Since resources will not permit every document to be translated, solutions need to be sought. Where there are large populations it may be appropriate to translate the majority of documents. Alternatives for smaller groups include leaflets which summarise a number of services and give information on how to access further support in their own language and summaries on the cover of English leaflets, again referring people on for further information. Carers' organisations need to ensure that general leaflets or summaries on subjects such as community care do not neglect information about carers.

Sometimes a more sophisticated analysis will be needed in order to ensure that information is targeted correctly. For instance, it is futile providing written translations to a community which is unable to read the language. It can be useful to ask communities how they would prefer to have information – some may prefer audio or video information rather than written information. Organisations requiring translation which do not have the capacity to undertake this themselves can commission a service from translation units in areas where there are large ethnic minority populations. Any practitioner involved in commissioning such a service needs to spend time talking with the relevant community and with workers experienced in social care translations in a variety of translation units.

Pitfalls in translations can be considerable; care should be taken to translate the language relevant to the local population rather than a national language which no one may speak. There may be considerable disagreement between translators about the right way to translate technical health or social services terms; sometimes even obvious mistakes can be made, such as that of the translation unit which omitted to translate the title page of a leaflet into the language, leaving it in English only. Similarly, one organisation's department had leaflets translated into a number of languages with no English explanation which meant that when the worker responsible left, no one in the organisation knew what they were about. Particular care should be taken over translating the term 'carer' which will not have a literal translation in many languages. Generally, information leaflets should appear in both English and the translation in order to avoid the problems mentioned above and so that families from ethnic minorities, where there may be both English and original language readers, have the maximum chance of understanding the information. It is also useful to consult with local communities about the style of any written material to ensure that it is acceptable. For example, Wing Kwong and Kerrie (1992) indicate that publicity material for Chinese people should not be in blue and white which are funeral colours.

Written information needs to be circulated in places where people from ethnic minority groups spend time, such as community centres, religious buildings, restaurants, businesses and workplaces as well as general locations of relevance to all carers. The snowball or grapevine effect can have a prominent role to play and it can be useful to ask members of local communities to pass information on to other people that they know. Information can also be spread through ethnic language media such as newspapers and radio programmes. It is important to have posters with summaries of information in reception areas of locations such as hospitals and social services departments. An interesting finding is that a number of studies have shown that the proportion of black people approaching their GPs is higher than that for white people (Butt and Mirza 1996), which suggests that primary care may be a positive location for informing carers from ethnic minority groups.

However, while written information is a positive start to informing people from ethnic minorities, it should not stand in isolation. 'It is not sufficient just to inform people about what is available; parents need to be in contact with someone who understands their needs and who can give them the support they require to assist them in arranging to receive benefits and services to which they are entitled' (Shah 1992). A service in which people can have face-to-face discussion with people who speak their language is a vital part of any information strategy in order that questions can be asked, and issues clarified. Ethnic minority community workers, health or social care practitioners or volunteers, have an important role in this. Close links should be made between carers' organisations and ethnic minority communities to ensure that information is shared.

Finally, special events can be organised to raise awareness in ethnic minority groups about aspects of health and social care. Again, where there are large numbers of people in the area it may be appropriate to have an event solely on the subject of carers; where numbers are few, a general event, perhaps about community care, in which the issue of carers is included is likely to be more effective. Events can be extremely successful, but need a great deal of work and commitment from practitioners and members of ethnic minority communities. In order to attract interest it can be useful to link them in with cultural, entertainment or social events with refreshments.

Practitioners and information

Finally, it is important that all practitioners should be aware of information that might be relevant to carers and accept the responsibility for passing this on. The problems in achieving this are that sometimes workers may have a blinkered approach to information and not investigate what is available beyond the confines of their own particular area of work; also workers may be so familiar with their subject there can be a tendency to assume that other people have a fuller understanding than is in fact the case. This is not confined to workers; sometimes carers who have become familiar with care systems will also assume knowledge in other carers. If giving accurate information is a priority for organisations they will need to ensure that workers understand this. This approach should also not be confined to operational staff, but extended to workers such as receptionists who may have high levels of contact with carers. Training in information giving is important for all levels of staff and volunteers.

Involving carers in the planning and delivery of services

The involvement of users and carers in community care and other services is based on the premise that users and carers have a great deal of expertise, knowledge and understanding about their own needs and what should be done to meet them. Rather than being passive recipients of care delivered by experts, they should be active participants whose views should be taken into account and acted upon. Consumerism has also had a great influence on the user and carer movement. With this model, social care can be seen to be an essential commodity, such as water or fuel, with users and carers being customers with all the rights to a high standard of service that this entails.

It is worth noting that a distinction has been made between consultation and involvement. At their point of greatest contrast, consultation can generally be taken to mean that people's views are sought at a late stage of any planning process. Involvement implies a more active role, with the carer having responsibilities and advisory or decision-making power. For example, in consultation carers may be presented with a draft document for their comments; with involvement they would have taken part in producing the document.

User and carer organisations may stress the importance of full involvement, while individual users and carers may not wish to give a large time commitment but may be prepared to give their views as part of a consultation process. Therefore both of these approaches are useful for any planning strategy but it is important that organisations understand the distinction. Research indicates that there is a lack of clarity in local authorities about the variety and levels of involvement of users and carers (Office for Public Management 1993).

Carer and user involvement, when operating well, offers a service truly based on people's needs, enhancing choice for individuals and creating an environment in which workers, users and carers are treated with equal respect and consideration. As we shall see, when operating badly, it becomes a system distinguished by recrimination, anger and acrimony, in which professionals pull up the drawbridge, carer groups lay siege, and choice for users and carers decreases. The positives and negatives of user and carer involvement are equally balanced; therefore it is essential that the process of developing involvement is managed in a way which avoids or minimises the potential for damage. Also, the involvement of carers is one strand of the wider service user empowerment movement, and sometimes the role of carer involvement is subsumed by this. It is important to maintain the distinction between the involvement of users and carers because, as we have seen, they may have different needs and priorities. At this level, the same potential for harmony and tension exists as in personal relationships between users and carers. Generally, user and carer groups work together to common goals, but occasionally they may come into conflict.

Carer involvement is not a simple concept, rather it operates on a number of levels, from individual care planning to departmental strategic planning. In this section we will examine these levels, general principles for effective carer involvement, and practical methods for achieving this.

Individual care plans

This level of involvement concerns the relationship between practitioner and carer in the areas of assessment and care planning. It entails working in partnership with the carer, respecting and acting upon their views, planning services with them rather than for them and ensuring that so far as possible services should fit flexibly with their personal needs. It has been the intention to emphasise the importance of establishing this way of working throughout this book. Arguably this is the most important way of involving carers, because the majority express the desire for appropriate and unobtrusive services to enable them and the people they care for to get on with their lives. It is also the most widely embraced; in research, 39 of 42 local authorities who replied to a survey had established user/carer involvement at this level (Office for Public Management 1993).

On an individual level, the ability of the practitioner to establish this form of relationship with the carer is vitally important, but this does not stand alone and needs to be based on organisational structures. The following are signs that an organisation is committed to promoting carer involvement:

- Self-assessment forms are available
- Users and carers have the opportunity to complete their own forms
- Users and carers have the opportunity to co-ordinate their own packages of care
- Carers are involved in hospital discharge
- Users and carers sign assessment forms and care plans and have copies of these
- Training is provided for practitioners in how to involve users and carers.

A further development is the Community Care (Direct Payments) Act 1996 which, currently, gives adults under 65 who are eligible for community care services, and indirectly their carers, the opportunity for a factor which all the good practice in the world may fail to provide – true choice. The direct payments legislation enables local authorities to allocate finance to eligible people so that they can organise and purchase their own package of care, including employing support workers. Direct payment is not a way of paying carers for what they do and payment cannot be made to relatives, but it can cover support for carers such as respite care if that is part of an assessed need (Department of Health 1996c).

Care purchased by the local authority may be confined to in-house provision or to particular service providers with whom the authority has a contract, both of which may involve limitations in flexibility. With direct payments it is possible for disabled people to purchase services which are customised to their needs and those of their carer. The drawback to this approach from their point of view may be the mechanisms which authorities will require to ensure that people are accountable for funding they receive.

Alternatives to direct payment are initiatives such as the voucher scheme for respite care which operates in Bradford Social Services Department, in which carers are given vouchers which can be redeemed from a variety of independent sector residential homes. This enables the carer to purchase respite when and where they want, rather than constantly referring to the care manager. Such a system could certainly be extended to other areas such as respite in the home (Nuffield Institute for Health 1994).

Assessing the quality of services

Consulting carers on the quality of the service they receive is a fundamental component of improving those services. People who actually experience services are in the best position to point out which areas work well and which could be improved. Surveys of carer satisfaction should be carried out regularly by all service providers. As with all forms of consultation, it is good practice, and a way of ensuring that people continue to respond to surveys, if the results are shared; in particular, people appreciate information on how services have been improved following consultation.

At the same time, carer involvement in evaluating the quality of services can go much further. Carers can be involved in the development of standards by which services can be assessed. For example, as part of a consultation exercise, a number of carers commented that there were no standards for respite services in the Wirral Community Care Charter and subsequently these were included. They can also contribute to service specifications – documents which describe in detail the service which an agency wishes to commission. On a more formal level, carers can directly take part in the inspection or monitoring of services. Lay inspectors of residential homes are an example of this, and such developments could easily be extended to other areas of service provision. For instance, carers could be recruited to carry out a monitoring exercise of respite agencies.

Carers as trainers, consultants or representatives

Carer involvement in the training of social care practitioners is now well established as good practice. My experience from teaching on social work qualifying courses is that sessions involving users or carers have a greater impact, and a stronger hold on the attention of the participants, than any other part of the course. Carers can give practitioners insights into the experience of caring and can encourage them to confront how it feels to be on the receiving end of their interventions. Care should be taken that this is not just an isolated part of a course which is quickly forgotten; carers cannot be present for every session, but these can be run as if they were.

As a *representative*, a carer would have a mandate from other carers to take forward their views, concerns and suggestions. For instance a carer representative may speak on behalf of a group of carers of people with mental health problems; alternatively someone may represent carers in a local area or even carers on a national basis. Representatives do not promote their own perspective, rather their role is clearly to speak for their catchment group, and to be accountable to them. A carer representative does not have to have been a carer; they may be volunteers or workers chosen to represent this group. As *consultants*, carers would generally be involved in discrete pieces of work such as reviews or development of particular services. Rather than representing other carers, they would be expected to contribute their own expertise, based on their background as a carer and other abilities such as research or facilitation skills. Their role would generally be to promote the needs of carers.

Arrangements for carers to be trainers, consultants or representatives can range from the informal, in which local carers may be involved on a goodwill basis, to the formal, in which suitably trained or experienced carers are commissioned and paid for their services (Department of Health 1996e). There are both advantages and disadvantages to each of these approaches. As informal representatives or consultants, carers with minimum training or support may not have the experience to be able to take an objective view point and understand the principles of working towards constructive change. In contrast, skilled carers can be invaluable as facilitators for other carers, and in moving workers on who may be stuck in their approach. On the other hand, there may be a feeling that 'career carers' may be too remote from the needs of local carers and too close to the perspective of professionals. Such issues can be addressed by having a mix of carers involved in any process.

Strategic planning and decision making

Carers can also be involved in the development of services at the level of strategic planning both within single agencies and in a multi-agency setting. At this level carers can influence the overall direction of policies. For example, research could be carried out amongst carers to establish their highest priority needs. If the consensus was that there should be more respite care within the home, resources could be targeted in this direction. Gaining this type of information is particularly important where resources are limited, because determining the priorities of service users and carers will help to ensure that the most appropriate services are commissioned.

Taking this a stage further, carers may also be involved in decision making at the strategic planning level. Where carers have power to make decisions at this level, there needs to be tight accountability. The carer's role, mandate and extent and limits of responsibility must be clarified. In many voluntary organisations carers take an active role as part of the management committee. Within a local authority or health setting their role is likely to be more advisory than decision making, due to the structure of the organisation. Nevertheless, their influence can have far-reaching effects. One senior manager described the process in which a carer representative attended regular meetings as like having 'an angel on my shoulder – just by being there she brings us back to thinking about the real issues, which are carers' needs'.

Operational management

Carers may contribute towards the operational management of services in a number of ways. In terms of statutory organisations, involvement tends to focus on advisory committees attached to day or residential settings which have a catchment of membership. However there is no reason why similar mechanisms could not be established for services such as home care. The purpose of these vary, from groups which fund-raise and take responsibility for organising social outings and holidays to those which contribute to decisions about management of budgets and recruitment and deployment of staff. Such arrangements may not be easy for workers who might find themselves caught between the demands of carers and their own-line management structures. Any such development would need to be established with forethought and sensitivity, with clear roles and responsibilities for all concerned.

Similar care needs to be exercised in the relationship between user and carer involvement. Since most services tend to be focused on the needs of users, it is appropriate that where there are user committees, carers should have representation on these. An alternative model is to have both a user and a carer committee, which occurs in some day centres for adults with learning disabilities. However, unless both groups have distinct areas of responsibility, there are, perhaps, more opportunities for conflict within this model, than in an integrated approach.

Carer-managed services

In many ways the 'purest' form of carer involvement is in services run by and for carers. Examples of these are services such as self-help groups or support networks. More extensive arrangements may take the form of: a drop-in run by carers for carers of people with mental health problems; social events to include carers and the people they care for; and sitting services in which carers group together to organise a system of mutual help – one carer looks after two dependants to enable the other carer to have an evening out and vice versa. Such initiatives are extremely helpful to carers in providing 'carer-friendly' respite and support. They should, however, be regarded as additional to mainstream services which provide the sort of ongoing, extensive support which is generally beyond the scope of self-help. Also, not all carers are willing or able to get involved in organising self-help services on top of all their caring responsibilities.

In some cases, carers have formed organisations to provide more direct services such as home respite or sitting services. The management committee of such organisations is likely to have a majority of carers or former carers as members. Some might be run along the lines of a carers' co-operative. The more formal these organisations become and the more they are dependent on funding from sources such as social services departments or health authorities, the more they will find themselves drawn into the contract culture, with the need to satisfy the requirements of statutory purchasers of services.

Principles of involvement

Carer and user involvement is rarely without its tensions for both carers and the agencies with whom they are involved, an issue which has become increasingly recognised. The range of difficulties which may result from involving carers in an unplanned way include: carers who have their own personal agenda rather than representing the views of carers; carers who are unable to separate personal interests from a planning vision; carers who are unprepared for working in organisations, the time and money needed to plan carer involvement appropriately; the attitudes of staff who may be resistant to involvement; and difficulties in achieving flexibility in bureaucratic organisations (Office for Public Management 1993).

My personal experience of a poorly conceived and poorly planned move towards service user involvement was that it resulted in anger and frustration among users who demanded immediate changes and total power, and similar emotions from workers who saw that the users were operating in an even less democratic way in relation to other users than the workers themselves. If users are not supported to behave in ways which enable them to work towards constructive change the results are likely to be poor. In contrast, a user or carer who is reasonably articulate and backs up what they have to say with sound arguments and the results of research will be a powerful instrument of change. Often one of the main reasons these difficulties arise is because of lack of clarity, on the part of all the individuals involved, about this new type of relationship. If adhered to, the following principles should greatly minimise the potential for such problems.

PARTNERSHIP, NOT CONFLICT

Harding and Oldman (1996) point out that 'the split between service users and professionals is in many ways a false one'. Service users have a life beyond services and workers will have a variety of personal experiences of illness and disability within their own lives. Certainly a high number of workers will have experience as carers and the claim 'you can't really understand' may be less accurate in this area than any other. It is only by establishing an atmosphere of mutual support, respect and partnership that involvement of carers will engender positive change.

EQUITY BETWEEN CARER GROUPS

Maintaining equity between carer groups in relation to carer involvement is important, and becomes increasingly so the more influence or decision-making power that carers have in issues such as strategic planning. Clearly, while there may be many issues that are common to all carers, there will be other situations in which decisions about resource allocation become choices between service user groups. For example, a carer representative who is from a particular group, say people with mental health problems, is likely to find it difficult to agree with cuts in mental health services to promote support for older people with dementia. Similarly, the promotion of specialist services to black carers may be at the expense of the development of general home care. In a wider context some carers' groups are clearly more organised than others: parents of adults with learning disabilities tend to be small but cohesive groups focused around day centre services; carers of older people will outnumber these greatly, but are much less likely to have strong representation. This could lead to interesting dilemmas in terms of carer involvement. There are two main ways of promoting equity in carer involvement which can be combined or used separately. Either there should be representation from all the main carer divisions in terms of service user groups, plus young carers and carers from ethnic minority groups, or the representative should be clearly impartial.

CLEAR, WRITTEN AND PUBLICISED STRATEGY

Authorities should have a strategy for involving carers which is clearly written, detailed and widely publicised. Needless to say, carers should be involved in planning the strategy.

CLEAR ROLES AND RESPONSIBILITIES

Ideally, carers would be involved at all levels of service planning and delivery. These levels should be clearly differentiated and the role of carers must be clear to all parties and agreed in advance, including the extent and limit of their responsibilities and those of other people involved. A clear purpose to meetings and the numbers of carer and user representatives at meetings must also be agreed. There should always be more than one carer or user representative at any meeting in order to provide mutual support and so that there will be less danger that they will be marginalised and ignored.

In particular, there should be clarity as to whether or not a carer is representing a group of carers. Not being representative is a common criticism of carers and users. If representatives are involved in any process, the following need to be in place:

- Mechanisms for that person to consult and give feedback to the group they represent

- Agreement on their accountability to the group

- Information about how many people they are representing

- Publicity about their role.

This enables agencies to gauge the extent and level of carers' opinions about a particular issue — especially important when making decisions on allocation of scant resources. Carers who do not represent other carers, for instance a carer who is a consultant, should generally not speak on behalf of carers, nor should workers in agencies which provides services for carers. Exceptions would be if they are referring to research findings or have had discussions with a specific group of carers.

LONG-TERM INVOLVEMENT

Carer involvement can be both short-term, such as a one-off questionnaire, or ongoing, such as a carers' forum. While a mix of short and long-term mechanisms is likely to be useful, a strategy made up of short-term involvement will be less effective. Involvement thrives where time is given to build up trust and working relationships between participants (White 1994).

FAIR PAYMENT

Carers who are invited to attend meetings should, at the least, have their expenses paid. It may well also be appropriate to remunerate them for their time. Not only is this fair to people on low incomes but it also formalises the arrangement. On the other hand, some carers have stated that they would not wish to receive payment because it would compromise their independence, and organisations may state that if they had to pay for involvement they would simply be unable to afford it.

Both may agree that resources should be targeted towards services; however, this issue should be discussed.

TRAINING

Training should be made available to carers to equip them for involvement with subjects such as: principles and practice of user/carer involvement, managing meetings, representational skills, mechanisms for effecting change, presentation skills, assertiveness; and information about the structure and purpose of organisations. There should also be opportunities for carers who may have unresolved personal feelings about services to talk these through so that they do not bring personal or emotional baggage into formal meetings. A list of people who have undergone this training could be maintained, so that they can be contacted for specific areas of involvement. Most importantly, training should also be organised for staff who may be unfamiliar with working with carers in a participative way. This training could cover all the areas mentioned above. In both cases it is essential to have carers or former carers involved in the delivery of training to emphasise the message of empowerment and involvement.

GROUND-RULES

While workers may complain that sometimes users or cares behave inappropriately at meetings, a counter claim would be that workers have subtle methods of ignoring their contribution. Ground-rules should be established for meetings, which would include participants exhibiting mutual respect, courtesy, confidentiality, polite behaviour and interest in each other's opinions. If there is likely to be conflict within the group, strategies for dealing with this need to be clear in advance, such as mechanisms for recording and managing differences of opinion.

ESTABLISHING A BUDGET

There are significant resource implications to carer involvement, and the more detailed and sophisticated the structures the more expense there is likely to be. Workers' time is likely to be a major factor in this, quite apart from direct costs such as payment to carers. In times of resource constraint, organisations, users and carers will need seriously to consider the relative merits of direct services and mechanisms for involvement to determine which is most appropriate. One way of ensuring that the direct resources involved in consulting with carers are taken into account is to establish a separate budget for this.

For detailed discussions on the relative merits and drawbacks of methods of involving users and carers see *Encouraging User Involvement in Commissioning* (Department of Health 1996d).

Mechanisms for consulting with carers

The following are some of the most effective ways that have been found for consulting with service users and carers at all levels of involvement. These approaches are complementary, rather than exclusive, and taken together offer a thorough approach to involving carers in planning.

CARER LISTS

A number of areas have developed lists of carers who wish to receive information and who are often willing to be involved in consultation.

FOCUS GROUPS

Focus groups are time-limited groups which are formed to consider specific areas of interest. For example, a focus group may meet with the aim of discussing and forming recommendations on carers' assessments. Such groups have agreed membership and agendas.

OPEN MEETINGS

General meetings can be arranged with a wide invitation to carers, their groups and organisations. The advantages of these are that a large number of people are invited to attend meetings and will have the opportunity for face-to-face contact. The disadvantages are that few people may actually turn up, and if the meeting is large it is difficult to keep it to a tight agenda. Such meetings are generally places to air initial views rather than undertake planned work.

QUESTIONNAIRES

Questionnaires can be used to gain information from a large sample of a population where it is not possible or suitable for meetings to be arranged. They also provide an opportunity for carers to give more consideration to their response. Ideally questionnaires will contain a mixture of questions which give quantifiable answers, such as yes/no or multiple choice, and also spaces for people to give comments and suggestions to ensure that a qualitative feel for the subject is gained. Anyone undertaking a questionnaire survey should familiarise themselves with good research practice so that their efforts will result in relevant information.

INTERVIEWS

Semi-structured interviews can be used to gain qualitative or in-depth responses from a small sample of people. Perhaps using a questionnaire or series of questions as a basis, they enable people to talk through what response they wish to give with an objective individual. These methods are time-intensive and require the interviewer to have good interpersonal and research skills.

FORUMS OR REGULAR MEETINGS

Carer forums are ongoing groups which meet on a regular basis to discuss and act on issues which are of interest to carers. For consultation purposes they may agree to read and comment on a document at a meeting, or to devote a number of meetings to a particular topic, thus in the short term becoming a focus group.

Checklist of considerations for informing and involving carers

Information

- Is there a written multi-agency strategy for providing information to carers?
- Is there a named person responsible for the strategy in each agency?
- Where are the distribution points for information?
- Who keeps the information in stock?
- Is there a strategy for monitoring take-up?
- Which of the following methods are used on a regular basis: service brochures, leaflets on carers' issues, carers' packs, helplines for carers, newsletters, the internet, special events?
- What special arrangements have been made to inform carers from ethnic minorities?
- Is training on informing carers available for practitioners, including reception staff?

Involvement

- Is there a written strategy for involving carers?
- Which of the following evidences of carer involvement are in operation: self-assessments, carers as co-ordinators of care packages, written copies of assessments and care plans being given to carers, carers signing documents, involvement in hospital discharge, direct payments schemes?
- Which of the following levels of carer involvement operate regularly: service satisfaction surveys; involvement in standard setting and inspection, strategic planning, operational management?
- What mechanisms are in place to inform carers of the results of surveys?
- Does the organisation have principles of good practice for involving carers?

- Which of the following mechanisms of involvement operate regularly: questionnaires, forums, focus groups?

- What training is in place for carers and workers in relation to carer involvement?

10

Young Carers

'My mum is in a wheelchair and can't walk to the shops. Sometimes my dad goes and sometimes I go with a list. When I'm older I'm going to push her.' (A young carer)

If understanding of carers' issues is still in its early days, the topic of young carers is embryonic. Interest in young carers has mainly developed in the health and social care field in Britain since the 1980s. At the same time, media interest in the topic has grown, with a number of articles and programmes alternatively lionising young carers as having 'hearts of gold' or decrying the 'scandal' of a system which allows young people to take on such responsibility.

Just as with carers in general, there is certainly nothing new about being a young carer – children have been undertaking this role for centuries – but it is only recently that young people with caring responsibilities have been formally recognised as requiring support, and that research into their needs has been conducted. What has already emerged is that, of all the areas of work with carers, this is one of the most involved and most contentious. As we shall see, debates take place around a number of topics such as: should a child be a carer? If so, to what extent, and what are the relative rights and responsibilities of parents and young carers? Work with young carers can also find itself awkwardly in the middle of the divide between children's and adults' services.

Who are young carers?

Basically this definition applies to carers who are children and young people under 18. Generally the person needing care will be a member of their family, often a mother, sometimes a father, sibling or grandparent. Within this general definition there are a number of distinct sub-categories.

Some young carers are the primary carer, providing care for an adult; often this situation involves the child supporting a single parent.

Example

Angela is 12; her mother is divorced and suffering from multiple sclerosis. Angela has always contributed to household tasks, including cleaning and shopping. Now 'on mum's bad mornings' Angela helps her mother to get washed and dressed and prepares her breakfast. When she comes home from school she cooks the meal her mother has been preparing. Angela and her mother feel the amount of care that she provides at the moment is acceptable, but are worried about what will happen when her mother's condition deteriorates.

It can also involve the young carer supporting other children in the family.

Example

Sam is 14; his mother is divorced and suffers from mental health problems. She is agoraphobic, unable to leave the house unless accompanied by her sister who lives a distance away. She keeps the house spotlessly clean and tidy and spends much of her time cooking meals and doing household tasks. Sam is responsible for doing the shopping and any other errands which take place outside the house. He takes his sisters, of six and eight years, to school and picks them up from an after-school club. He also tries to make sure that they do not make a mess at home and 'upset mum'. Sam's mother is worried that he is missing out on social activities, but feels she compensates for not being able to leave the house by making sure that the family are well cared for and have as much money as she can spare. She is concerned as to what will happen to her when her children have grown up. Sam has ambitions to join the army. He and his mother have not discussed his future career.

Young carers may be part of a family where an individual requires care and may undertake some tasks for this person but not have any overall responsibility.

Examples

Carla is ten and lives with her parents and her grandmother who has suffered a stroke. Her parents work and Carla comes home from school at lunch-times to make sure her gran is all right, to help her with a meal and to get to the toilet. Her parents do not get home from work until after five, therefore Carla comes straight home from school and checks on her gran. Carla loves her gran, but she does wish she could spend more time with her friends at school.

John is six and has a brother of four who has severe asthma and requires substantial periods of hospitalisation. John is responsible for playing with his brother and for protecting him if they are playing with friends. John knows how to help his brother with his inhaler and that he must contact an adult or dial 999 if he has breathing difficulties.

Other children or young people live in families where an individual requires care, but are not themselves responsible for undertaking any caring tasks. Strictly speaking, these individuals cannot be considered young carers; however, the effects of living in this environment can certainly be as stressful as for children undertaking actual caring tasks.

Example

Laura is five and her older brother abuses drugs. She is aware that home has changed. Her mother shouts a lot at her brother and sometimes at Laura. She knows her brother has done something bad and that her parents do not like his friends. Her father spends a lot of time away from home. Laura has cleared up after her brother when he was sick in the bathroom so he would not get into any more trouble. Laura is trying to make herself very, very small.

The extent of young caring

Current estimates of the numbers of young carers in Britain are based on local area samples or extrapolations of data from other large-scale surveys. Figures tend to be contradictory, therefore they should be taken as approximations only. Estimates from the Office for National Statistics (ONS) suggest that there are over 50,000 young carers in Britain (Downey 1997). Previous estimates include a population of 10,000 *primary* young carers (Page 1988) and between 15,000 and 40,000 young carers (Mahon and Higgins 1995).

One of the areas which is still unclear is the extent to which young carers have substantial caring responsibilities. An interesting feature is that only 14 per cent of young carers in the ONS sample were primary carers in single-parent families – those likely to have the highest caring responsibilities. Previous research had indicated that up to 60 per cent fell into this category. It appears likely that while the number of children providing some care within the family is reasonably large, those at the heavy end of caring comprise a much smaller group. Indications about the numbers involved clearly have implications for the allocation of resources; however, as we shall see, to take a narrow view of young carers may mean failure to address needs of other children on the edges of care.

Young carers can be found in all age groups, from children at primary school to those above school-leaving age. A study of young carers projects showed that the average age of young carers in contact with the projects was 12 (Dearden and Becker 1995). Young carers may be involved in the range of tasks for which adult carers take responsibility, including providing supervision and personal care. While the image of a young carer is as a child of a disabled person, there are many young carers contributing to the care of people with mental health and substance abuse problems. In a review of three young carers' projects, almost 50 per cent of the children involved had parents with mental health problems (Mahon and Higgins 1995).

Concerns about young carers

The image of the young carer can be particularly emotive and induces concern in those who are aware of the responsibilities they may undertake. On one level, concerns about young carers focus on all the areas which have been highlighted as problematic for adult carers. These include lack of opportunity for social contacts, leisure time and education, and stress factors such as isolation, emotional problems, conflict of needs and overwork. In respect of children, however, these are seen as having much more serious implications for child development and for potential psychological damage.

In terms of development, young carers may be losing out on key opportunities which may affect their lives as adults. Social isolation may mean they do not develop social skills and have difficulties establishing relationships; spasmodic school attendance or lack of time for homework can result in poor academic achievement and lost opportunities in future years; physical strain may lead to health problems in later life, while emotional stress may lead to mental health problems. Furthermore, as children, they are much less able to choose whether or not they wish to be involved in caring activities and, even if they have expressed a choice, may not be making an informed decision.

Young carers have also indicated areas which are of concern to themselves which differ subtly from those of adult carers. The majority of children do not have caring responsibilities; therefore young carers feel different from their peers. It is likely that most young carers will not have friends or even acquaintances in similar situations which leads to the anxiety of feeling out of the ordinary and the belief that nobody understands them. Young carers also have less skills in dealing with authority figures than adults and indicate that they feel that professionals disregard them while paying attention to the adult with care needs (Aldridge and Becker 1993). A concern for the future is also apparent as young carers get older and begin to balance their caring responsibilities with the desire to have a life of their own.

Beyond lack of opportunities for appropriate development are concerns about the active damage that can occur to young carers or to young people who are part of particular households where someone requires care. This is not the family where a child cuts their time with their friends to look after a much loved parent, or where a young person is ashamed to invite friends to their generally happy home because of a grandparent with dementia, but rather situations which are potentially abusive to that child. The father with alcohol problems who is violent towards their mother; the deaf couple who wish to teach their hearing child at home so that they remain part of the deaf culture; the mother with a disability who feels that that her eight-year-old has a duty to provide as much care for her as she requires.

Interestingly, it is being found that a number of children with special needs within the education system appear to come from family backgrounds where there is an individual requiring care (Social Services Inspectorate 1995d). Appropriate intervention with young carers, in the widest sense, appears essential in order that today's young carers do not become tomorrow's users of services.

Young carers and families

In relation to developmental issues at least, it can be perceived that these areas are based upon a culturally specific view of childhood which is prevalent in western cultures, where there is a belief that certain work tasks and responsibilities are age-appropriate and not suitable for children. 'REMEMBER children must be allowed to be children' (Department of Health 1996b, p.12). However, even with this general acceptance about the role of children in society, it has proved difficult to come to a consensus on the extent and type of care that is deemed suitable for young carers. Some situations would be clearly seen as inappropriate – a child under ten toileting an opposite-sex parent, a child of six being asked to keep an eye on a sibling in an acute schizophrenic episode. But what of a ten-year-old toileting a same-sex parent recovering from an operation or a twelve-year-old spending time with their depressed relative? Here the ethical issues are less obvious and the decision could go either way. It is interesting that the idea that children and young people should not undertake caring tasks is rarely proposed. The consensus appears to be that caring should be appropriate to their age and abilities and should not have a detrimental effect on their lives.

Obviously the younger the child, the more demanding the task or extensive the responsibility and the more this interferes with educational and social opportunities, the clearer the issues are, but it has proved difficult to reach any general principles on what is and what is not appropriate care. Rather, practitioners need to view every situation as unique, taking such factors as the wishes of the child, maturity, culture, family relationships and effects on the child's development into account. It is important to remember that caring is not necessarily a negative experience for children. Some young people feel proud of the responsibilities they undertake, view themselves as more independent and mature than other people of their age and enjoy being needed and useful to someone they love. Many more accept the role with the same resignation that they may have for any unwelcome responsibility, such as having to do the washing-up or tidy their room.

A slightly different perspective on young carers' issues has been expressed by some people with physical disabilities and their representatives. There is anxiety and annoyance that the emphasis on images such as a young carer 'raising themselves' in the absence of adequate parenting, or taking on responsibility for a parent and other siblings, portrays disabled people as incapable of undertaking the parenting role. A disabled person is equally able to provide an environment of good parenting skills, appropriate discipline and love as someone without a disability. The emphasis on young carers undermines the abilities and competence of disabled parents. What is needed is not to create a new social care category of young carer and specific services for this group, but services to enable the disabled person to live more independently and facilitate their ability to be a good parent.

It is probably only at the extremes of the disabled persons'/children's rights ideological spectrum that true conflict exists. The central tenet, that appropriate services should be provided for the person requiring care, to release the young carer from inappropriate responsibilities, would be agreed by all concerned. Undoubtedly some people with physical disabilities need only some practical support to be able to have a full role in bringing up a child. However, other people who need care might live in an environment of stress and uncertainty which can have extremely detrimental effects on any child living in that family. A Social Services Inspectorate report on young carers makes the following point to practitioners. 'Parenting – recognise that while most ill or disabled parents and their children do not need help with their relationships, some do – be alert' (1996, p.3). It is clear that practitioners in this area need to be experienced and exercise great sensitivity.

Legislation and assessment

There are a number of subtle differences in approach between assessment of adult carers and assessment of young carers in the Carers (Recognition and Services) Act 1995. Initially, children and young people have the same right of access to an assessment as adults, through an assessment or a review of the adult who is eligible under the NHS and Community Care Act 1990. They also have the same right to have their views taken into account and to have a separate assessment. However, the guidance to practitioners has additional features which apply to young carers.

Practitioners should be mindful of the relationship between young carers and their parents. They must be careful not to undermine the parent's ability to care and should consider providing services which would help the parent to fulfil their parental responsibilities. At the same time they need to assess what support the young carer is giving to the parent and to consider whether providing services to the parent could benefit the carer, by relieving the amount or changing the type of care that they undertake. Workers also need to assess whether the young carer's development is being adversely affected by their caring role and, if so, should consider services, either for the parent or the young person, to address this. There is no sense in which young carers should not be able to provide care, rather 'it should not be assumed that children should take on similar levels of caring responsibilities as adults' (Department of Health 1996a, p.11).

Consideration should also be given to the needs of young carers who do not provide substantial and regular care. Furthermore, practitioners should take into account the needs of children who might be detrimentally affected when a parent has an illness or disability but who do not have caring responsibilities. Practitioners should consider whether these young people or young carers themselves may be 'children in need' under the Children Act 1989. A child is viewed to be in need if:

(a) he is unlikely to achieve or maintain, or have the opportunity of achieving or maintaining, a reasonable standard of health or development without the provision for him of services by a local authority; or

(b) his health or development is likely to be significantly impaired or further impaired, without the provision for him of such services; or

(c) he is disabled.

(The Children Act 1989, 17 (10))

Through this legislation local authorities are empowered to provide services to families to 'promote the upbringing' of the children, which can include services specifically for the child or for the parents.

Thus agencies are able to provide services which benefit young carers either through community care or children's legislation. In light of this, it is essential that agencies ensure that young carers do not fall into a gap between children's and adults' services within social services departments. To achieve this, procedures must be in place so that appropriate intra-agency referrals can be made. First, care managers who are undertaking assessments must have awareness about the needs of young carers. Wherever young family members are involved, as part of their assessment they should try to ascertain whether they are taking on a caring role. They should inform the adults involved and any young carer about their right to an assessment and should take their needs into account when designing the package of care. If it is felt that the young carer may be a child in need then a referral to their children's division will be appropriate. In the reverse scenario, children's social workers may wish to refer the parents of young carers who have been highlighted as children in need to a care manager for a community care assessment. Procedures should also cover arrangements for co-working and agreement on financial accountability between divisions. It will also be useful for one division to take on the lead responsibility for young carers. Usually this will be children's services, due to their expertise in working with children and young people and their families.

However, even if such arrangements are in place, one worrying factor is that young carers may have significant needs but not be eligible for support by either route, because they do not meet tight priorities. The Greater Manchester Black Young Carers Working Group (1996) cites an example of young carers receiving no support from social services because they were having to operate eligibility criteria at the level of children at risk rather than children in need because of resource problems. In such circumstances, young carer projects can prove a valuable support.

In Scotland there is a difference in the Carers Act in relation to young carers. Here young carers are ineligible for assessment due to the Age of Legal Capacity

(Scotland) Act 1991, which does not allow people under 16 to enter into legal transactions. Therefore a parent or guardian would have to request an assessment on their behalf. An alternative way of assessing their needs is through the Social Work (Scotland) Act 1968 section 12(1) which specifies a duty to promote social welfare (Scottish Office 1996). The irony of young people being deemed able to take on the responsibilities for caring but not to have a right to ask for their own assessment is apparent and while this limitation may be a technicality rather than having any practice implications, carers' organisations have sought to have this anomaly addressed.

Practice issues

If we examine the implications of the Carers Act and its guidance in relation to young carers, we can see that it is treading a line between the rights of the child and those of the parent. It is likely that the main potential for tension will come if the views of children about their situation differ from those of their parents. Conflict between young carers and those needing care is likely to be more problematic than those involving adult carers, due to the complexities of the power relationship. It has been highlighted that children may undertake activities that distress them but do not acknowledge this because of loyalty to their parents. In their turn parents may not wish their children to be carers but may allow this to take place because they have no alternative. Also both children and parents may not express any true problems because of fear of interference by professionals, the ultimate fear of course being that the child might be removed. This may be particularly relevant where children are primary carers, in which case there may be collusion between children and parents to keep their situation private. Interestingly, one study found that young carers who had contact with social services or carers' projects did not express any concern about being taken into care (Mahon and Higgins 1995). It appears likely that it is mainly families who do not have contact with services who have this fear.

It is important, therefore, that practitioners supporting young carers are able to work to a high level of expertise. In many ways, young carers' issues highlight a weakness in practice which has been apparent for many years and which needs to be addressed. Adult carers often cite how they feel ignored by the worker's concentration of attention on the person requiring care. How much more might this occur when the carer involved is a child or young person? With the focus on the individual needing care, it is all too easy not to consider what is happening for children involved in any situation. However, talking with children and young people indicates that they are far from passive observers in family situations, rather they have a variety of emotional reactions and active responses. For instance, they may try to 'fix' a problem, or may deflect attention by negative behaviour.

Many of the methods of supporting carers which have already been discussed will be useful to young carers; in particular they require access to services to enable the people they care for to live as independently as possible. At the same time there are a number of approaches which will be particularly relevant to young carers.

Strategies for young carers

Since work with young carers is a recent development it is particularly important that practitioners should have guidance in this. All authorities need a strategic plan to show their overall direction in relation to support for young carers, and policies, procedures and practice guidance in order to carry this out. A Social Services Inspectorate report (1996) indicates that 55 out of 71 authorities already have policies in place. Any strategy for young carers should include the following elements.

MULTI-AGENCY APPROACH AND LEAD RESPONSIBILITY

Appropriate support for young carers is totally dependent on a multi-agency approach. The problems that can be found in agencies attempting joint work are likely to be compounded in the case of young carers; this is because of the number of agencies which have a responsibility in this area and the fact that these are across the adult/children service division, compounded by the fact that young carers are a relatively new area of work.

It is essential that a multi-agency approach is adopted by all relevant organisations, primarily social services, health, education, youth services and the voluntary sector, with agreement and understanding at all levels, from senior management to individual practitioners. A lead officer with responsibility for strategy on young carers' issues should be appointed in each agency. It can also be helpful for each team or locality to have a named contact person who has developed expertise in this area. Without assigning responsibility in this way there is a danger that the needs of young carers will be lost within the high level of demand for statutory services. The multi-agency approach should be reflected throughout all the following points.

OUTLINE OF PRINCIPLES

The principles which inform support for young carers should be clearly outlined in order to give practitioners an overall framework in which to carry out individual work. Such principles might include a commitment to supporting families to keep together and to the rights of a child to access educational, social and leisure activities. Consideration could also be given to the definition of 'young carer' to which an authority is working. For instance, the decision may be taken to offer a service to young carers within the widest definition. Alternatively, where resources are limited, those who provide the greatest levels of care may be the priority.

IDENTIFYING YOUNG CARERS AND MAKING APPROPRIATE REFERRALS

Education services and primary health care teams are particularly well placed to identify young carers. The Social Services Inspectorate (1996) suggests that organisations should agree protocols with agreed triggers to identify young carers who may be under stress. In schools, examples of such triggers include: lateness, absences, leaving school early, going home at lunch-time, a drop in standard of work, general exhaustion, falling asleep in class, poor academic performance, and a variety of behaviour problems. Obviously these characteristics may apply to young people with any number of problems, and education workers will need to look into their home circumstances to make the connection. Teachers should always bear in mind that caring responsibilities could be a relevant factor in problems at school.

In addition to identifying young carers, schools are in a good position to give support. Recognition of the needs of young carers can lead to practical help such as flexibility on work requirements, offering extra tuition at appropriate times, permission to use the telephone to check on their relative, and permission to leave school premises if necessary. Education practitioners can also involve parents in dialogue about problems their child might be experiencing and ways of overcoming these. In a number of areas, young carer projects have started after-school groups. There are advantages and disadvantages to such an approach – groups within schools can show young carers that they are not alone and create a convenient support network; on the other hand, there may be insufficient people of a similar age to relate to each other and some young carers indicate that school is somewhere they can be like everyone else, so they do not wish to draw attention to themselves. *Teachers – Young Carers Need You!* is a useful leaflet from the Carers National Association (1994) to enable teachers to identify and support young carers.

Primary health care, particularly GPs and community nurses, may also have an important role in identifying young carers and should, in their turn, have procedures to help them to do this. Most importantly, they should be aware of families where parents have long-term disabilities, particularly where there is a single parent, and inform them of the support which may be available for young carers. Additional factors which they should be mindful of are possible stress-related illnesses in children, and physical strains caused by lifting.

Both health and education departments should have clear information about eligibility criteria and how to refer people to social services for assessment.

INFORMATION FOR YOUNG CARERS

One of my first experiences of services for young carers was a project worker informing me that the Community Care Plan was entirely inadequate for the needs of young carers, who would not read such a boring document, and that this needed to be redesigned in a way that would be attractive to them. While it is unlikely that many young carers would ever have much interest in an entire Community Care Plan, however enticingly presented, it is important that information relevant for young carers should be in a form appropriate for them. Young carers themselves should be consulted in relation to what they feel is relevant and how they would like this to be presented. Posters and a leaflet specific to information on young carers, available through schools, are particularly effective. These should include colour, cartoons, contemporary references and topics which are of interest to young people in order to engage their interest. It is also useful to design two forms of information relevant to the interests of particular age bands, perhaps for children under ten and for young people in adolescence.

Young carers from ethnic minorities

At the time of writing, little research has been undertaken into young carers from ethnic minorities. Although numbers of black young carers are not known there are indications that they may be proportionately greater than white carers because of the levels of poverty and health problems in some black communities. At the same time they are under-represented in young carer projects (Greater Manchester Black Young Carers Working Group 1996). Black young carers may face similar problems to those of black adult carers, with their disadvantages compounded by the fact that as young people they are likely to find it more difficult to access support than adults. On the other hand, generally they will not experience the language problems of elders in their communities.

Approaching issues of young carers in some Asian and Chinese communities may be particularly difficult for workers, in that the communities' views about what is appropriate for young carers may be different from those of British culture. For instance, there may be expectations that very young children should take on tasks or that girls should give up their education. Practitioners will need to work with great sensitivity in this area, not imposing their own cultural judgements on a family situation, but still safeguarding the child. A danger can be that workers will not intervene in what they view as an issue for a particular community. 'Workers will need to make an assessment about the relationship and cultural context within which caring occurs, being mindful not to justify age-inappropriate responsibilities as culturally appropriate' (Greater Manchester Black Young Carers Working Group 1996, p.13). A helpful framework can be to consider generally agreed principles of child care, such as those in the United

Nations Convention on the Rights of the Child, 1989, which indicates that children have a right to play, education and health care.

Young carer projects

Recent years have seen the development of a number of special projects which provide support systems for young carers. Carers Impact (1997) has estimated that approximately 90 young carer projects exist in Britain. These projects are usually based in a centre and will employ paid workers and volunteers to support young carers. The main components of this support generally involve the following services:

- Individual counselling or groupwork with other carers of a similar age, the purpose of which is to give emotional support and to enable the young person to work through their feelings, to develop coping strategies and to be able to make informed choices about caring. Anecdotally, workers indicate how young carers exhibit greater maturity than other people of their age, particularly in group situations.

- Organised leisure/social activities, such as groups of young carers going ice-skating or on a picnic. This is to give them the opportunity of developing social skills, making social contacts and generally having fun. Obviously, respite care may need to be organised for the person requiring care to enable some young carers to join in these activities. Reactions from users of the Sefton and St Helens projects indicate that older young carers tend to appreciate one-to-one support, while the younger group benefit from activities (NHS 1994).

- While the focus remains on young carers, projects also need to work closely with parents and establish positive relationships with families as a whole. On one level, parents will need to give their permission for younger children to join in project activities, while on a deeper level, good relationships can mean that young carers' workers can provide support for the whole family which will in turn benefit the young carer.

- Advocacy and practical advice on issues such as welfare benefits are also provided. Young carers may have particular difficulty in voicing their own needs and advocates can support young carers in their dealings with practitioners and also, on occasion, with their parents. In particular, advocates can ensure that young carers receive appropriate information and services.

- The involvement of former young carers to provide support from someone who has been through a similar experience. This is particularly appreciated by young carers who are able to see positive role models.

• In addition, where young carers are assessed as being children in need, they will receive support from social workers, which is likely to involve work with the whole family to address the child's needs.

The majority of these special projects have been funded to take place within voluntary sector agencies. Undoubtedly this has had the benefit of making them more accessible to young carers and their families. There is less stigma attached to the voluntary sector, and less fear of compulsory intervention than with statutory authorities. Users of the Sefton and St Helens projects indicated that they appreciated their centre being in offices which were not associated with official services (NHS 1994).

On the other hand, projects need good connections with statutory organisations. Links with education departments will enable them to target new young carers and gain support from teachers and other education professionals. Similarly, contact with social services will mean that issues of children who are at risk can be swiftly addressed, and that projects will have a better understanding of what services are available. To operate effectively, voluntary sector projects need formalised links with statutory services, such as officers being members of advisory committees.

One problem of young carer projects being at arm's length from statutory agencies was shown in the funding crisis in 1997, in which a large number of projects found their future in jeopardy as statutory agencies failed to renew contracts (Thompson 1997). The continuance of such projects is by no means assured, as the statutory sector is compelled increasingly to target its resources on legally required services. Indeed, there is a question mark about the role of specialist young carer projects. In particular, it is felt that resources to fund mainstream services should not be diverted into specialist projects since it is these mainstream services which truly offer relief to carers. Also, by creating small-scale, specialist projects, authorities may feel their duties have been discharged and may fail to continue to address the needs of this group. While many young carers benefit from specialist services many, also, prefer to get on with their lives like adult carers, and simply require the services to enable the person they are caring for to be more independent.

However, the balance appears to be that young carer projects have an important role in profile-raising activities and giving specialist support which should be allowed to continue. 'In an ideal world there should be no need for young carer projects but until the wider issues are addressed we need the focus of the projects' (Social Services Inspectorate 1995d, p.7).

Checklist of considerations for supporting young carers

- Is a multi-agency strategy for young carers in place?
- Is there a lead officer for young carers?
- What information, suitable for young carers, is provided?
- Are there procedures for co-working between adults' and children's divisions in relation to young carers?
- What specialist services exist for young carers?
- Do practitioners receive training in working with young carers?

11

Carers of People
with Mental Health Problems

'My son Sean is schizophrenic. They got in touch with us from the university and we went up to see him. He was in the health centre, talking nonsense, believing someone was putting something in the water to control the students. We thought it was just the stress of the course and he would get over it. That was ten years ago. Sometimes for a few moments we'll be sharing a joke or watching something on TV and it's the old Sean again. Even now I still have hope. Then he says something strange and it's back to normal. I lost my son ten years ago.' (A carer)

As we have seen, many people who require the support of a carer, and carers themselves, often suffer emotional problems such as depression and anxiety. Here, however, we will be chiefly addressing the most serious and chronic mental health problems such as schizophrenia, manic depression, clinical depression and other conditions which generally require periods of hospitalisation or intensive psychiatric support.

Carers of people who are experiencing mental health problems have traditionally been at a remove from 'mainstream' carer activity. In many ways these carers are a distinct group with an identity of their own which predates the development of interest in carers. This is reflected in the fact that the language which is used to refer to them involves different concepts from other carer groups. For instance, there is an emphasis on family or relative involvement, rather than the role of an individual carer, with, as we have seen, the term 'family burden'. This distinct identity is also shown by the fact that mental health carers' groups tend to be focused on mental illness and the problems facing people experiencing this, rather than the needs of carers themselves. This trend is mirrored in the majority of research into the role of families of people with mental health problems; again, the needs of the carers are mainly considered in terms of how far they can support individuals in improving their mental health. As the concept of the carer as someone who has needs in their own right gains increasing recognition, it will be interesting to see to what extent this influences the field of mental health.

The reasons behind these differences in approach have their origins in a number of interlinking factors, most importantly theories about the role of the family as a cause of mental illness, the development of community care, and differences in the nature of the caring role in relation to people with mental health problems. One significant effect of these factors has been a particular tension in the relationship between professionals and carers of people with mental health problems which often still needs to be addressed. Another is that work with families in this field is particularly well developed and can inform practice in other areas of social care.

Causation and blame

Unlike factors causing the majority of conditions that require the support of a carer, the causes of mental illness are by no means clear. This fact alone has had an immense impact on the interactions of the families of those with mental health problems with professional workers. The medical and social models of mental illness are polarised explanations of the cause of these conditions. In the medical model, mental illness is believed to be caused by physiological disturbances, including genetic and biochemical factors. In contrast, social models eschew the term 'mental illness' and seek explanations for disturbed behaviour in the influence of social factors such as friends, environment, culture and, most significantly, the family.

Both models have had enthusiastic and exclusive proponents, but many take a middle position between the extremes in which it is believed that individuals may have a physiological predisposition to illness which is then triggered by environmental factors. So it is possible for someone with the physiological potential for illness to live in a supportive environment and never develop psychological problems. Alternatively, someone with a high propensity for illness may experience this even though living in circumstances which do not appear overly stressful. Research into this area indicates that there is strong evidence in support of physiological causes for schizophrenia, and significant evidence to indicate that personal experiences and the social environment also play a role, particularly in relation to relapse rates.

There are a number of classic social theories which have passed into the mythology of mental illness and are still affecting practice today. Here there is only space to describe a few of the most influential theories. The idea of the schizophrenogenic mother proposed by Fromm-Reichmann (1948) portrays an emotionally cold and distant mother who is nevertheless demanding and dominating. She provides an intimidating atmosphere which affects her child's ability to develop emotionally. Some years later, Laing (1960) widened the concept to include the pathogenic family in which the dynamics of all family members need to be taken into account. With some members overly involved, others too withdrawn and none supportive, the child may try to make sense of an impossible situation by reacting in disturbed ways. Similarly, one child may be the scapegoat for the rest of the family and live out their collective emotional disturbances.

Another prominent idea has been double bind theory (Bateson *et al.* 1956), which is one of the range of theories which point to confused and confusing communication within a family with a member with schizophrenia. The term 'double bind' refers to a situation in which someone repeatedly receives contradictory messages, either verbal or behavioural; for instance a parent may tell a child 'I love you' but accompany this with a punishment. The child grows up unable to make sense of the 'reality' around them and falls into a personal and skewed world view such as schizophrenia.

The problem with many of these theories is that most fail to conform to empirical testing. For example, Hirsch and Leff (1975) undertook research into the concept of the schizophrenogenic mother and found no supporting evidence for it. Despite this, such theories continue to exert influence on how workers may view carers of people with mental health problems. One reason for this is that it is all too easy for practitioners to be swayed by anecdotal evidence which supports these theories. There can be few mental health workers who have not come across a number of parents who conform to every characteristic of being schizophrenogenic. Similarly, many workers will have experienced a situation where an individual lives alone in relative stability, but returns from a holiday visit to their family in a state of anxiety or disturbance. In these cases, the image in the mind of the worker is not of a supportive carer, but someone who contributes to the deterioration of the service user's condition. However, for every family with difficulties there will be many which, however deeply one investigates, exhibit no characteristic which should trigger mental health problems.

At the same time, there is a substantial amount of evidence which indicates that factors in the social environment, including the family, can have negative effects on the condition of people with mental health problems. Much of this research has shown the individual with schizophrenia as someone who is overly sensitive to life events. Thus, an unstimulating environment can lead to withdrawal and de-skilling, but one in which the individual is forced to interact can also have this effect or may lead to acute symptoms of disturbance. In terms of relapse rates it has been found that, in comparison with people leaving hospital to live alone or with distant relatives, there is a higher relapse rate in people who return to spouse or parents (Brown, Carstairs and Topping 1958). This is generally attributed to the higher expectations close relatives may have for individuals, the investment they have in their return to health and the stress that they may themselves be experiencing through the problems of their family member.

The theory of Expressed Emotion (EE) has had a significant impact in this area. Based on the results of research, the theory of EE indicates that it is in families which have a strong emotional content in their interactions with each other that the individual is most likely to suffer relapse and re-hospitalisation (Brown *et al.* 1962; Brown, Birley and Wing 1972). But again, such factors need to be seen in the light of other research which indicates the positive effects of families, such as that which suggests that being married is one of a number of positive factors in the prognosis of people with schizophrenia (World Health Organisation 1979).

Positive approach from workers

So what is the practitioner to make of this confusing situation? Is the carer of someone with mental health problems a supportive ally or someone from whom the individual needs protection? Perhaps most importantly, we need to ensure that we do not slip into stereotyping but view each situation as involving distinct individuals. I have encountered mental health workers who have a blanket view that all people diagnosed as schizophrenic should not return to live with their families because of a failure to understand the implications of the research into Expressed Emotion, a clearly absurd and dangerous position to take.

Workers in the area of mental health need to spend time reviewing the way they interact with families of service users to ensure that they are treating them with consideration and respect and are not, consciously or unconsciously, viewing them as responsible for their relative's problems. Within mental health there is a particular need for workers to focus on the needs of carers, rather than carers in relation to service users or service users alone. It may be helpful to view carers of people with mental health problems as potentially belonging to one of the following categories:

- Carers who support people with mental health problems
- Carers who provide support but whose interactions with the individual can exacerbate their problems
- Carers who provide support, but themselves may have mental health problems.

These categories serve in no way to separate carers in terms of responsibilities they undertake but as a way of enabling workers better to assess their needs and decide on the most appropriate course of intervention. All of these carers may benefit from the general support for carers described earlier in this book, however those in the third category may require specialist help in their own right, while those in the second could benefit from a programme to work on the relationships in the family. Whatever the needs of the carer, it is essential that a supportive, non-blame approach is taken.

Mental health and community care

A further factor to be taken into account is the history of the care and treatment offered to people with mental health problems. The rise of institutionalisation from the nineteenth century to the mid 1950s arguably focused most strongly on mental illness. At one stage this was clearly to protect society from people who did not conform to the norm, however, as knowledge and skills with regard to mental illness advanced, institutions took on the role of providing treatment. A system of mental health expertise developed and it was these 'experts' who were able to treat people and restore them to health. Institutions took on the responsibility for their residents and only rarely were relatives involved in this process. In fact the concept of 'asylum' started to take on the meaning of protecting people from the rigours of community life including family members.

With the onset of anti-psychotic drugs which, to some extent, could control extremes of behaviour, and with the development of the policy of community care, there came a decisive change. The irony of a situation in which families were suddenly given back the responsibility of caring for their relative is clear. Without training or experience they were expected to cope with responsibilities which had previously belonged to qualified ward staff. However, although people with mental health problems have returned to the community, in a number of areas the psychiatric profession has maintained its expert role, from the slightly more accessible venue of the community hospital. Generally the approach remains of concentrating on the needs of the patient. The carer is often not involved and, as we have seen above, in some situations may be viewed with indifference or hostility.

> Sometimes psychiatrists and nurses behave as if the only important bit of their [the patients] lives is the time they spend up at the hospital. I don't know what they think happens when their patients walk out of the door. We have them the other 20 hours a day but nobody seems to understand this. (A carer)

Positive approach from workers

Again, mental health workers need to focus on the needs of carers in addition to those of services users and, importantly, systems need to be in place within organisations to encourage this. In particular, all mental health services need to ensure that consideration is given to the home circumstances of an individual and how the carers and families are affected by living with someone with mental health problems. Similarly, procedures should require that carers are involved as far as possible in decisions about interventions to support someone or help them improve their mental health. The ethos of the organisation should be such that assumption of the role of 'expert' by practitioners should be seen as inappropriate in all workers including medical practitioners.

The nature of the caring tasks

Carers are likely to play a large role in the life of someone with severe mental health problems. Research indicates that up to 70 per cent of people with schizophrenia are living with relatives (Atkinson 1986). The majority of carers are elderly parents, sometimes single mothers, and about 10 per cent have been patients themselves (Kuipers and Bebbington 1994). While the tasks a carer of someone with mental health problems may need to undertake have similarities to those of other carer groups there are also differences which are quite distinct. Most obviously, the carer is unlikely to be involved in the most intimate physical tasks of personal care. It is unusual for someone with a mental health problem to need hands-on help with toileting, feeding or personal hygiene. If such support was required, it would be likely to be when the individual was in an extremely disturbed state, in which case the main problem would be achieving compliance rather than providing the physical help necessary. On the other hand, it may be that although the person does not need practical help to do these tasks, they may require considerable prompting which may be equally time-consuming.

Since we are discussing people who develop mental health problems in late adolescence or adulthood, most individuals will already have developed some skills to enable them to be independent from their families. Generally they will have experience in caring for themselves, in studying, working, travelling and coping with the practical tasks of life such as budgeting. Even if people have not had personal experience of, say, cooking for themselves or tackling the benefit system, because their intellectual ability is not impaired it could be assumed that they will be fully able to develop these skills. But with the onset of mental health problems any or all of these abilities may be impaired. Someone suffering from chronic depression may not have the energy to take care of their finances and may fall into monetary difficulties which, in turn, can cause more anxiety. A person experiencing a psychotic episode may neglect to eat properly which can further affect their mental and physical health. Carers, therefore, may find themselves *supervising* the individual, undertaking tasks that the person is unwilling or unable to do or trying to persuade them to do these for themselves.

One of the most problematic areas for carers is that people with mental health problems are likely to have a different view of reality. Depending on the severity of their condition they may have extremely strong but unrealistic views about what they want to do and what is best for them. The depressed person may sincerely believe that they are unworthy to live and may attempt suicide. The person on a high may think it is perfectly reasonable to order three new computers on their friend's behalf to help their business. In contrast, the carer's perspective is likely to be one based in accepted reality which will be in conflict with the person they are caring for. Unlike other groups, there may be little sense of co-operation and working towards a common goal. Rather there will be tension and stress as both parties struggle to impose their reality. An area which is often the focus for this is over taking medication. Similarly, service users might resent the support of a carer and think of it as interference; they may not recognise that they have a problem and become suspicious of their relative's actions.

People with mental health problems can present very challenging behaviour. The extremes of this include aggression, violence and suicide, all of which will obviously have an extremely destructive effect on carers. However, other behaviours, while less dramatic, will also have serious effects: refusing to leave their room; demanding the family undertake rituals such as washing or cleaning in a certain way; neglect of self-care; becoming nocturnal and sleeping all day; lack of care for property; extreme inactivity; restlessness; alcohol or drug misuse while taking medication; suspicion and paranoia all contribute stress to families. As we have seen, carers often become the focus of an individual's discontent. Either because they feel secure enough within the family to show how they feel, or because a family member is triggering a negative reaction, it is common for extremes of behaviour to be found within the home environment.

Another factor which is often highlighted is that the needs of someone with mental health problems may fluctuate. An individual may be functioning well for a period of time and people may start to believe that the person's mental health has improved. Then there may be a slow, and at first hardly noticeable, deterioration in the person's mental health, or alternatively a sudden crisis. Long-term carers will not have a sense of a settled role, rather they become constantly alert, waiting for the next crisis situation.

Impact on carers' lives

While the practical or restrictive impact on the carer's life may be less than for other groups of carers, the emotional pressures may be greater. Generally the carer will be more able to leave the person they are caring for alone and will rarely need to arrange a sitter so they can have an evening out. On the other hand, research indicates that these carers' ability to socialise and have contact with people outside the family may be just as limited as other carers (Fadden, Bebbington and Kuipers 1987). Embarrassment about the behaviour of their relative is a common feeling reported by carers who may prefer not to go out than to accompany a relative who does not conform to expectations about social behaviour. Stigma about mental illness remains prevalent in society, and is an added stressor. Feelings of being trapped and helpless are also often expressed. Carers often see no end to their problems, rather a deterioration of the situation. Helplessness comes when they feel powerless to alter their circumstances. For instance, an individual may be showing signs of disturbed behaviour following a decision to stop taking their medication. The carer will see the deterioration and how it becomes reinforced – without medication the person may start to neglect eating which can lead to further problems – however, they are often powerless to help. It is in such circumstances that carers often feel extremely frustrated with statutory services, which they feel ought to be able to intervene more readily.

Carers may experience feelings of guilt about their relative's condition. In close relationships it is, perhaps, natural and reasonable to question whether you have contributed to a person's problems. As after a bereavement, people may be tormented by worries about what they did or did not do or say. Were their parenting skills adequate, were they too strict or too lenient, too distant or too protective? Conversely they may also have feelings of anger and blame towards the individual. Some relatives find it difficult to understand that their relatives with dementia are not in control of their actions. How much more difficult it must be to be understanding in regard to a condition whose origins are even more obscure and where there seems no physical reason why the person should behave in such ways.

Sadness and loss are also factors which need to be taken into account. Just as with any individual who suffers a disability in adulthood, people with mental health problems will be the subject of other people's hopes and dreams. Parents will have an image in their mind of their child's future. Spouses will have plans for their future lives with the individual. In particular, partners or spouses are likely to experience a difference in the quality of their relationship. Just as with other groups where a partner suffers mental disability, such as through brain damage, those in a relationship with people with mental health problems may find that they no longer have a feeling of support or closeness with that person (Perring, Twigg and Atkin 1990). Possibly this is made more difficult by the fact that in so many ways the person is like they used to be. Skills and abilities may remain intact, manner and characteristics will be similar; the difference may be subtle, but overwhelmingly apparent to those closest to them.

A number of studies have indicated that carers of people with mental health problems have significantly higher levels of psychiatric disturbance and physical ill health than the rest of the population. As with other groups, the most stressful time appears to be when people have not been in the caring role for a long period of time. There are also high numbers of family breakdowns, indicating that some families are not willing or able to continue in their situation. 'Those families that do survive intact do so in part because they are able to accommodate to a distressing situation, but probably only at a cost of higher than normal levels of psychiatric distress' (Perring, Twigg and Atkin 1990).

At the same time we need to be aware of the complexities of working with relatives in the field of mental health. The role of carer is perhaps more ambivalent in the area of mental health than any other user group. Sometimes there is a very clear carer/cared for distinction: a son or daughter develops a psychotic illness or a spouse severe depression. While the relationship between these individuals may be complex there is a clear supportive, carer function. In many cases, however, the roles and relationships between members of a family are less clear. It is not unusual to work with a family in which a number of individuals, sometimes across generations, are involved in mental health services. Alternatively a person with mental health problems may appear to have power and control over their relatives who adapt their behaviour to the demands of the individual. For example, a person with a powerful phobia about travelling by public transport may not allow family members to go on a train. Although any of these relatives may at times take on caring tasks, their role could not be defined as a carer, rather they are participants in the events which occur around a focal individual.

Supporting carers of people with mental health problems

Carers of people with mental health problems will benefit from any of the general methods of support for carers covered in previous chapters. At the same time, such individuals often have specific needs that may not apply to other carer groups because of the nature of mental illness. The following approaches have been found to be particularly useful for carers of people with mental health problems.

Information on the individual's condition

Carers of people with mental health problems find it particularly difficult to obtain information about the nature, prognosis and treatment of their relative's condition. In one respect this is an understandable reaction on behalf of practitioners, since it is particularly difficult to predict the nature and outcome of mental illness. There can be dangers of alarming people unnecessarily – although in many situations people experiencing psychotic incidents will develop chronic mental health problems, some people recover completely. Similarly, there may be concerns about self-fulfilling prophecy in that if people expect a condition to deteriorate, their behaviour may alter to bring this about. However, this should not be an excuse for failing to give relevant information. Lack of information leads to high anxiety and confusion on the part of relatives which can only be detrimental for all concerned. Undoubtedly, practitioners need to be extremely careful with the information they give out and ensure that it presents a balanced view. Mental health practitioners could benefit from having written information to be given to relatives which has been agreed by all major agencies *and by users and carers themselves* so that mixed messages are not being received from different quarters.

At the same time, tensions between the views and aspirations of service users and carers can be particularly apparent in the field of mental health. The user movement has become increasingly dissatisfied with workers being considered experts in mental health if this implies that they know best and that they have the right to unilaterally impose treatment on individuals. Some carers might also espouse this view, however there may be more of a tendency to welcome anyone who indicates that they have answers to the problems that the carers are experiencing. At the same time, they will inevitably become frustrated if the experts do not involve them or adopt a critical attitude.

Carers' dissatisfaction with practitioners often focuses on the area of ongoing information about their relative. Carers' organisations may state that it is their right to have access to all relevant information. If they do not, it is argued, then they as people who provide the greatest input of care, and whose lives are most affected, may have less information about their relative than the most remote social worker or ward staff member. The dilemma for practitioners is that in terms of confidentiality, the service user must agree to information being shared. This is often a particular problem in the area of mental health where it is not uncommon for people to say that nothing must be told to their relatives, but then not to admit that they have given this instruction, because they do not wish, or are not able, to address this with their carer. To clarify these issues, agencies need to acknowledge this dilemma and to have clear procedures on confidentiality and the transmission of information which are written and freely available to users and carers. Such procedures should cover situations when workers may break confidentiality, such as in cases of potential risk to the individual or their carer.

Dealing with stigma

As we have seen, the lack of clarity about the origins of mental illness and the behaviour of some people with mental health problems mean that there is a definite stigma attached to these conditions which can result in avoidance and fear from other people. Carers are faced with coping with this stigma and the lack of understanding and sometimes hostility from people with whom their relative has contact. Often this results from ignorance about mental illness, and the general experience of carers indicates that, provided their relative agrees, they can reduce this negativity by being open about the person's condition, and giving basic information about mental health issues. For instance, it might be appropriate to approach people in local shops to explain that their relative may sometimes appear troubled and talk to himself because of his condition and explain that if the shopworkers engage him in everyday conversation this may help him to feel more safe and welcomed. This course of actions tends to reduce suspicion and fear in people in the community and also encourages them to be more supportive of the individual concerned. Atkinson (1986) indicates that practitioners can be of use to families in helping them select the information they wish to share and to rehearse how they might approach this.

Carers' denial

One of the areas in which carers often get stuck is with the image of the person as they were, before their problems started. Sometimes holding the image is like a shrine to a person from the past – such as the parents who have many pictures of their daughter on her graduation day, but none since her first hospitalisation. Families may hold on to this image and spend their time waiting for their relative to 'change back'. Because there is no obvious physiological cause for the change, it is particularly easy to believe that this might occur. The problems involved in this are that it may be unlikely that such a change will take place and in the meantime there is a danger of failure to accept what the person has become. This means that the family are living in the past or future rather than the present, and sending obvious messages to the individual that they are no longer good enough.

A related issue is that of 'if only' – unrealistic hopes about the future which may be shared by both carer and the person with mental health problems: 'If only I had a job I would be OK'; 'If she could get herself a boyfriend she would be normal'. The converse to this is the belief that any change in circumstances will result in the individual's condition deteriorating: 'If I try to go to work I'll only get myself in a state'; 'She couldn't cope with a boyfriend'. Similarly, families may become so anxious about the situation that they believe any 'negative' behaviour is a manifestation of their relative's condition. Any anger, irritability, sadness or independence is seen as a mental health issue rather than a normal emotional reaction; in some situations people with mental health problems are compelled to behave in an unnaturally passive manner due to family concern.

The role of practitioners in such situations is to work with families on the reality of what is. There could be specific work around acceptance of the individual, looking at their strengths and potential as well as problem areas. Work can also be done on helping families to distinguish between elements of the mental health problem and normal expressions of feeling. Individual counselling may be appropriate where carers have problems coming to terms with personality changes in the person they care for.

Managing challenging behaviour

One of the most pressing issues for carers of people with mental health problems is the matter of how they should treat their relative when his or her behaviour is disruptive to the family environment. The questions most often asked concern how to manage bizarre thoughts, withdrawal from social contact, anti-social behaviour and aggression. It is important that workers have suggestions of how to address these problems and can work with family members to develop strategies to deal with them.

Carers are often caught between the dilemma of challenging bizarre statements, or accepting them and entering into the person's frame of reality, thus reinforcing psychotic thought patterns. Generally it is believed that a middle course – neither actively challenging or colluding with delusions – is the most appropriate method since it avoids stress on both sides. Statements such as 'I accept what you are saying, but I don't see it that way,' or ignoring what is said and changing the subject can both be effective. In group settings carers can be encouraged to share strategies that have worked for them.

In terms of behaviour, it is helpful if relatives can find a balance between giving the individual licence to behave as they wish, which could be intolerable for the family, and insisting on 'normal' behaviour which may be both unachievable and so stressful for the individual that their behaviour actually deteriorates. It appears that both under and over-stimulation can be detrimental to people with mental health problems. Thus if an individual is left in their room and ignored by the family this may exacerbate their condition, but this may also be the result if people repeatedly pressurise them to come out. Since people with severe mental health problems are sensitive to stress in the environment, perhaps the key phrase to bear in mind is encouragement without pressure. Through this approach people are gently encouraged to alter their behaviour. In the example above the individual could be invited to come out of the room at a particular time, either when all the family are to be together, or, if more appropriate, at a quiet time in the home. 'I hope you will be able to join us for tea' or 'The kids are going out tonight, why don't you come and watch some TV' could be the approach. However, any pressure or insistence should be avoided.

At the same time, families cannot function without all members taking some responsibility for their behaviour and there being some boundaries as to what is and what is not acceptable. Just where those boundaries lie may involve negotiation and compromise between all parties. It may be that the family have a strong culture of getting up early, whereas the person with mental health problems is nocturnal. In this situation, where it is the family's value system which disagrees with the person's actions it may be that this has to be compromised. On the other hand, if they are not simply awake at night, but playing loud rock music, then the compromise will have to be made by the individual. Of course, it should not be imagined that such compromises happen spontaneously or easily in all family environments. The need for professional support so that families can learn how to negotiate solutions is perhaps greater in the area of mental health than any other.

Where behaviour is threatening in nature, carers will need specific training in managing aggression and violence. This includes learning skills in how to avoid triggering aggressive outbursts and how to deflect anger. Such training needs to be specific for the needs of carers rather than being general training for staff members. For instance, it would be an extremely tolerant carer who, having been faced by physical violence, accepts the euphemistic professional terminology of 'challenging behaviour'. Of course, tendencies to aggression and violence are situations about which carers will have to make serious decisions in terms of what they are prepared to tolerate. If problem solving or behaviour modification approaches to improving the situation have not effected change, then the worker can help the carer explore where their boundaries should lie and what options they have if the situation is untenable.

Practitioners need to be mindful that carers' organisations have pointed out that people who are prone to violent outbursts are usually the least welcome in any form of service and that in these situations, where help is most needed, workers may be less willing to help. There is also a huge gap between what carers feel that workers should be able to do about disturbed behaviour and what workers are legally able to undertake. For instance, it is not uncommon for carers to indicate that an individual should be detained under the Mental Health Act 1983, but for the approved social worker to feel that this is not appropriate. While it is likely that this tension cannot be resolved to the carer's satisfaction, this is another instance where clear information can at least dispel myths and give some understanding of the parameters within which the worker operates. In such situations it may also be advisable for carers to discuss this with an independent person, perhaps a carers' advocate. Living situations for some carers of people with mental health problems may become intolerable and if they decide that they can no longer continue with this, they may need support in encouraging the relevant organisation to make alternative arrangements which are appropriate for their relative.

Carers as therapists

Involving carers in the therapy or rehabilitation of the person they care for is a practice which takes place in some mental health settings. While describing this in depth goes beyond the purpose of this book, it is a significant development for carers. There are a variety of ways in which relatives may be involved in therapy. Examples include behaviour modification for people who have phobias and programmes for people suffering from eating disorders. Carers can also have a role in working with patients to detect early signs of relapse so that appropriate intervention can be taken. Whenever relatives are involved in such processes there are basic principles which should be adhered to so that the intervention has the maximum chance of success.

The carer should have a thorough understanding of the situation and the aims and implications of the intervention. The worker will need to ensure that they explain what is involved with great clarity. The carer's agreement should always be sought and there should never be any sense that they are being pressurised or compelled into action. They should be involved at all stages of the process and have full explanations for what is asked of them. In short they should be active partners rather than passive recipients of an 'expert's' instructions. Equally important is that the service user should also have an understanding of what is involved and should agree to it taking place. The whole context of the family should be taken into account when deciding on this intervention, and consideration should be given to implications for other family members such as children, the time the family has to devote to undertaking this and the chances for a positive outcome.

Mental health and ethnic minorities

Studies into mental health in relation to ethnic minority groups are well documented and have consistently indicated an over-representation of young Afro-Caribbean males in compulsory detention and in being diagnosed as schizophrenic. Racist assumptions by mental health practitioners have been one reason to which these differences have been attributed. The picture in relation to Asian people is less clear, some studies indicating that there is little difference from the white population, and others that there is either more or less involvement (Butt and Mirza 1996). Problems of determining mental illness in a variety of different cultures have also been highlighted, as has the fact that some cultures have a different concept and vocabulary of mental health. For instance, there is no equivalent of depression in Asian languages, rather people might describe themselves as having a pain in the heart.

It seems also as if some people from ethnic minorities may experience high levels of mental health problems due to the stressors of racism, conflicts of culture, and communication difficulties. Community workers often indicate that mental health is an underlying problem in many of the people they encounter in their work. Accordingly, organisations need to develop services which take into account the needs of carers and sufferers from ethnic minority groups, especially in terms of information, interpersonal support and services which are culturally sensitive.

Working with carers who may exacerbate the service user's condition

In the above situations we have considered support for carers to enable them to cope better with living with someone with serious mental health problems. However, as we have seen, the behaviour of relatives can contribute to deterioration in the individual's mental health. The concept of High Expressed Emotion (HEE) is a way of describing families who demonstrate high levels of hostility, criticism and emotional over-involvement towards a member with schizophrenia. These indicators are determined by a standard assessment method – the Camberwell Family Interview – which has enabled extensive research to take place with families across cultures (Falloon, Boyd and McGill 1984). They have also been further defined in terms of the characteristics of families – HEE families are more likely to express anger and distress concerning the individual; they will be intrusive into their relative's personal space through actions such as talking for them, making their decisions and being over-protective. They will also be intolerant towards the person's condition and behaviour and may believe that the relative could control their actions if they really wanted to. This may lead them to have high expectations of the individual and to be impatient about their progress. In contrast Low Expressed Emotion families tend to be emotionally calm, give the individual more space, and have more understanding and tolerance of their condition (Vaughn and Leff 1981). If, through therapeutic intervention, families can reduce their level of EE, then it has been shown that the chance of relapse amongst patients is significantly reduced. Of all the psychosocial approaches, EE has most consistently been shown to be effective. For instance, Tarrier showed that reducing EE could have beneficial effects up to nine years after the intervention (Tarrier et al. 1994).

It can be seen that here there is a shift in emphasis from supporting the carer, to encouraging them to amend behaviour which may be their natural way of interaction and which the practitioner sees as being detrimental to the person with mental health problems. Obviously this is an issue which needs to be approached with sensitivity and Hatfield warns against falling into the trap of using EE to once again label and judge families (Hatfield and Lefley 1987). Reducing EE is usually approached as a method of supporting service users, however there is also a strong rationale for pursing this from the point of view of carers, in that it will almost inevitably have an accompanying improvement on their own lives.

Programmes for reducing EE generally fall into a category of intervention known as psychoeducation which has many elements in common with those discussed in earlier chapters, such as information giving, problem-solving, improving communication, and coping strategies such as establishing time apart. Indeed, many of these useful approaches originated in the field of mental health. Within this, there will be a focus on effecting changes on the HEE characteristics above. It is perhaps useful to make distinct those situations in which a clinical assessment of HEE has been made within a family, in which case it is likely that individual family work is the most appropriate intervention. Alternatively, issues involved in EE could be approached, albeit in much less depth, within the setting of a mental health carers' group.

Carers' groups

Support groups for carers and families of people with mental health problems are well established both nationally and locally and are essential for helping people manage in what can be extremely difficult situations.

However, as might be expected, some organisations representing families of people with mental health problems tend to support a medical model of mental illness. Some groups are formed exclusively from this perspective and will take actions such as vetting written information to make sure it supports their party line. Psychiatrists and medical researchers, rather than psychologists or social workers, tend to be preferred guest speakers at meetings. Instead of being given a range of views about mental illness, new members will receive information which conforms to the ideology of the group. Established members may work extremely hard at improving the lives of people with mental health problems but the developments they support will tend to be along practical lines, such as schemes to help people into employment, or to improve leisure and social outlets. In some groups there is resistance towards interventions which focus on improving the family environment, especially those which encourage family members to examine their own role and behaviour.

This can lead to tension with local practitioners who may feel that the emphasis on purely medical causes may mean that carers will become unwilling to consider whether addressing their own interactions with the person with mental health problems may improve the situation. They may also be reluctant to refer carers on to the group in case they receive biased information. In order to address this, some practitioners establish support groups connected to their organisation which subsequently take on a self-help format. Therefore it is not unusual to find a variety of different carers' support groups operating in any area.

Services requested by carers

Finally, while carers of people with mental health problems generally wish for similar types of services as other carers, there is a difference in emphasis.

Easy access to emergency services is particularly important for these carers, since the nature of mental health often involves a series of crises. This involves 24-hour access to workers who can provide support – some carers indicate that if they were supported, rather than being left alone in times of crisis, they might be able to cope without the need for hospitalisation. This suggests a need for workers able to undertake intensive, short-term interventions within people's own homes. Just as important is 24-hour access to safe and secure accommodation for their relative. Latterly, there has been a re-emphasis on the importance of 'asylum', a place for people outside the community where they are safe from the complexities of life and so that, in some cases, society can be safe from the individual. While there is agreement from user groups on the need for this service, the emphasis is perhaps slightly different, in that carers may be more inclined to view this as a long-term measure, while service users may see it as time out, facilitating return to the community.

In terms of therapeutic intervention, carers as well as service users emphasise the need for therapies to enable the individual to lead as 'normal' a life as possible. They also stress the need for meaningful activity geared to the level of functioning of the individual. This is likely to include supported employment and training schemes.

While many of the approaches discussed in this chapter have substantial benefits for carers and sufferers of mental health problems this has been no guarantee that they have been embraced by mental health organisations.

> The reduction of EE in the family, the provision of adequate and suitable non-family based accommodation and a flexible and tailored mental health management plan, which involves the patient's family are all implicated. And yet there is little evidence that such approaches are widely adopted in contemporary psychiatric practice. (Rogers and Pilgrim 1996)

Rather there is a focus on management through medication and crisis. The challenge for mental health services is to develop a wider perspective which takes into account the importance of the role of carers and services outside the hospital environment.

Checklist of considerations for supporting carers of people with mental health problems

- What measures are in place for ensuring that mental health workers adopt principles of involving and encouraging carers?
- Is there an information strategy for carers of people with mental health problems?
- Is there a training strategy for carers?
- Do mental health organisations undertake family work with carers?
- Is a 24-hour mental health crisis support service in operation?
- What services are in operation to meet the needs of carers from ethnic minorities?

12

Parent Carers

'It's constant hard work, like looking after a small child but without the joy or fun.' (A carer)

Here we consider the needs of parent carers, people whose children have disabilities, either from birth or acquired during childhood. There are a range of conditions which require a caring, in addition to a parenting, role; probably the most common of these are learning disabilities, physical disabilities, autistic spectrum disorders and sensory impairment. An OPCS survey in 1989 estimated that there are 360,000 children with disabilities in Britain, half of whom will have a severe disability (Atkinson and Crawforth 1995). While parent carers have many needs in common with other carers, there are also a number of distinct differences. Many of these stem from the dual role of being both parent and carer which means that they will have a large range of demanding responsibilities additional to parents of children without special needs, and many parenting responsibilities which other carers do not experience. In this chapter we consider the most significant issues that parent carers face and how services can be adapted to meet their needs.

Significant life stages for parent carers

One way of considering the needs of parent carers is to view their experiences as a process with a number of significant transition points which require them to adapt to new circumstances in the life of their disabled child. Within this, while there are recognised patterns which parent carers may experience, practitioners must be aware that everyone will react in an individual way and beware of any preconceived ideas or stereotyping. There have been a number of models which describe what parent carers may experience. For instance, Cunningham (1979) cites the following stages which parents may pass through when they have a child with a learning disability: confusion and disbelief; sorrow; anxiety; denial; guilt; starting to come to terms with the situation; and planning for the future. Bayley (1973) outlines five levels which parents may go through as part of the process of accepting the situation. These are: fantasy; going through the motions; doing tasks through duty; accepting that caring is a personal responsibility and, finally, loving the child. Here a chronological approach will be taken, corresponding to stages in the child's development.

Discovery

There are many graphic accounts of how parents first discover that their child has a disability. With modern scanning techniques, this may now be before birth; sometimes it becomes obvious at the point of birth, while in other situations it may be a gradual discovery, as babies and small children fail to respond or to meet developmental milestones. More rarely, there may be a disabling illness or accident in early childhood. At whatever stage this awareness occurs, it is obvious that for nearly everyone this will be a devastating experience.

Parent carers and researchers indicate the following common reactions and emotions at discovery. Guilt is mentioned by many parents, especially mothers.

> I felt guilty when I found Gill was handicapped. Carrying a baby from start to finish…it's something I did wrong. I produced a defective child. I wanted to be close to Steve, to talk to him, to hold his hand when we found out, but he didn't want to know. I felt really hurt… (A mother)

It seems that experiences such as bonding with the baby during the pregnancy may leave the mother particularly prone to feeling that any problem is somehow her fault. Guilt may be ascribed to genetic factors, concern that they have done something inappropriate during pregnancy, such as smoking, or just a general feeling that they are somehow responsible. Guilt may also be accompanied by anger, an emotion which may be extremely difficult for parents to acknowledge. This feeling may be directed against oneself, the other parent and sometimes the child itself. A secret wish that the child had died is experienced by some parents, a feeling which can further fuel feelings of guilt. This feeling may be prolonged if the baby is born with a medical condition which requires substantial treatment – for instance, the family may watch the baby undergo a series of operations, with uncertainty about how he or she may emerge. Sometimes there may be a desire to save the baby at all costs; in other situations, feelings may be more ambivalent, with a wish for events to take their natural course without medical intervention.

Another significant factor is the realisation of the loss of the child's expected future. Whether parents have made plans involving choice of school, hobbies and career or have the simple wish that their child will live healthy and happily, they will have some image in their minds about their future. Inevitably, this image will have to be adjusted, in a process which has been compared to the grief following a bereavement and which may take months or years to come to terms with.

Practical concerns for the future will also lie heavily on parents. They may be faced with the possibility of a lifetime of care and may have numerous worries about what might be involved. It is likely that only those who have experienced a similar situation with friends or relatives, or who have worked in health or social care, will have a conception of what might be involved in the care of their child. Furthermore, not only will their image of the future life of their child be changed, but also, like other carers, they will be faced with addressing the fact that their ideas for their own future and that of other family members will alter. There will be an increasing realisation that their whole life will now be different.

Depending on circumstances, parents may experience complicating factors which lead them to experience even more stress. For instance, the child may have a reduced life expectancy, perhaps he or she is not expected to survive more than a few months or years, which means that family members are constantly living with the possibility of their imminent death. Alternatively, the child may be suffering from a condition which medical professionals are unable to diagnose clearly. This can lead to a great deal of confusion and uncertainty, with parents veering between hope and resignation on the prognosis for their child.

Starting life together

Following the realisation of their child's disability, parents will be faced with the first choices about their role in relation to looking after the child; while many will decide to care for their child themselves, some will be unable to take on these responsibilities. It is essential that parents have the opportunity to discuss what options are open to them in depth and to take time over their decisions. The accommodation of children with disabilities in residential homes has substantially decreased in recent years, and is now mainly confined to children with severe disabilities, although a number are looked after on a semi-permanent basis through fostering. However, the vast majority will be looked after at home by their parents. Only 5000 children are estimated not to be living at home (Atkinson and Crawforth 1995).

For parents who take on the responsibility, once they begin the process of looking after their child there may be a period of time in which they can experience relative stability in which to adjust to the situation. Babies with a disability may not have much greater dependency levels than other newborns. At the same time there will be a number of additional pressures. This is the stage at which relatives and close friends who were expecting to welcome a new baby need to be informed that he or she has a serious disability. It is not unfair to say that many people find it extremely hard to know how to react in such circumstances. As well as sensitivity and support, parents may experience avoidance, awkward sympathy, people making unintentionally hurtful comments, people giving unwanted advice and even accusation, such as when an in-law feels that one parent is to blame. These experiences may be similar to those of carers looking after people in older age ranges, but are, perhaps, more acute when a baby or young child are involved.

Parents do not operate in a vacuum and inevitably the reactions of those around them will have an effect. High levels of negativity from those close to them will affect their perception of their child which in turn may jeopardise their ability to cope. Because parents may be unprepared to deal with the reactions of others, they may benefit from support in how to manage this situation, such as advice sessions on what to expect, when their child is still in hospital. By a positive approach to the people around them, parents can change the attitude of other people to become more supportive and sensitive to their needs. Without this, some parents may increasingly withdraw into a small, self-contained environment. Grandparents have been found to have a key role in supporting the family. Positive grandparents can be a significant help with the care of the child, particularly in offering a sitting service and respite care. It is worth noting, however, that as they get older, input from grandparents is likely to reduce (Brown and Hepple 1989).

The role of siblings may be particularly problematic for parents in terms of ensuring that all their children get the chance for equal time, attention and resources from the family when one member's needs are so much greater than the others. Specific dilemmas involve such issues as how to introduce the new child to its brothers and sisters – existing children may have had ambivalent feelings towards a new arrival which can only be increased when this is accompanied by so much disturbance and depth of feeling in their parents – and how far it is appropriate for siblings to take on caring duties. In a study by Barnardos, children were involved in caring for their disabled sibling, mainly through playing with them, baby-sitting and some household tasks (Brown and Hepple 1989). Practical problems may include dilemmas about whether the family should always go on trips out or holidays together, which may involve everyone focusing on the needs of the child with disabilities but emphasises family unity, or whether they should have some separate time, which may feel like excluding that child from the family. Parents are often aware of such issues but may lack strategies on how to deal with them and so can benefit from early support in this area.

As the baby gets older their disability will be increasingly apparent, since they remain dependent on physical care or supervision in ways in which their contemporaries do not. At this time parents will be developing skills in how to look after their child, learning techniques specific to their condition and also finding their way around the services which are available to help them. At this early age, children with disabilities who need care such as lifting present less problems to parents, for the simple reason that they are small and light. On the other hand, behaviour problems in relation to children with learning disabilities may be more acute at a young age than when they become adults and learn some social skills (Richardson and Ritchie 1986).

As their children become old enough for school, either special or mainstream, parents experience some respite during the day. School is an event which happens in the lives of most children and can be a comfortingly 'normal' experience. On the other hand, it can also mean interacting with a range of new professionals, an assessment process for the child who will receive a statement of special educational need under the 1981 Education Act, and possibly fighting battles to achieve access to the school of their choice. Families who have led a self-contained and private life will need to adjust to greater contact with other people. This may bring opportunities for support and development but also problems such as concern about being judged by professionals and other parents (Anderson 1982).

Adjusting

These early years will give signs as to how the family are adjusting to having a child with a disability. In the Barnardos study parents reported that the most significant effects on their lives involved practical restrictions, emotional effects such as anger and shock, and physical exertion/health problems (Brown and Hepple 1989). There is no one way of reacting to this situation; below are a number of common patterns which practitioners might encounter.

Some families appear to experience few major problems – there is a good bond of affection between all family members, the disabled child is supported in developing as fully as possible, while other siblings and the parents' own relationship are not neglected. There can be no easy way of assessing which families are likely to cope in this way, but it is likely that those who already have positive relationships, who create a low-stress lifestyle and a positive outlook, who are reasonably affluent and who have strong support networks, will find it easiest to cope. It is important not to overestimate the stress that can be involved in caring for a disabled child and focus on the element of burden. Many parents indicate pleasures that the relationship can bring in terms of closeness, being needed, and a long-term relationship of care and support. In the study referred to above, the main reason parent carers gave for coping with their problems was the love they felt for their child.

Counter indicators for any family being able to cope with a child are situations in which the child has challenging behaviour such as aggression, frequent fits, lack of accepted social behaviour or withdrawal (Richardson and Ritchie 1986). Also where the existing relationship between parents is already shaky, where there are weak support networks and where there is a pessimistic outlook about the child.

In some situations, the relationship between parent carers may be adversely affected by the experience of having a child with a disability. One or other of the parents may find it difficult to cope and on occasion one parent, generally the father, either withdraws emotionally from the mother and child or leaves the home, meaning that the mother becomes a single carer. Sometimes this is attributed to an intense bond which has developed between the mother and the child which can become an exclusive relationship, in which so much energy is focused on the child that the other parent can become excluded. Not only can this lead to problems between spouses but also to difficulties for any siblings involved, in terms of their own self-esteem and development.

When very strong bonds are forged between parents and child there can be a sense that this is a permanent family relationship – parents are not giving time and care to their child in preparation for their becoming an independent adult, rather the child is expected to have a permanent role within the family environment. While this can have positive elements for those involved, it can also lead to areas of difficulty. A similar situation may exist where parents perceive their duty to be in providing a safe and loving environment for their child, protecting them from harm and avoiding any risk. Here, we enter an area which has the greatest potential for conflict between parents and practitioners, and between parents and children – that of developing independence.

The move to independence

The time when the individual with a disability leaves school or college is another important transition in the life of the family. This is the stage when children without disabilities will generally be making the move to more independence from their family. They may have physically moved out of the family home, taken a job in order to support themselves financially, established new relationships which have the potential of creating their own family and generally become more distanced emotionally. Obviously this time is rarely problem-free for any family, as the caring/independence relationship between parents and child is challenged; but where the young person has a disability it can be particularly problematic.

For one thing there is a transition to services for adults, a new set of staff to get to know, such as workers in day centres, careers guidance and health services. The young person may now be spending much more time at home, which can put additional pressure on parents. This is also a time when, for some people, true realisation about their child's condition strikes home. While children are very small or at school there is an expectation that they will be dependent. Leaving education is a signal for independence, but possibly not for the person with a disability. There will also be a need for emotional adjustment as the person makes the transition to adulthood and parents consider their role in the next years of their child's life. Dilemmas about how to deal with sexuality and relationships in relation to their child may also be an issue for parents.

A number of significant social factors can influence the stage of independence. In the area of learning disabilities, developments in professional practice, such as normalisation and social role valorisation, have emphasised the importance of enabling people to lead as independent a life as possible, maximising their ability to undertake mainstream activities within the community. At the same time, the user movement has emphasised the right of people with learning disabilities to make decisions about their own lives and the importance of supporting people to achieve this. Sometimes these two movements have taken a complementary stance, in opposition to the perceived role of parents. Voluntary organisations which have been formed by parents may have a philosophy and approach which is in conflict with user-focused groups. Generally the area in dispute revolves around the aspect of risk and ability, with parents perhaps more cautious, and the user movement more willing to address issues of risk. This issue is paralleled with people with physical disabilities, perhaps with the distinction that generally these individuals will be able to take on more of a lead role in establishing their own independence.

It is important that these issues do not polarise into a right/wrong conflict, and that a stereotyped idea of the parent of someone with a disability as unwilling to allow them to develop like other children is not adopted. Often, the attitude of parents towards the independence of their children will be complex and individual. Some parents adopt a philosophy of encouraging their child towards independence from an early age. This may not be a particularly easy approach, since, while children without disabilities will have an expectation of establishing a separate life, children with learning disabilities, in particular, may not aspire to this without encouragement. Parents, therefore, may be in the unusual situation of having to encourage their child to rebel. This can lead to uncertainty for the parent – whether to push, whether to let things go – and they may also doubt the advisability of taking this approach, perhaps fearing that they are over-hard on their child.

In contrast, some parents may take an approach which limits the potential of their children for developing skills and abilities. Perhaps they have a tendency to do things for the child rather than allowing them the time to do things for themselves. They may be over-protective and not allow their child the opportunity to make mistakes or take risks either through fear for their safety or through fear that they may become demoralised. Sometimes it may simply be the case that parents have low expectations for their child and do not give the necessary extra encouragement towards independence. It is quite common for parents to develop the belief that they are the only people capable of looking after their child and that things have to be done 'their way'. In a small number of situations a mother may enjoy having someone who needs looking after like a baby or small child and may seek to keep the person dependent. These situations can cause major dilemmas for practitioners involved with the family.

At the day centre they say she can travel independently, but I know what she's like. Anything might distract her attention and she might walk out into the road, and although she knows not to go off with strangers you never know what might get into her head. (A carer)

Interestingly, an 'over-protective' attitude is also found in parents of adults who became disabled in later life. Many individuals express great frustration at parents who are perceived as treating them like they were children again, or trying to wrap them in cotton wool. This often distresses parents who feel they are just trying to do their best for their child and save them from further harm.

Example

Jane was born with a serious physical disability which gave her no movement in her legs and limited movement in her arms and hands. She is of average intelligence and is able to communicate reasonably well – her speech being slightly indistinct. From her birth, both parents, Helen and Tony, decided that they would have no other children but would devote their lives to looking after Jane. Helen gave up her job and spent much of her free time with her daughter. As she got older all available technological devices were incorporated into the house to enable her to function as independently as possible.

Because of the severity of her disability she attended a special school where she obtained 5 GCSEs. Helen and Tony became very involved in the school's parents group and were responsible for successful fund-raising and social events. When Jane left school she spent two years in a special class in college and then attended a local authority day centre three days a week. Paid work had been ruled out as impossible due to the extent of her disability. Helen transferred her fund-raising energies to the centre, and began to attend most of the days Jane was present, helping out as a volunteer. Most of those attending were closer in age to Helen than Jane.

When Tony died at the age of 75, Helen began to be seriously concerned about Jane's future. Although she had asked her sister if she would take over responsibility for her, and had taken her 'that's a long way off' as a tacit agreement, she still felt uneasy. Helen found it increasingly difficult to physically manage Jane, now 30, and for the first time accepted home care support and Jane spending some time in respite in a residential home. While initially nervous about being separated from her mother, Jane came to enjoy respite. In the course of two years, she established a relationship with a disabled man, became engaged and announced her intention to marry. With her fiancé, she put pressure on social workers to establish them in their own accommodation.

Although seriously concerned about their ability to cope, Helen said she would look for, and purchase, a suitable bungalow for the couple. At this stage Jane refused to let her mother be involved. There was an extremely angry meeting in which she accused her of ruining her life and not letting her do anything she wanted to do. It was a year before Jane agreed to have contact with her mother again. Helen relied heavily on her support networks in carers' groups and the day centre to enable her to get over the anguish of the rift in their relationship.

As the example indicates, the interplay of parenting and caring can be a difficult balance to achieve. With entirely good intentions, Jane's parents crossed the boundary between support and intrusion. Their lifestyle was built entirely around their daughter and a relationship of mutual dependency was established. When Jane came to realise she had other options in life, one interpretation of her actions was that she was making a decisive statement of independence that people often make in adolescence. Past resentments and feelings of lost chances contributed to her need to have a decisive break from her mother.

When parents can no longer care

This final transition is one which people may find particularly difficult to acknowledge – what will happen to their child when they are no longer able to provide the care? Quite apart from any fears for their child, addressing this issue means acknowledging their own inevitable ageing, ill health and death. While this may not be particularly pressing when the parents are young, as they get older it becomes increasingly important and is consistently mentioned as a major fear in studies on this subject. People may have a number of means of coping with this fear. Some carers appear to deny that there is a problem, do not mention it openly and will not engage with people who do. Many quietly worry about the future, but are unable to see any acceptable solutions so become increasingly anxious. Some have an unspoken expectancy that other family members will carry on with the care. Others, who are able, take practical steps to ensure that their child's care will be as close as possible to the care they give, such as establishing trusts with people in a similar position or through organisations such as Mencap.

This issue is closely connected with that of maximising the child's independence. Where parents have supported their children to develop their skills and to forge links outside the family this transition has the greatest chance of running smoothly for all concerned. As we shall see, the best way to approach to this is through planning and preparation.

Practice issues

While parent carers will benefit from the general forms of support and services which can be useful to all carers, there are also a number of specialist approaches which can be helpful for people bringing up a child with a disability.

The role of workers

Parent carers generally have distinct preferences in how they wish practitioners to relate to them. Primarily they wish to be seen as parents first rather than carers, while their child should be treated as a child first and as having a disability second. While some welcome external support, others may view this as an intrusion into their private lives. An approach which is sensitive, and avoids any patronising 'expert knows best' attitudes is essential. In recent years the concept of 'partnership' has become accepted good practice; in this, acknowledgement of the abilities and experience of parents forms the basis for the parent/worker relationship. Parents and workers are both viewed as bringing particular attributes to a situation and as working together for the benefit of the child. Practitioners who are involved with the children should be experienced child care workers, but should also have specialist knowledge of children with disabilities. For instance, health visitors should have specialist training in this area of work. In common with most other service users and carers, parent carers appreciate establishing a relationship with a worker which will be continuous, rather than having a constant change of faces.

Initial information

The way in which the news that their child has a disability is given to parents is of crucial importance, as is their access to information and support in the following weeks, since their experience at this stage can affect their relationship with their child and their feelings about the future. The following are recommendations from parents as to how the initial disclosure can be made as positive as possible.

In common with other carers, parent carers want information as soon as possible. The discussion should not be rushed, rather parents should be given the chance to ask as many questions as possible. Practitioners should be honest and give full information – being evasive or trying to spare people's feelings is not appreciated. At the same time, of course, a sensitive and tactful approach is necessary, as is a positive and encouraging attitude. It is recommended that the baby should be present when the parents are told (Cunningham 1984). This is so that a psychological distance should not grow between baby and parents. Wherever possible, close family such as grandparents and siblings should be involved. Since it is not possible to take in all the information in the first meeting, there should be a chance for further discussions. Parents generally wish to speak to individuals who can give full information on their child's condition, particularly in the initial discussions, and non-connected people such as students should not be present. Parents should never be informed separately and expected to pass the information on to the rest of the family (Fairbrother 1991). Organisations which are involved in these initial information stages should have procedures on how meetings should be carried out. There should also be a checklist to ensure that all relevant information is given to parents.

Following these discussions, parents want access to counselling, for the opportunity to talk through their feelings, preferably with someone who has understanding of the issues involved in being a parent carer. They can also benefit from sessions with a worker who can explain in depth the practical issues involved in bringing up a child with a disability and who can give information on how to access the services which can give them support. It has been pointed out that sometimes the attention of practitioners will focus on the mother, to the extent of excluding the father. Workers need to ensure that both parents are involved as far as possible. Some areas have developed systems in which other parents may work alongside practitioners in these early discussions to share their own experiences and give peer support. It is important that parent supporters are appropriately trained and supervised in such situations and that the parents *wish for* this type of support. Some parents indicate that they would not have wished for contact with other parents in the early days (Cunningham 1986).

Helping parents cope with friends and relatives

The opportunity for a session on what to expect from other people when their baby leaves the hospital can be extremely useful for parents. Such sessions can include descriptions of common reactions, discussions of how parents feel their friends and relatives may react and strategies for coping with this. Particularly useful strategies include:

- Talking openly to other people about how they feel and how they would like the baby to be treated, generally, as a baby first and foremost
- Sharing information about the child's condition
- Using supportive friends or family members to 'fend off' others who are not supportive
- Spending time with siblings explaining about the new baby's condition and hearing their reactions
- Family meetings for in-depth discussions.

Of course, there may be a fine line between parent carers using strategies to improve the reactions of those around them and their becoming support mechanisms for other people. The last thing parents may wish to do at this stage is be strong for others. However, if handled positively, managing this situation can give some parents a sense of focus and purpose.

Assessment of need

Parents are entitled to an assessment under the Carers Act when their child is being assessed under the Children Act. In Scotland, the rights of parent carers to an assessment are covered by the Children (Scotland) Act 1995 rather than the Carers Act which is confined to assessments of people receiving community care services (Scottish Office 1996). While assessments for carers were carried out for adult services in many social services departments prior to the Carers Act, children's services have taken a different, but parallel approach. Authorities need to develop a system of assessment for parent carers which takes into account guidance on both the Carers Act and the Children Act, such as assessment of the needs of the child and family, ascertaining the wishes and feelings of the parents and children and working in partnership.

Support for siblings

As we have seen, siblings of children with a disability have particular needs of their own. Most studies into the effects on brothers and sisters show a great deal of love for their disabled sibling but also feelings of jealousy, isolation, and frustration. Siblings can be subject to ridicule from school friends about their relative and may feel different from other children. At the same time they often exhibit maturity and common sense beyond their years. It can be useful for parents to have support and guidance about the role their other children can take in caring for their child with disabilities since, as we have seen, they are often concerned about this. Young carer projects in which support is offered to children in the context of their family can be very appropriate here.

Parents from ethnic minorities

Parents of Asian children with disabilities may face particular discrimination from assumptions by practitioners. Shah (1992) outlines a number of stereotyped views, many of which are the opposite of the more usual stereotype of the caring Asian family: parents reject children with disabilities; they face discrimination from other members of the community and feel shame and embarrassment; parents do not play appropriately with their children to encourage their development; and they do not plan for the child's future because of the belief that God will provide. Shah points out that while the above points may indeed apply to some Asian parents they may equally well be found in white parents.

As with other services for people from ethnic minorities it is important that practitioners view people as individuals and that services are appropriate for their needs. In particular, in relation to children with disabilities, organisations need to ensure that they are committed to involving parents in services and taking the extra effort which may be needed to ensure that people who do not speak English fluently have a thorough understanding of the services their children receive. One specific service which is useful is to attempt to increase the number of ethnic minority foster parents who are interested in providing respite care, so that respite can be arranged within similar cultures.

Practical advice and support

Parents need practical advice and support on how best to support their disabled child through all stages of their childhood. Where multi-agencies are involved in supporting parent carers it is important that responsibilities for this process are clearly assigned. Particular areas of support include:

- Specific ways of coping with children with disabilities such as feeding problems, mobility problems and the like
- Ways of managing medical and behaviour problems such as hyperactivity, fitting, screaming, repetitive behaviours, aggression
- Practical methods of working with children to increase their motor skills, communication and intellectual abilities
- Support for carers themselves, such as strategies to maximise their chances of sleep – sleep disturbance being a major issue for many parent carers.

Developing skills and independence

While some children are severely disabled and are clearly always going to need high levels of care, many have the potential for developing skills and abilities to enable them to become more independent. It is important that practitioners operate with an ethos of developing children's abilities and with the goal of maximising their potential for independence from the earliest possible stage, so that this becomes a way of life for the family. To this end, practitioners need to work in partnership with parents on individual plans for the child, including elements such as risk assessment and setting realistic targets.

To take this approach from the earliest stages will clearly be more beneficial than for carers to be faced with agonising problems about what will happen to their child when they are gone. It has been found that younger parents are the most willing to consider this issue, while older, widowed parents of middle-aged children, who are also most at risk of the need for emergency care, are most resistant (Richardson and Ritchie 1986). With ongoing planning, carers will have a clear understanding of what their child is capable of and how their needs can best be met. As the individuals who are likely to be the constant figures in a child's life, in contrast to swiftly changing professionals, parent carers are ideally suited to take a co-ordinating view of their life plan.

Starting to work towards independence with parents when the person with a disability has become an adult may be more problematic, but should still be an integral part of any care plan in the same way as for a young child. The issue of when to address the issue of the parents becoming older and less able to cope with caring is a difficult one for practitioners who may fear to offend parents or cause them anxiety. This situation can reach an impasse if parents themselves will not broach the subject, whether through reluctance to put their worries into words or because they feel guilty for thinking about alternative ways of caring for their child. Some parents have indicated that it is a relief for them if the topic is raised by another person in a sensitive fashion since it gives them 'permission' to address it. Even those who may initially react with indifference or hostility may subsequently say that they appreciated that this had been done.

Parents in partnership with professionals

One example of the partnership approach is to involve parents in practical methods to promote their child's physical or intellectual development. It has been found that interventions at an early age can have significant learning benefits for children with disabilities. Such techniques might include parents undertaking physiotherapy tasks to continue a programme developed by a physiotherapist. They may also involve teaching educational or motor skills. An example of this is the Portage system in which practitioners support parents at home to work with their pre-school children on achieving agreed short-term learning goals. Similarly, children can be taught early forms of communication like MAKATON from a very young age with parent's help. Mittler and McConachie (1986) stress the importance of true partnership in these approaches – parents need to be fully informed and in agreement with the aims and methods of any programme rather than passive participants carrying out the instructions of a worker.

Parents bring knowledge and experience of their child to the partnership while practitioners bring knowledge and experience of working in the field, such as effective methods of teaching children with learning disabilities. They can also provide ongoing support and encouragement to parents and can give realistic and achievable targets to be reached. At the same time, workers should avoid any expectation that parents will undertake such work – not all parents will have the inclination or capacity to take on such a role. External pressure could lead to additional stress on the family and practitioners need to be skilled in working with parents to determine a level of involvement appropriate for individual families.

While the role of parents in teaching their children can be very beneficial, there is acknowledgement that as children with learning disabilities move into adolescence it may become less appropriate for parents to have a formal teaching role, since this may promote a continuing dependence. However, involvement in support in learning living skills tasks such as cooking and cleaning may continue to be appropriate.

Involving parents in services is intrinsic to any partnership model. This approach should start at the earliest opportunity and continue through subsequent services. Parent support groups could be attached to all services. It is now usual for special schools to have open access for parents and to include them in their child's progress through mechanisms such as regular meetings and home/school notebooks. This type of contact is even more crucial when children are away from home in residential schools. It enables parents to understand what activities their child is experiencing at school and to reinforce positive learning within the home environment. Since some parents may be diffident about approaching services, the onus is on practitioners to make these as accessible and welcoming as possible.

Other pre-school and respite/early learning services such as day nurseries and toy libraries generally operate policies of involving parents with activities such as parent and children groups. Such pre-school resources are essential for children with disabilities in order to give them a 'head start'. The extra time spent learning and playing in specialist resource centres can enable children to access mainstream nursery education at a later stage. They are also invaluable as a meeting place for parents and as a central location for appointments with specialists.

Respite

Respite care for young children with a disability is a different process from that for older people, in that the break from a known family environment can be much more traumatic, and children do not have the necessary skills to deal with this. If approached well, however, respite can be a pleasurable experience for the child as well as a relief to other family members. Generally respite for children takes place in specialist family placements – 'second families' or small residential homes. Children need to be introduced to these slowly to get to know the place and the people, perhaps attending for meals and extending this to half-days and eventually an overnight stay.

Moving on

Parents often indicate that appropriate resources need to be in place for them to agree to their child moving from home. Alternatives which tend to be approved of by parents are residential homes or hostels, and village-style communities. Group homes and individual tenancies may be less favoured (Richardson and Ritchie 1986). Things parents wish to see in any accommodation are love, safety, single bedrooms, high levels of personal care, and stimulation. Reservations are often expressed about issues such as frequent changes of personnel, insufficient supervision over personal care and lack of activities meaning that people spend too much time watching television. A range of facilities appropriate to different levels of disability are also seen as important.

From an emotional point of view, the stage at which the child moves on to more independent living can be extremely difficult for parents. Their lives may change from having many responsibilities to having unaccustomed time on their hands. Even more importantly they may be experiencing a huge void in their lives and feeling a lack of purpose. Wherever possible parents need to be closely involved in their child's move; however, in order to allow them to start to become more independent there will inevitably be a time at which they need to draw back. It is important that practitioners who may have worked closely with the whole family up to this time should not immediately withdraw contact from the parents. Expressions of interest in their welfare and how they are feeling will generally be greatly appreciated. This can also be a time when parent carers may benefit from talking with a specialist carers' worker about how they are feeling and how they see their future.

Checklist of considerations for supporting parent carers

- What procedures are in place to promote good practice when informing parents that their child has a disability?
- Are other parents involved as support to new parent carers and what training do these receive?
- Are parents informed of their right to a separate assessment of their needs?
- What measures are in place to emphasise working in partnership with parents?
- Are there parent support groups attached to all services?
- Do services for children encourage open access to parents?
- What measures are taken to work to an ethos of maximising potential and independence from the earliest stages?

CONCLUSION

The Future for Carers in
Policy and Practice

'Many of the authorities were concerned about future funding either because of changes in the special transitional grant allocation or because of the way the Standard Spending Assessment was calculated. The anticipated budgetary constraints which might affect their ability to continue current levels of resourcing' (Social Services Inspectorate 1995c)

So what of the future? What developments for carers are likely to take place over the next few years? Here we briefly examine options for the future in relation to social care policy and practice and in the wider context of society as a whole.

Social care practice

Approaches to working with carers on an interpersonal level are still at an early stage of development. There is still a great deal to be explored in developing good practice in areas such as assessment, care planning and direct work in relation to carers. As work with carers becomes adopted as a discipline in its own right, it is likely that the body of knowledge will increase, with practitioners in carers' projects developing useful techniques and methods. Knowledge and understanding from specific areas which have developed methods of working with carers, such as mental health, can be transferred to the field of carers in general. One of the challenges of working with carers will be in maintaining an overall view of the needs of carers as a group, while being aware of the differences between sub-categories and individual carers. Another will be to maintain professional standards in areas such as assessment, when pressure of work means that the time spent with each individual is limited and long-term relationships cannot be maintained.

Social care policy

It is likely that the intense activity in recent years will slow down and a period of consolidation will take place in which the advances which have been made can be built upon. An awareness of the significance of carers and their needs has been raised, and this now needs to be fostered and maintained. All local authorities have initiatives to support carers and for those that have not already done this, there needs to be a multi-agency strategy for carers in each area.

The quote at the beginning of this chapter has proved prophetic. In my current post as a commissioner of services, I have been struck at the contrast between some of what I have been writing and the state of social care provision at the current time. The difference between the ideal and the reality, between the expectation and the ability to deliver, is huge, especially in authorities which are particularly beset by budgetary constraints. Since the very first literature on social care, writers have identified resource problems, however I would suggest that the scale of the current problem is unlike anything that has been experienced in the past. The delivery of services to vulnerable people is seriously under threat, with services increasingly targeted at those in the most dire need.

If this trend continues, and at the time of writing there is nothing to suggest that it will not, what is the future for carers? On the positive side, the recognition of the role of carers means that they are now considered alongside the service user groups as a group towards which organisations have a responsibility to provide support. They are, therefore, operating from a much greater position of strength than would have been the case a few years ago.

From a negative perspective, it is likely that, as with other groups, it will only be carers at the heaviest end of caring, or those closest to breakdown, that receive support. An example of this is in the change of relationship between social services departments and voluntary organisations, in which the trend is for the latter no longer to receive grants for services that they wish to provide but funding to provide services that the authority wishes to commission. Organisations which are not self-financing will have to comply with service level agreements, service specifications and contracts. This shift has meant significant changes for carer-focused voluntary organisations such as Crossroads. There is a general feeling in the voluntary sector that they are now less able to be responsive to carers' needs. But from a statutory perspective it seems unfair for a limited number of carers to be able to tap into a voluntary organisation to receive a deluxe service, while others receive little or nothing. The dilemma for voluntary organisations is that with contracts for services they may find themselves increasingly unable to provide the type of service to which they would aspire. However, the strength of such organisations is that their ethos should determine that they respond to the needs of carers as closely as possible, which should guarantee their continued popularity with carers and purchasers of services.

In these difficult circumstances it is important that authorities take a clear and honest standpoint about service provision. One of the most frustrating situations for carers, service users and workers is for an organisation to fudge the issue of resource difficulties. An example of this would be to continue to make empty commitments about enabling carers to consider giving up care, when all the efforts of the organisation go towards making this as difficult as possible. This is a classic double bind situation and can mean that people involved become confused and disheartened. There is, perhaps, a move towards organisations 'setting out their stall' and being clear about the initiatives in which they are able to get involved and the level of support which they are able to give. While this may be an uncomfortable position, at least it means that people understand the situation and that resources can be clearly targeted at people with the highest levels of need. Nor is an aim of helping carers to continue to care in conflict with the majority of carers, who consistently indicate that they wish to continue as long as possible. Any dispute, of course, is likely to focus on the stage at which they require support and the level of need which triggers services.

Accompanying this approach, both organisations and carers will benefit from research which indicates what are the most effective services to support carers. Hitherto, research into services has largely tended to be qualitative, asking carers what they felt about services. The response has generally been positive; carers approve of most forms of support – their comments are usually that they require more. A move to selective research would examine which services are actually most useful.

The wider context

In the wider social context, campaigning for improved rights for carers will continue and their profile is likely to remain high. Carers are extensive in number and low level carers or 'helpers', who comprise the majority of the 6.8 million carers, may come to take on much greater levels of care in the future. The combination of carers and older people is likely to be a force that no political party can ignore. Furthermore, carers as a group find favour in public opinion. A MORI poll asked which group people would support if they had won the lottery and had £1 million to give to charity and 69 per cent indicated they would support carers (Warner 1995). While this may not be strictly representative – there were no children's causes on the list – people did have the opportunity to make their own choice. Perhaps the fact that any one of us might become a carer has a significant effect on support for this group.

Such factors are likely to have a direct relation to future policies in regard to carers and the resources that are targeted to support them. Perhaps at the very minimum we will see changes in training and employment legislation to facilitate carers in gaining employment and in receiving sympathetic treatment when employed. However, the possibility of demographic and social trends creating a 'gap' in care – meaning that there may well be insufficient people to take on the role of caring in the future – is a cause for concern. Pitkeathley (1996) discusses this possibility and the solution of 'investing' in carers – encouraging people to take on and sustain caring responsibilities – which is seen as a potentially cost-effective mechanism of maintaining informal caring. In this scenario, support for carers is pitched at a much higher level than is seen currently, but is still a lower cost than the option of organised state care. If there is indeed a gap in care, this will undoubtedly be a trigger for government response to increase support for carers.

Useful Contacts

Carers National Association
20–25 Glasshouse Yard
London EC1A 4JS
Tel: 0171–490 8818

Young Carers Research Group
Dr Saul Becker
Department of Social Science
Loughborough University
Loughborough
Leicestershire LE11 3YU

References

Aldridge, J. and Becker, S. (1993) *Children Who Care: Inside the World of Young Carers.* Loughborough: Loughborough University.

Anderson, D. (1982) *Social Work and Mental Handicap.* London: Macmillan.

Arber, S. and Gilbert, N. (1993) 'Men: the forgotten carers.' In J. Bornat *et al.* (eds) *Community Care: A Reader.* Milton Keynes: Macmillan/The Open University.

Atkinson, J.M. (1986) *Schizophrenia at Home. A Guide to Helping the Family.* London: Croom Helm.

Atkinson, N. and Crawforth, M. (1995) *All in the Family. Siblings and Disability.* NCH Action for Children.

Baker, P. with Hussain, Z. and Saunders, J. (1991) *Interpreters in Public Services.* Birmingham: Venture Press.

Bateson, G., Jackson, D.D., Haley, J. and Weakland, J. (1956) 'Towards a theory of schizophrenia.' *Behavioural Science 1,* 251–264.

Bayley, M. (1973) *Mental Handicap and Community Care.* London: Routledge and Kegan Paul.

Biggs, S., Phillipson, C. and Kingston, P. (1995) *Elder Abuse in Perspective.* Milton Keynes: Open University Press.

Brown, A. (1989) *Groupwork.* Aldershot: Gower

Brown, A. and Hepple, S. (1989) *How Parents Cope: Caring for a Child who has a Handicap.* London: Barnardos.

Brown, G.W., Carstairs, G.M. and Topping, C.G. (1958) 'Post hospital adjustment of chronic mental patients.' *Lancet 2,* 685–689.

Brown, G.W., Monck, E.M., Carstairs, G.M. and Wing, J.K. (1962) 'Influence of family life in the course of schizophrenic illness.' *British Journal of Social and Preventive Medicine 16,* 55–68.

Brown, G.W., Birley, J.L.T. and Wing, J.K. (1972) 'Influence of family life on the course of schizophrenic disorders: a replication.' *British Journal of Psychiatry 121,* 241–258.

Butt, J. and Mirza, K. (1996) *Social Care and Black Communities.* London: HMSO.

Caplan, G. (1964) *Principles of Preventive Psychiatry.* London: Tavistock.

Carers Impact (1997) *Bulletin No. 2.* (March) London: Kings Fund.

Carers National Association (1992) *Speak Up, Speak Out.* London: CNA.

Carers National Association (1994) *Teachers – Young Carers Need You!* London: CNA.

Carers National Association (1994/95) *Annual Report.* London: CNA.

Carers National Association (1997) *Still Battling? The Carers Act One Year On.* London: CNA.

Caring Costs (1994) *Carers Deserve a Better Deal Campaign Pack.* 20–25 Glasshouse Yard, London EC1A 4JS.

Caring Costs Alliance (1996) *The True Cost of Caring: A Survey of Carers' Lost Income.* London: Caring Costs.

CENTRA (1994) *Customs and Cultures: A Flexible Training Pack.* CENTRA, Duxbury Park, Duxbury Hall Rd, Chorley, Lancashire P7 4AT.

Clarke, M. (1997) 'Viewpoint: feel the force.' *Community Care.* (13—19 February)

Commonwealth Department of Health, Housing and Community Services (1993) *Carer Support: Practical Support on Caring at Home.* Queensland: Commonwealth Department of Health.

Coulshed, V. (1991) *Social Work Practice.* Basingstoke: Macmillan.

Cunningham, C. (1979) 'Parent counselling.' In M. Craft (ed) *Tredgold's Mental Retardation.* London: Balliere Tindall.

Cunningham, C. (1984) 'Down's syndrome: disclosure and early family needs'. *Down's Syndrome 7, No. 4*

Cuthbert, V. (1996 unpublished) *Respite Care for the Elderly: A Survey of Client and Carer Needs.* Wirral Health Authority.

Dearden, C. and Becker, S. (1995) 'Young carers: the facts.' (Special report). *Community Care Magazine.*

Department of Health (1989) *Caring for People – Community Care in the Next Decade and Beyond.* Cmnd 84,9. London: HMSO.

Department of Health (1990) *Community Care in the Next Decade and Beyond: Policy Guidance.* London: HMSO.

Department of Health (1991) *Carer Support in the Community: Evaluation of the Department of Health Initiative 'Demonstration Districts for Informal Carers' 1986–1989.* London: HMSO.

Department of Health (1996a) *Carers (Recognition and Services) Act 1995 Policy Guidance.* London: HMSO.

Department of Health (1996b) *Carers (Recognition and Services) Act 1995 Practice Guidance.* London: HMSO.

Department of Health (1996c) *Community Care (Direct Payments) Act 1996 Policy and Practice Guidance.* London: HMSO.

Department of Health (1996d) *Encouraging User Involvement in Commissioning: A Resource for Commissioners.* London: HMSO.

Department of Health (1996e) *User Involvement: Community Service Users as Consultants and Trainers.* West Yorkshire: NHS Executive Community Care Branch.

Downey, R. (1997) 'Survey exposes scale of young carers' burden.' *Community Care* (19 December 1996–8 January).

Eastman, M. (1984) *Old Age Abuse.* London: Age Concern.

Equal Opportunities Commission (1980) *The Experience of Caring for Elderly and Handicapped Dependants.* Manchester: Equal Opportunities Commission.

Ernst, S. and Goodison, L. (1981) *In Our Own Hands: A Book of Self Help Therapy.* London: Women's Press Limited.

Evandrou, M. (1990) *Challenging the Invisibility of Carers: Mapping Informal Care Nationally.* London: LSE Welfare State Programme.

Fadden, G., Bebbington, P. and Kuipers, I. (1987) 'Caring and its burdens: a study of relatives of depressed patients.' *British Journal of Psychiatry 10,* 660–667.

Fairbrother, P. (1991) *The Special Needs of the Under 5's and their Families*. Brussels: International League of Societies for Persons with Mental Handicap.

Falloon, I., Boyd, J. and McGill, C. (1984) *Family Care of Schizophrenia: A Problem-Solving Approach to the Treatment of Mental Illness*. New York: Guilford.

Finch, J. and Mason, J. (1993) 'Filial obligations and kin support for elderly people.' In J. Bornat *et al.* (ed) *Community Care: A Reader*. Milton Keynes: Macmillan/Open University.

Fromm-Reichmann, F. (1948) 'Notes on the development of treatment of schizophrenics by psychoanalytic psychotherapy.' *Psychiatry 11*, 263–273.

Glendinning, C. (1992) *The Costs of Informal Care: Looking Inside the Household*. Social Policy Research Unit. London: HMSO.

Grad, J. and Sainsbury, P. (1968) 'The effects that patients have on their families in a community care and a control psychiatric service – a two year follow-up.' *British Journal of Psychiatry 114*, 265–78.

Greater Manchester Black Young Carers Working Group (1996) *Working with Black Young Carers: A Framework for Change*. London: Carers National Association.

Green, H. (1988) *Informal Carers: General Household Survey 1985*. OPCS. London: HMSO.

Griffiths, R. (1988) *Community Care: Agenda for Action (The Griffiths Report)*. London: HMSO.

Haffenden, S. (1991) *Getting it Right for Carers. Setting Up Services for Carers*. London: HMSO.

Harding, T. and Oldman, H. (1996) *Involving Service Users and Carers in Local Services: Guidelines for Social Services Departments and Others*. London: National Institute for Social Work and Surrey Social Services Department.

Hatfield, A. and Lefley, P. (1987) *Families of the Mentally Ill. Coping and Adaptation*. London: Cassell.

Health Advisory Service (1996) *Heading for Better Care*. London: HAS

Help the Aged (1995) *Coming Clean on Caring Costs*. London: Help the Aged.

Heron, C. (1995 unpublished) *Consultation on Wirral Community Care Plan*.

Heron, C. (1996) *The Relaxation Therapy Manual*. Bicester: Winslow Press Limited.

Hirsch, S.R. and Leff, J.P. (1975) *Abnormalities in Parents of Schizophrenics*. London: Oxford University Press.

Jackins, H. (1965) *The Human Side of Human Beings*. Rational Island Publishers: Seattle.

Jamieson, A. and Illsley, R. (eds) (1990) *Contrasting European Policies for the Care of Older People*. Aldershot: Gower.

Kuipers, L. and Bebbington, P.E. (1994) 'The social management of long-standing schizophrenia II: social-psychological techniques for helping patients and carers.' *Clinician 12*, 1, 30–37.

Laing, R.D. (1960) *The Divided Self: A Study of Sanity, Madness and the Family*. London: Tavistock Publications.

Lamb, B. and Layzell, S. (1995) *Disability in Britain: Behind Closed Doors – The Carers Experience*. London: Scope.

Levin, E., Sinclair, I. and Gorbach, P. (1989) *Families Services and Confusion in Old Age*. Avebury: National Institute for Social Work Research Unit.

Lewis, J. and Meredith, B. (1988) *Daughters Who Care*. London: Routledge.

McLaughlin, E. (1990) *Social Security and Community Care – the Case of the Invalid Care Allowance*. DSS Research Report No. 4. London: HMSO.

230

Mahon, A. and Higgins, J. (1995) *'A Life of Our Own' – Young Carers: An Evaluation of Three RHA Funded Projects in Merseyside*. Manchester: Health Services Management Unit.

Mittler, P. and McConachie, H. (1986) *Parents, Professionals and Mentally Handicapped People: Approaches to Partnership*. London: Croom Helm.

Moffat, F. (1997) 'Carers raising the profile.' *Community Care* (July 24–30).

Morris, G. (1996 unpublished) Birkenhead: *Consultation on Wirral Carers' Pack*.

Morris, J. (1993) '"Us" and "Them"? Feminist research and community care.' In J. Bornat *et al*. (eds) *Community Care: A Reader*. Milton Keynes: Macmillan/Open University.

NHS (1994) *St Helens and Sefton Young Carers. Young Carers Projects on Merseyside. Some Guidelines for Practice*. St. Helens: North West Regional Health Authority.

Nuttall, S.R. *et al*. (1993) *Financing Long-term Care in Great Britain*. London: Institute of Actuaries.

Office for Public Management (1993) *Initiatives in User and Carer Involvement – A Survey of Local Authorities*. Occasional Papers no. 4. From Margin to Mainstream. London: Joseph Rowntree.

Office of Population Censuses and Surveys (OPCS) (1982) *General Household Survey 1980*. London: HMSO.

Office of Population Censuses and Surveys (OPCS) (1987) *Population Trends*. London: HMSO.

Office of Population Censuses and Surveys (OPCS) (1990) *The General Household Survey 1988*. London: HMSO.

Office of Population Censuses and Surveys (OPCS) (1992) *The General Household Survey 1990: Carers*. London: HMSO.

Page, R. (1988) *Report on the Initial Survey Investigating the Number of Young Carers in Sandwell Secondary Schools*. Sandwell Metropolitan Borough Council.

Pahl, J. (Winter, 1994) *Discovering the Carer*. National Institute of Social Work Noticeboard. http://WWW.dircsa.org.au/pub/docs/2 camp.txt.

Parker, G. and Lawton, D. (1994) *Different Types of Care, Different Types of Carers: Evidence from the General Household Survey*. London: HMSO.

Perring, C., Twigg, J. and Atkin, K. (1990) *Families Caring for People Diagnosed as Mentally Ill*. London: HMSO.

Pitkeathley, J. (1996) 'Carers.' In *Community Care Research Matters: A Digest of Research in Social Services*. April–October.

Powell, T. (1992) *The Mental Health Handbook*. Bicester: Winslow Press.

Preston-Shoot, M. (1987) *Effective Groupwork*. Basingstoke: BASW/McMillan.

Priestly, P. McGuire, J., Flegg, D., Hemsley, V. and Welham, D. (1978) *Social Skills and Personal Problem Solving*. London: Tavistock.

Pritchard, J. (1995) *The Abuse of Older People: A Training Manual for Detection and Prevention*. London: Jessica Kingsley Publishers.

Qureshi, H. and Walker, A. (1986) 'Caring for elderly people: the family and the state.' In C. Phillipson and A. Walker (eds) *Ageing and Social Policy*. Aldershot: Gower.

Richardson, A. and Ritchie, J. (1986) *Making the Break: Parents Views About Adults with a Mental Handicap Leaving the Parental Home*. Policy Studies Institute. London: Kings Fund.

Rogers, A. and Pilgrim, D. (1996) *Mental Health Policy in Britain*. Basingstoke: Macmillan.

Scottish Office (1996) *Community Care in Scotland Carers (Recognition and Services) Act 1995 Policy and Practice Guidance.* London: HMSO.

Shah, R. (1992) *The Silent Minority: Children with Disabilities in Asian Families.* London: National Children's Bureau.

Simmons, M. and Daw, P. (1994) *Stress, Anxiety, Depression.* Bicester: Winslow Press.

Social Services Inspectorate (1993) *No Longer Afraid: the Safeguard of Older People in Domestic Settings.* London: HMSO.

Social Services Inspectorate (1995a) *Caring Today. National Inspection of Local Authority Support to Carers.* Wetherby: Department of Health.

Social Services Inspectorate (1995b) *A Way Ahead for Carers. Priorities for Managers and Practitioners.* Wetherby: Department of Health.

Social Services Inspectorate (1995c) *What Next for Carers? Findings from an SSI Report.* Wetherby: Department of Health.

Social Services Inspectorate (1995d) *YOUNG CARERS: Something to Think About: Report of Four SSI Workshops May–July.* Wetherby: Department of Health.

Social Services Inspectorate (1996) *YOUNG CARERS: Making a Start.* A Summary. Wetherby: Department of Health.

Squires, A. (1991) *Multicultural Health Care and Rehabilitation.* London: Edward Arnold.

Tarrier, N., Barrowclough, C., Porcedduk, K. *et al.* (1994) 'The Salford Family Intervention Project: relapse rates of schizophrenia at 5 and 8 years.' *British Journal of Psychiatry 165,* 829–832.

Thompson, A. (1997) 'Where to now?' *Community Care* (6–12 March).

Twigg, J. (1989) 'Models of carers: how do agencies conceptualise their relationship with informal carers.' *Journal of Social Policy 18,* 1, 53–66.

Twigg, J., Atkin, K. and Perring, C. (1990) *Carers and Services: a Review of Research.* Social Policy Research Unit. London: HMSO.

Twigg, J. and Grand, A. (1996) *Contrasting Legal Conceptions of the Role of Relatives in the Support of Older People: France and England.* Unpublished paper presented to Social Policy Association.

Unell, J. (1996) *The Carers Impact Experiment.* London: Kings Fund.

Vaughn, C.E. and Leff, J.P. (1981) 'Patterns of emotional response in the relatives of schizophrenic patients.' *Schizophrenia Bulletin 7,* 43–44.

Warner, N. (1994) *Community Care: Just a Fairy Tale?* London: Carers National Association

Warner, N. (1995) *Better Tomorrows: Report of a National Study of Carers and the Community Care Changes.* London: Carers National Association.

White, J. (1994) *User Involvement in the Planning of Services within Social Services Departments.* Social Services Research No. 4. University of Birmingham.

Wilson, J. (1988) *Caring Together: Guidelines for Carers' Self-help and Support Groups.* Cambridge: National Extension College.

Wing Kwong, L. and Kerrie, P.K. Lin, (1992) *Working with Chinese Carers: A Handbook for Professionals.* London: Health Education Authority and Kings Fund Centre.

World Health Organisation (1979) *Schizophrenia. An International Follow-up Study.* Chichester: John Wiley and Sons.

Subject Index

Author Index